To Mum
Wishing you a very happy
60th Birthday. So glad we're
here to celebrate it with you.
With all our love
Katy, David & Benjamin
xxx
15.1.87.

OLD DAYS: OLD WAYS

Mary Gilmore

Mary Gilmore

OLD DAYS: OLD WAYS

A Book of Recollections

WITH NOTES
ON THE LIFE OF
DAME MARY GILMORE
BY BARRIE OVENDEN
AND
ILLUSTRATIONS BY
ROBERT AVITABILE

ANGUS & ROBERTSON PUBLISHERS

Unit 4, Eden Park, 31 Waterloo Road,
North Ryde, NSW, Australia 2113, and
16 Golden Square, London W1R 4BN,
United Kingdom

First published in Australia
by Angus & Robertson Ltd in 1934
This illustrated edition first published in Australia
by Angus & Robertson Publishers
and in the United Kingdom
by Angus & Robertson (UK) Ltd in 1986

The publishers gratefully acknowledge Jo Barnes, John Ovenden and the Estate of Barrie Ovenden for permission to reprint extracts from "Biographical Notes on the Life of Dame Mary Gilmore" published in Dymphna Cusack, T. Inglis Moore and Barrie Ovenden, Mary Gilmore: a Tribute *(Australasian Book Society, Sydney, 1965).*

National Library of Australia
Cataloguing-in-publication data.

Gilmore, Dame Mary, 1865–1962.
Old days, old ways.

New ed.
ISBN 0 207 15016 8.

1. Frontier and pioneer life — Australia. 2. Australia — Social conditions — 1851–1901. I. Title.

994.03

Typeset in 12/13 Baskerville
Printed in Tokyo, Japan

CONTENTS

PREFACE
to the first edition

THE writing in this book is so personal that at times it seems almost something of an impertinence to thrust it upon others. Yet it is put forward for a reason, and that is the hope that before it is too late it may cause some who are near the passing to look back and remember, and others to gather up and keep that remembering.

So far, this country's writers of reminiscence and recollection have shown events rather than people, have detailed historied hours rather than life. I have written here of life as I knew it, and with the desire to show, not the miles walked, but the feet that walked them; not the oven, but the bread baked in it, and the talk of those who buttered (when there was butter) and ate that bread.

That errors will be found in what I have done is inevitable. Memory cannot hold everything. Yet, if like Don Quixote I ride a sorry steed, better to ride a sorry steed than none at all. So I have here brought together something of the individual as well as the general that is so rapidly sinking into the passing, there to be lost forever if, as I have indicated, intentional collection is not soon made. One man is doing this, though not in my way; and that is Vance Palmer. He calls his books novels. They are more; they are life such as the people he represents do still live and have lived it. His characters are more than characters, his incidents are more than incidents. They are time, which is creative, even if they are "times"—which is the created. I have long wished to pay this tribute to Mr Palmer for his work, and I am more than pleased to do it here in this book which, I hope, gives to Australia some things not found in anything else that I or others have written.

For the rest, there can be no blame for any who feel that I wander too loosely altogether in the chapters immediately following. I admit the fault. But because with one single thought of recollection come whole battalions, and because there is so much to do and so little time in which to do it, I have forgiven myself. I hope that others who come to judgment will temper judgment by the light of these conditions.

MARY GILMORE
Sydney, October 1933

"The morning meal was porridge, with or without salt . . ."

When butter was sixpence a pound

When butter was sixpence a pound children ate dry bread, or bread and dripping. Money was so scarce that property and produce had but small cash value, so that earnings were very low, and people working for wages lived very hard. A doctor for a sick child was unheard of anywhere except in a squatter's family. "Father" had to have the doctor if he could not be saved without, as "father" was the protector. A woman without a man was defenceless against womanless men once the aboriginals had been destroyed. The man wooed it is true, but his allies in courtship were the danger from worse men, and the need of a provider for children when they would come. A woman only had a doctor when she could no longer stand on her feet, or when she had a kinder husband than most women had. In roughing it she was expected to endure what a man endured, bear with man, and then have and rear her children. Yet amid all the indifference and brutality of the times there were wives who were happy, and men who thought of them. As to children, if they lived they were an asset; if they died (and the death-rate was terrible) God took them. It was the "Will of God" that they died; and on the "Will of God" callous men rested, and women were forbidden to grieve.

But the bush was full of meat even if butter and eggs were scarce. If you could not afford or were not allowed station beef, there were always kangaroos and possums. And many have hungered for possum after beef and mutton became the portion of man, greedily catching a stray one, and roasting it in its fur on the coals. Sometimes there followed disappointment, the habit of salt and ordinary meat-eating having changed the palate, so that "the taste had gone out of the possum." "Joey," however, was different. "Joey" was grass-born, was always tender, and had not the strong taste of eucalyptus that the tree-dweller had. Yet many a time a child grew strong on well-sucked possum bones. Many children had bread only once a day. The morning meal was porridge, with or without salt or black sugar, and no milk; at midday there was a hunk of meat or a leg of possum; at night with sop for the little ones, there was bread and dripping (or

more meat) for tea. Sop was bread soaked in black tea and sweetened. With settlement, goats, cows, and even sheep were milked. But on the old-time frontier of our inland settlement no one but the landowner and his station employees had these.

A man engaged by the year boundary-riding or as stockman would have a hut provided him, and would be allowed a cow; a shepherd might have a goat or two, or he would milk ewes when they were in milk. I even recollect a mare being milked for the tea of a nursing woman, with the elder baby scarcely weaned before its successor came. So hard was the bush that there was a case where even pig's milk was tried to keep a sick child alive. The only thing on the place that had milk was a sow, and when the distracted father said the child was dying (bread and possum being almost all the fare the family had) my father said:

"Any milk is better than none," and a few spoonfuls were procured. I told this once to a townswoman:

"But what did they feed the pigs on?" she asked in astonishment. She could not understand a pig finding food for itself. But pigs foraged for themselves as the hordes of wild pigs in northern Queensland do today. The earth was still a natural, centuries-old storehouse to great roots of grass, to yams, grubs, and worms. Pig meat was almost as lean as kangaroo, but sows littered, and their young had milk to drink. My townswoman friend never quite accepted my story. "If people had pigs they must have had food; and if they had food, how could a child want milk?" her easily read thought ran.

It was at this naked place that I saw the woman's family graves on the hillside behind the house, each grave roofed with a sheet of bark set on four small forked stakes as posts.

"It isn't good for her to have them always before her eyes; it keeps her mind on her loss," my father told her husband.

"She must have them near," was the husband's reply. "She couldn't part with them."

And he went on to tell how, when the first baby was buried, and the rain came in the night, the mother had got up and gone out and covered the grave. After that he had had to roof each little place as each child went. There were four little ones, and three larger mounds with bark laid over them where her father and mother and a sister lay. The earth all round was swept and the space kept as clean as a house floor. Flowers there were none. Geraniums had not reached out so far, and geraniums travelled farther than any rose could because geraniums might be kept indoors and safe. Out of doors possums, kangaroos, and stock ate everything green where a house stood usually unfenced till it fell.

When again I saw that hillside it was spring and the graves were covered with branches of wild flowers. The next time, a year later, the house was empty, neglect was on the hillside. The last child lay there, its little mound naked and uncovered. With its death the mother's mind had broken; the man, childless and wifeless, had given up the struggle and had abandoned the place.

Yes: when butter was sixpence a pound children ate dry bread or dripping, and nothing was lonelier than man.

And musing over those lonely, naked days—specially naked for women—it seems strange to think that there was a time when thimbles, scissors, needles, and pins were nursed and minded as though they were treasures. As indeed they were! I have seen pine-splinters used as pins; and a woman who had for a thimble an open-topped strip of hide that went round her thumb like a sailor's or a tailor's thimble. The hide was soaked to soften it, then holes were made in the ends of the strip and a lacing of kangaroo or emu sinew joined it into a ring. When knotted together, it was left to dry hard in the sun on a round stick the size of the thumb or finger that was to use it.

As to scissors! During the Great War I remember talking to one of the Newells from Lismore about "early days;" she told me that her grandmother took the first pair of scissors to the North Coast. The scissors were so precious that all the way up in the boat the old lady nursed them for fear she might lose them. Yet, when she was landing they slipped and went down into the sand. For days men raked the shore and dived for them. When such things went there was no replacing them. This pair of scissors was never found. The sea had taken them.

Once as children we went to a place where there was a woman who had one blade of a scissors, keeping it in the hope that some day someone might come across her path who had a second. Still, she was not the worst off, as her husband had a pair of shears and she had learned to use them. In this present era when even children play with death in the use of electricity, or wreck in the case of motor cars, and court injury in the multiplicity of machines, it may seem strange that it was thought too dangerous for a woman to cut-out with shears, or to trim children's hair with them. Yet it was so. Shears belonged to a man's life, and a woman could not walk in the way of a man. It was still believed that man had one less rib than woman. On the authority of the Bible story of the Creation I heard this declared from the pulpit many a time.

People also said that a woman breathed differently from a man, and that "no female" could ever be a doctor or a lawyer, as only men could reason or had the faculty of logic. That woman was inferior was a regular Church doctrine; and man was constantly told to shun woman as the agent of the devil. As a matter of fact, in looking back, I think that men regarded the devil as a much less venal being than woman. The devil was male, and that made a lot of difference. "God made men kings and in likeness to Himself; but women were not made in the likeness of God and could only be queens as the daughters or wives of kings" would be thundered at us.

As to thimbles and needles, I recollect when we paid a penny a piece for pins, threepence for a sewing-needle, and up to a shilling for a darner. Only stations bought needles by the packet and pins by the paper. The head of the house, if he saw the house-list before it went to town with the supply teams, would cut three of each to one, and that to last a year. I have yet an old pin of the early seventies. It has a trunk like a small tree, and the top is a wire twist. It was made by hand before America ran pins out by a machine that stamped the head; as it stamped the heads of the shingling-nails that also came from there, and were so different from the long-pointed, hammered English nails.

Hairpins were another trouble, being just as scarce as scissors and needles and pins. They also were thick and enduring. And what a price! Once my mother lost the last one she had, and my father tried to make her wooden ones. It was one of the few occasions in which he did not make a success of experiment. Then he brought in the aboriginal women to show her how they kept their hair up, which they did by a twist on each side of the neck, a cross-over and a turn-in of the ends at the back of the head. Their hair stayed up all day no matter what they did. But my mother never mastered the art. I tried to do it for her, and I failed, too. So she had to go back to the bag-net she had discarded as unfashionable.

But hairpins and needles were not all. I have known people make wooden forks because they had no others, and even use a piece of blade-shaped fire-hardened wood for a knife. The only knife in a household would be a butcher's knife, and if the father had that away there was nothing in the house to cut with. Plates were often made of bark, or the sawn-off end of a board. I have eaten off one of these

". . . these frontier folk . . ."

myself when we were travelling and our things packed up; but it created no sense of hardship, people were so used to using whatever would do. The only thing regarded as really a hardship would be shortage of food or want of water. In regard to the former, bread would be the trouble, for this was not a land of wheat then. Nothing was watched so anxiously as flour.

Meat did not matter. There were plenty of cattle till the runs were fenced and made ownership obvious and vindictive. When that came there were people who, it was said, ate horse. My father had some once at the hut of a notable Riverina character called Bill Nye, of whom I shall say nothing more here, as a book could be written of him, his scamp of a dog, his shifts, and his escapades. My father did not relish the horse-flesh, though he said that if he had been a

Frenchman it would not have mattered. But one thing he certainly did; he took a dose of medicine when he got home. He said that after it did its work he would feel less like a cannibal.

Wooden spoons were another thing that people made—with a pocket-knife, of course. Because for his building contracts we had plenty of chisels and other tools, father was often asked to deepen a spoon, or to rasp the wood smooth so that it would not be rough at the edges.

In all this I refer to the frontier people, the real carriers of this country in its early movement towards settlement. There were the people who had mahogany tables, sat in easy chairs, and had their supplies up by teams, if only once a year. They were not a few, and they did their part, even if it was in a rude plenty and comfort. But the people whom I wish to record are those who travelled in drays and carts, or who went on foot driving a pig, a calf, or a goat ahead of them, the mother helping to carry the bedding, the children bearing the pots and pans; the people to whom a hairpin, a thimble, or a needle mattered, and to whose children a shining American nail was a wonder. I remember babies who cut their teeth by the rubbing of these nails, and little girls who dressed and nursed them as dolls. When they lost one (or it was taken by the boys or their father) they broke their little hearts for it, hunting the grass for days in case it had been dropped in play or when running home when called.

The stations have been written of again and again; but of these frontier folk, nothing, except as farce, has ever been written.

The biscuit-eater

They lived clean in their little huts, so austere in their naked whitewash and the bare scant possessions, the early settlers of our Inland. And though life in looking back through the plenty of these later years seems to have been hard, it had not as much continued toil for the frontier housewife as it has for the housewives of today. A woman then had time to sew with a needle and thread as she cannot hope to do even with a sewing-machine in modern times. Take the life. The day began with sunrise, and ended with dusk. The house or hut had bare walls, whitewashed if possible; dark in their native bark or split slabs if not whitened. Often the dwelling was of bushes alone, and there one slept, fenced securely in, and yet in the air.

There were no windows to clean in the house, no floors to wash even if there were water to spare for it, no curtains or hangings to pleat and iron. If the primitive room were large enough the table stood in the middle of the floor; if the space were small the table abutted on the wall at either side of the house. There was no furniture to move when cleaning up. The table-legs were driven into the earth, as were the bed-posts. There were no chairs to polish, no covers, no table-cloths, table-napkins, or mats to worry one. The seats were either blocks cut from logs, or slab stools. As a rule there was a block at each side of the fire-place for the children. These were used by the father and mother when they wanted to sit at the side, and not in front of the fire. Then the children had the stools. There were women so habituated to blocks that they did not feel safe on a chair, the frame seemed too light because they were so used to the solid wood. They would refuse to sit on a chair while they nursed a baby. "If it broke the baby would be hurt," they would say, excusing themselves; anxiety even in the safest of places pursuing woman where there was helplessness.

Along the front of the fire-place ran a log as a fire-step. (How long is it since you heard that word fire-step?) On the fire-step the children sat to eat; otherwise they stood at table. The only other furniture would be a shelf for the few plates, some nails or pegs for the pannikins and frying-pan, and a cradle for the baby. There would be a clothes-box, and now and then, but very rarely, a small chest of drawers.

". . . no chairs to polish, no covers, no table-cloths, table-napkins, or mats to worry one."

The cradle would be a gin-case on rockers. The gin-case was universal because it was of soft wood and had no splinters. Also it was just the right size, easy to obtain and light to carry. Over it a tilt was made with a bit of gauze or tarlatan to keep the flies from the child's face.

But once in a while some man, tender for the woman who was to bear his child, and grown self-forgetful because tender, would make a cradle such as she had rocked in the old land, or similar to one in which his mother had laid one child after the other till the whole twelve, fourteen, or even sixteen, had slept in it in turn. The first one of this kind that I ever saw was made of boree, the beautiful, darkly patterned wood polished till it shone like old wine in amber glass. The curiously shaped ends were high, so that (the husband said) the wife would not have to stoop to rock it. The wife told us that the original from which it had been copied had come down either in her husband's or her own family from the time of Alfred the Great, and was still in the family.

Both ends of this cradle were carved, the head very ornately. And it had all been done with a pocket-knife. But because of the smallness of the knife and its great value owing to scarcity of the times (for if broken it could not be replaced, and because life itself in stress might depend on it) the surface of the hard wood had to be charred, inch by inch, before the knife was put on it. Even then one of the blades had been snapped at the point. The charring had been done by the slow process of tiny fire-sticks. There were no pokers for poor people in those days, iron was too scarce. Every scrap of iron was saved for mending chains and making horseshoes. Till the increase of machinery came with its natural waste of worn-out bolts, rods, and nuts, a country farrier often had to allow only two shoes to a horse, because he had not scrap-iron enough to afford one man any more.

Speaking of iron, there was never a time, as we drove from pine forest to pine forest, or into or out of town, that we did not stop to pick up any piece we saw, even hoop-iron from a broken case, that was found along the road. The only iron people had in plenty in the conquest of the frontier, conquest by foot and hoof, was in their own iron resolve, and in the stoutness of their own hearts; so that, even if they sometimes looked back, still they pushed forward. And as they pushed they took the cradle with them.

After the first conquest by foot and hoof came that of the furrow. The furrow meant carts, sickles, reaping-hooks, and scythes, as well as ploughs, though some of the ploughs were still of wood, even to the share. My father often made shares of wood for people who were

too poor to buy iron. Indeed, in that period the Australian frontier pegged its slabs to make walls; pegged its roof down so that it would not blow away, or curl and the rain pour in under the bark; and pegged its doors which were oftener of bark than of either stubs or slabs. In addition it hung its hat and its poor pots and pans on pegs. And in doing this it pegged down the corners of the earth in settlement, making it a place to which those who followed might come in safety, and sit down in comfort.

When the first cradle was made it too was pegged. Only gin-case cradles had nails. And when nails were needed, one that could be spared would be carefully drawn from the cradle and a shaped splinter pushed into its place.

"What has become of my cradle?" my father inquired of a woman who was putting her baby to sleep in her arms.

"Tom wanted the nails," was her reply.

It seemed the extreme of poverty to us, equally poor; for, as a builder's children we lived in a welter of nails.

"I'll bring some over next time I come, and put it together again," he said.

I have wandered from my initial subject. But the baby is the beginning of us all, so I will leave it at that.

In the days of the wooden cradle, when a visitor came, one of the homely customs was for the hostess or one of her daughters to untie the new-comer's bonnet-strings or hat-ribbons, and take off the hat, hood, or bonnet that was worn when she was visiting. "Put it on the bed!" was always the direction to whoever took it off.

When this was done the visitor was brought to the fire and her hands rubbed if it were winter, or she was sat "in the cool of a draught" and fanned if in summer. Attentions were fussy, and fuss was expected.

At night slippers were provided; if you had no slippers the guest wore your light Sunday boots. These were either prunella or lasting. Both had elastic sides and a "tag" (loop) back and front for pulling them on. But while prunellas were of thick soft cloth, quite often purple in colour, flat-heeled, and on the broad side, lastings were French in origin, and, being French, were either smart, fast, or wicked, according to who wore them and the mind that considered them. They were made with a slender shape, high arched instep, and high heels. Sometimes toe-capped, sometimes not, they always had a double row of white stitching in an involuted pattern up the front. Sometimes they had six, eight, or more buttons on the instep,

"*. . . the new-comer's hat-ribbons . . .*"

sometimes a double or a single row all the way up from the toe to the top. The buttons were black when stuff-covered, or white, black, or smoked pearl when not covered. Anything more pretty on a foot was never seen, for the seam up the front shaped the boots so that they fitted snugly. The high instep and the narrow foot on the high heel just peeping from the full long skirts and petticoats, together with the tightened ankle, gave an impression of delicacy of feet and of movement entirely lost in modern times.

We all thought such feet beautiful. But it was with a sense of shock I lately saw just such a foot and ankle on an old lady at a Sydney Peace Society meeting. She must have her boots made on the same last she used when she was a girl. She cannot buy them ready-made. It would be impossible to get them, for no shop now stocks them. I must confess that her tight ankle looked as unnatural and as unshapely as her laced-in waist. Judging from her figure she wore one of what I once saw advertised as: "the last lot of old-fashioned corsets to be sold in Sydney, as they are not made now."

Besides the removal of the bonnet, and the special seating of the visitor when she came, there was the glass of wine and a biscuit if your wealth ran so far, or cake if you could not afford "stores." These I might say were not shop's; they were your own personal or family provision against the period known as "between the teams." People had not the water-supplies, artesian and sub-artesian, that they have today, and the teams could only set out when the seasonal rains provided water. We read of the breaking of the ice in Canada and of the melting of the snows on the Rockies as the periods of activities there and in the United States of America. But we had just the same eager stir and the same field for romance in Australia when the creeks ran, the billabongs and soaks filled, and in the towns the gathered army of the teams could start. Then the whips cracked and the voice of the teamster went out into the wilderness; then "the stores" came out back, and there were wine and biscuits for the visitor.

There were no bridge afternoons then; instead, the visitor would ask for a piece of sewing or some mending, or "receipts" would be talked, and an orgy of cooking would be indulged in. No visitor was so discourteous as not "to offer" to do something. An equal courtesy required the acceptance of the offer. "She did not offer," condemned any woman. *Her* things went on the bed once, but never again!

A woman once lived near the Narrandera Berry Jerry when Mr Leitch owned it. She was a lover of biscuits. This was regarded as an unnatural appetite, bread being natural and not biscuits. So everyone said she would have something wrong with her if she continued to eat biscuits instead of bread. It was not a proper thing, they said, to eat biscuits instead of bread. Bread was in the Bible, biscuits were not. I recollect, then being about seven, that I remarked that "cake" was in the Bible, and that biscuits were like cake. I was sternly told that it was "cakes" in the Bible, *not* "cake;" that the word only referred to the form and not to the material in the thing baked, and that that was unleavened bread baked on the coals or on hot bricks like a damper in an oven. So damper was legitimate, biscuits were not, and cake did not exist in the Bible. Whether the biscuit-eater died, or "perished at the waist," as she was expected to do, I know not. Later, my doubts of things accepted were strengthened, but my bewilderment was not lessened, by finding that another neighbour ate biscuits, and she remained plump! The funny thing about it all was that it was customary to eat biscuits with wine. My own people had cracknels with port, arrowroot biscuits with sherry, and a "plain" biscuit with sweet Madeira and Malaga. So that's that!

There was another usage of the day that I might mention but that was neither of cradles, bonnets, or babes. It was the use of silver and gilt cages for small birds. Because in England in the time of the first Georges it was etiquette to have a silver cage for a lark and a gold one for a finch, it was still a *faux pas* in Australia to have two silver or two gold cages at the same time for the one room. "Two gold cages?" A vulgarity. "Two silver ones?" An insufficiency. To remedy the latter, but not enough to obliterate the fact, one cage could have a blue bow, or a blue cord and tassels, and the other could be all white if both were silver. But a blue bow was all one might have on a gold cage. With canaries the male bird as the songster had the gold cage; the hen bird, paler and less the singer, had the silver one. "As moonlight is to sunlight. As water is to wine . . ." Yet there were times, even then, when an astonished mistress found that the singer had laid an egg.

Such a finding was as dumbfounding as to learn that a woman (George Eliot, Harriet Martineau, Adah Isaacs Menken, and one or two other strange creatures excepted) had written a book. Indeed it was as strange as a baby without a cradle, or a man who did not make a leg when he bowed; that is if the man were a gentleman. Others bobbed the head or pulled the forelock; sometimes it was the brim of the hat that was pulled. I have seen many forelocks tugged in greeting. And many a bushwhacker and many a swan-hopping farmer's son my father taught to make a leg, so that he could curve his right hand to his breast, where his heart was supposed to be, and bow properly in a dance!

As to birds . . . But perhaps it is best not to begin on birds, except to say that people brought other of their home customs to this country; the tongues of caged birds were slit with the idea of making them better vocalists or talkers, and little birds were blinded by the bird-catcher's red-hot wire to make them sing (so they said) as birds with sight did not.

When hoods were hats

Among beautiful things found unexpectedly sometimes there were antique fans. The only ones I remember were a couple of French fans, one of which was said to have belonged to the Empress Josephine. Both had delicate figures painted on silk or satin. One of these belonged either to the John Stinsons of Kindra or to the Meurants, Mrs John having been a Meurant. Who owned the other I have forgotten. But the ordinary everyday fan was the sun-bonnet, a spray of a bush, or a turkey's wing. The "turkey's" wing might be that of the domestic variety, of the scrub turkey, or of the brolga. Sometimes a magpie's wing was used, and sometimes an eagle's. But an eagle's wing always seemed too narrow for its length and for that was disliked. Small birds' wings were not of much use, unless a number were mounted together as in the case of parrots' wings and tails.

To keep away flies (and there were clouds of the little black fly), a bush, an emu's wing, a brush-chopped horse's tail, or a cow's swisher was employed. I am talking of the country between the Darling and the Murray, where flies followed man and horse in pillaring hosts in the fly-time of the year. Men wore netted veils and women had gossamers. Besides the veils there were the dingle-dangles of cork. As a protection against the sun turbans came in, and later on pugarees. A turban was a long loosely woven white or coloured cotton scarf, with bright stripes across the ends, and a short fringe. If white, the stripes would be alternately red, green, blue, or possibly plain black. Some turbans were striped throughout, and some at intervals. They were worn on flat straw hats, broad felts with flexible steel rims, hard-hitters, and even, if travelling, on top hats. The pugaree, on the other hand, was not coloured, was usually of silk or else of a strong cream or ecru-coloured thread almost like a strong linen. It had a long fringe knotted to a pattern where it joined the material, and came from the East—probably India. It was twice as wide and three or four times as heavy as the turban. When by degrees the turban went out (for people in mourning I forgot to say there were black ones) it went for good. But the pugaree still survives.

The light turban going out, the heavy and broader pugaree which displaced it was found to be too hot for general summer use, and a shaped back-fall or shade of open woven silk tape, or even of cotton braid, came in. This, shell-shaped at the back, hung down from a narrow band which went round the hat. Being of an open mesh it gave shelter and allowed the circulation of air. All these turbans, pugarees, and shades were washable, except that the pretty colours of the turbans went in the washing. The turbans were starched to keep them wide on the neck, the pugarees did not need starch, being made of good China or Indian silk.

As to the hats that men wore, they were either the tall Yankee gallon hat, the cabbage-tree (which was an imitation of the other) or a low-crowned cloth, felt, beaver, or velvet hat. This had a broad brim and was shaped much like the Puritan hat of the Miltonic period. It had but little stiffening in it, so it softened and flopped when wet. The commercial farm animals were still a limited quantity in the world—a world that had not yet begun to mass-breed and mass-collect for factory production—so that glue was a consideration, if used at all. To make up for the want of a permanent stiffening in the material itself, a flexible steel hoop edged the brim of these broad-leafed hats. This was either top-sewed in place, or secured by a binding of ribbon, braid, or a coloured tape. The tall hat was like that shown in the cow-boy pictures today. It was of palm-leaf, woven Indian fashion, or as the aborigines did their bags and nets of leaf, that is, from the centre of the crown down, and then outward to the edge. The straw hat worn at this time, was like a sailor-hat, and like a sailor it had tails. For Sundays and formal occasions there were the beaver and the bell-topper. All hats lasted till they fell to pieces; but the beaver and the bell-topper often came down from father to son—as women's silk dresses and shawls did, too.

Men fastened their hats on with a ribbon under the chin, with plaited bootlace, or with elastic. Some used a small brass chain, the rich used a silver one. The ways of wearing any of these fastenings varied before they finally went out, for they were worn under the chin, under the bottom lip, upon the chin, and (like the troopers) under the nose. All but the chains went behind the ears. Toward the last, when elastic came in, it was caught under the hair, which was long and reached well down over the collar at the back. For this style the hat was well tilted forward over the face, so that to see, when riding, a man had to fasten the hat-brim up in the front.

Hats of all ordinary kinds had ribbon-tails that fluttered and flickered in the wind. The rustle and ripple of these was a matter of

pride. "You could hear his tails *louder than anyone else's* when you were out riding!" young sparks said. So they cut tails with the utmost care in order that they would rustle. Square ends were no good, and the economical wife or mother who pointed the ends with a seam, and turned in corners, was no man's idol.

Yet when the tails went and the flat bow set close to the crown at the back came in, it *had* turned-in corners; and also a tiny button on each pointed end with three on the cross band. The first tight bows after the tails were very narrow, a quarter-inch rep ribbon being used. This had the edge corded over a linen thread. These hat-ribbons were valued and were always saved as an emergency cord for tying a break in harness or any other horse-trapping. There was no vegetable silk then. Silk was silk, and lasted. Even cotton stood a pull such as it does not today. After these narrow rep ribbons came smoother ones of cotton and silk, and with the bow at the side. Later years set the bow at the front, then again at the back, but the modern years have been faithful to the side.

Here I might interpolate a rather curious incident. Girls have two terrors always subconsciously rooted in their being, men only one. Both have the fear of death, but girls have the additional instinctive fear of sex. A man is free of this. So girls grow up with the idea that men and boys, because they have not this second burden of dread laid on them, are without fear. And it comes with a devastating shock in later years to find that men, though safer, are just as fearful as women. That is, in general. There are the exceptions.

As showing this, there was in the seventies a big stockman we knew, who, going into town, bought himself a brand new hat with tails, and such as he had never worn before. Coming home late through the then wholly untenanted bush (and ten o'clock was very late then, night being a time of ghosts) he suddenly heard on the air a mysterious sound, that belonged neither to heaven nor earth. It came and went, and was something he had never experienced before. For a while it went; then it came again, and even his horse responded to the sense of shock the man felt. Still there was nothing to be seen, and nothing to account for it. A third time it came; and, unable to stand his terror any longer, the rider put spurs to his horse and rode for his life to escape whatever it was. But no matter how fast he rode the pursuer was still at his ear.

"It was something like a hissing, and something like fingers rubbing together," he said when he came to our house and told us of his fright, adding that nothing would induce him to ride through that place again at night. "I would not do it for all the gold of Tay," he

"Hats of all kinds had ribbon-tails that fluttered and flickered in the wind."

said. My father laughed and said, "It looks like a case of Tam o' Shanter over again;" and added, "she nearly had you that time, Jack!"

It was the unaccustomed tails of his new hat that he had heard hissing on the wind as he rode; and though my father afterwards took him through the place to prove it, that man never again went that way alone if he could help it.

Of the hoods that women and girls wore there were as many fashions as there were in flounces. (But used we not to see that word spelled flownces when trousers were trowsers, when an axe was an ax, a basin a bason, and assuage was asswage as in the authorized version of the Bible? I think so.)

The old-fashioned sun-bonnet that Kate Greenaway revived in her drawings of children used to be made of calico or print. I never saw a silk one in my young years; but winter ones were made of red flannel; sometimes even of grey flannel. Jean (nearly like the denim of today, and properly called "jane") was made up for the heat of the harvest-field when women reaped and raked with their men. Women also used the same thing for the cow-yard.

The head part of the hood was double, corded, frilled, and puffed, if of light material, and finished with a curtain at the back of the neck. It was starched till it shone under the iron. Some astonishing people even had a goffering iron. Then the frills were indeed something to stare at.

"Try with three round sticks," said a woman to my mother. But the sticks did not work; so my heart ached on, for I never had a goffered frill. In doing up hoods some people simply doubled the puffs and ironed them flat. But these showed their plebeian origin. They had a crease along the top when pulled out. The cunning who could afford piping-cord (even candle-wick did, but you did not advertise your use of it) cut the cord long enough to allow of the hood being drawn out flat for ironing. Then what lovely puffs one had when the hood was drawn up again and the ends of the cords tied. No crease showed on these envy-producing puffs.

With the strong materials the head-piece would be heavily corded, the fronts cut scoop or spade shaped, and the neck portion buttoned on with white bone, pearl, or red or blue buttons. The front over the face, and the hem of the curtain, would be bound or piped in red or blue to match the buttons. Buttons were also used on print hoods, but I never saw them on hail-spot muslin.

When I was about fifteen there came in a fashion for mob-caps

for growing girls. Even women wore them. They were of lawn, cambric, or muslin, pleated or drawn in to a black velvet band made to fit the head, and with a black velvet bow at the front or the side. Velvet seemed the only black band used on them. If they had a white band and a frill, either of lace or of the material, they had coloured bows of ribbon, but not of velvet. Whether this fashion was universal or local I cannot say.

Just after this the pique hat took the place of the sun-bonnet for girls. It had either a circular, octagonal, or oval brim, with a crown sewn or buttoned down to it. It too had a black velvet band and bow, but it could also have ribbons and coloured pipings. Sometimes the crown and brim were buttonholed and laced together with a cord or ribbon. The last person I saw wearing one of these was Topsy Stephen. She was only eight or nine years old when I saw her first in one. She was a married woman with greying hair when I last saw her, and she still wore one—not because it was a revival but because she liked it.

Of course, all these were for daily wear. For high days and visiting there were poke bonnets and mushroom hats, with later on Dolly Vardens and the minute bonnet made of a flower or two and a quilling of lace, and which had long strings of quilled ribbon and lace ending in a flat bow resting away down on the well-raised bust of the wearer. Ruches of sarcenet trimmed the pokes and the mushroom hats. Case-bonnets were very "genteel" wear; with them went a deep, flowered, Spanish-lace veil through which you had to peer if you wanted to see. The poke had ostrich-plumes—plumes like a hearse, *not* just feathers!

"They had but their hands and feet, and their bent backs . . ."

As for the bonnets of poverty—poor poverty had no choice. It wore moleskin as a hood, cut from the legs of father's worn-out trousers, and tied with kangaroo-skin bootlace. Boys, having no faces to consider, went bare-headed quite a lot. Besides they were more wilful than girls. But in spite of that there were boys who were made to wear half-hoods, and rag hats, when straw could not be bought, and there was no grass suitable for sewing into shape for their unruly heads, such grass hats as Mrs Rickly's boys had.

Mrs Rickly, of Rickly's Farm, had twelve children, six boys and six girls, and she made hats of grass for all her boys. Wheat and stock being at their beginnings, straw had to be saved for cattle-chaff and house-thatch. Patiently each summer she went out and picked the stems of the fine Riverina grass, and (this being her only time of rest) in the early dusk of winter, or at daylight in summer, she sat and sewed, sewed, sewed them into hats.

In the early morning as she bent to her stitching, her Bible lay open beside her. She had just light enough to read, and her eye would catch a word and memory supply the rest as she worked. In the evening when the dusk did not allow of reading she verbally taught the family the texts and the lessons she herself had learned. There was no reading at night, as there were no candles. They had a few wooden matches—the old sulphur-headed matches—and when they had used the last of these they had to go out to the fire for a light when one was needed in the night, as was the case once when one of the children was ill. My father finding it out gave them a box of vestas—wax vestas as the new wax match was called.

In the night the sick child had waked up crying, and just as Mrs Rickly sat up to get out of bed she heard a snake in the room. There was no way of getting light except by the father shouting to the eldest boy, outside, to bring a fire-stick. The boy was a heavy sleeper and they called long before he woke.

This eldest was a lad of nineteen, followed by two girls. These three had worldly names—the old German names of Victorian splendour. But, after these were born, there had come a religious revival, and with it conversion to one of the strict Evangelical creeds. So all the younger children had scriptural names, together with the names allowed in the Puritan period—Faith, Mercy, Love.

Mercy and Love were twins, and during the Great War, asking a friend for news of the family, I was told that it was dispersed and that not even the corner post of the old home was left to mark its place.

When I first knew the Ricklys in the early seventies their house was

a house of stubs with a thatched roof. And as they could not afford much thatch the top was sodded over with earth, to weight the straw and to keep out the rain. The boys slept under bags, a tree their shelter; the father and mother had a possum-rug; the girls had patchwork. One quilt had been made by Mrs Rickly's great grandmother, one by her own mother. Both had been given her for her wedding. What beautiful everlasting sewing, and what slender starry patterns they both had! More than ancestral, they were racial. Now they are lost to us here, though revived in Europe and the Old Country as a result of a new world's search, first in ancient chateaux in France, and then across the Channel.

The girls, as soon as they could hold a needle, were set to work on new patchwork. But the new was not the old. We, in Australia, had not the patterns in prints that would make them. So the square, the triangle, and the diamond had to be used, with the colours set out as best one could arrange them. My mother, taking over a bag of patches, they were gone through; the woollens where big enough were set aside to make patch-hats and caps for the use of the little boys; the muslins were of no use for quilts, and the cambric and prints had the wrong colours. Still they would be used. The muslin trimmed the girls' hats; cambric pieced-up, made handkerchiefs; the print and other odd pieces were sewn together for petticoats. Being unseen their patterns did not matter.

The family so far had never gone to school. There was no school within six miles it is true, and the days of compulsory education had not begun. Nor had free education. We paid a shilling a week then. But in any case there was too much for the Rickly children to do to spare time for school. Almost with bare hands the farm had to be made. There was no money for more than the annual free-selection payments to make the property freehold. English, the family had the land-hunger of the land-starved English farm-labourer. They had seen that ownership gave standing and stability, and ownership they must have. Indeed they told us this themselves; and they were but one case among many. So everywhere families paid the price of land in premature ageing through overwork after birth, and through parental overwork before they were born.

Parents having survived by sheer tenacity of life in the homeland where they had meat only at Christmas (or at most on Sundays, and only otherwise as a charity when sick) throve and added strength to strength on the lean red meats of Australia—possums, kangaroo, and wallaby. As it was with others so it was with these of whom I write. Their meat was possum. No possum was allowed to be killed for sport

". . . as soon as she was milking . . ."

in any of the trees near the house.

When I best remember the Ricklys, they had a cow and a calf, an old horse, a pig, and a few fowls. Before they had the cow they had had a couple of goats. When they killed a spare billy kid they had a change from possum meat. They could not afford shot, so any game that could not be caught in a gamekeeper's rabbit-snare, knocked down with a stick like a possum, or caught in a covered crow-pit, was beyond their reach. It was said that they ate the crows they caught. With the cruelty of the times people called them "crow-eaters," and they were despised accordingly by those who lived in the altitudes of "killed meat."

When they got the cow—an old one given them by a neighbour kinder than most—as soon as she was milking the whole yield was set for butter to sell. The family ate none of the butter; and most of the

skim milk when skimmed went to nourish the growing pig. Only the girls, the mother, and the very little boys, had milk when they had tea, and it was only on Sundays that they all had tea. Perhaps indeed it was only when strangers came that they had milk; for I remember (and now with what grief) how little went into the girls' tea, and how much went into ours when we visited there.

For the first slender handful of wheat sowed the earth was turned up for it with a spade, a heavy home-made wooden spade, the man himself being his only working animal.

I think it was my father gave the horse that followed. I know my father made the first plough, which was of wood. The next year my grandfather, Hugh Beattie, buying a new one, gave his old share to go in place of the iron-bark or boree point my father had made. So the following year the family made money; it had a bag of wheat to sell. But it was the man and the woman who, as horses, had pulled the harrow over the seed when it had been sown. They had gone out in the dusk to do it; but a neighbour somewhere near had seen them and deridingly told it. Yet we all knew that they had to do it because the horse was old and must be spared; and we all knew they waited till late dusk hoping to be unobserved.

Still this harrowing was not wholly unusual. When land was everything, money hard to get (some full men's wages were only five shillings a week) and when horses had not multiplied, or had been killed off as brumbies by in-coming frontier settlement, in the first wheat plantings in Riverina, many harrows were hand-pulled, and sometimes, as in the present case, women had to do it.

Years later I saw the parallel, also in Riverina, when the wave of Victorian families came over and selected largely on the dry areas. These families, German-taught from South Australia, put in wheat by the paddockful instead of by the patch, talked dry farming as a cult; and made wealth where people had, till then, said wheat could never pay for putting in in quantity. But the women—in this case daughters, not mothers—drove machines, had a seat to sit on, wore veils, had gloves, and set umbrellas up to shelter them from the sun. The earlier women had none of these things. They had but their hands and feet, and their bent backs. When I think of them I see them as Millet saw them; when I write of them I write with tears.

Snuff-box and rosemary

Life had something very distinctive about it when even in Australia every man's county, shire, and even his town spoke in his dialect. But more than dialect spoke, for where language remained unchanged generation after generation, narrowness of material possession and restriction of use also uttered themselves. Consequently it was the day of the hoarded, so that if one's clothes wore out one was obliged to go without, or dress in skins. But other things than clothes were guarded. Women had to keep their marriage-lines; because if these were lost they became in a way automatically unmarried, and the children of another might inherit, their children being disinherited for the stranger. Of course, witnesses to a marriage counted. But it was only in Scotland that a woman's word and one witness was enough, or that a woman, called by a man's name as his wife, held that status in law, unless an earlier undivorced wife existed and was produced.

Besides marriage-lines, families hoarded their "parchments," that is, the family-tree and pedigree. There are several of these yet to be seen about Goulburn, Taralga, and the Crookwell, where remain the last of the one time wide settlement of the Scots there. And along with these things, snuff was hoarded—and with what care!

Snuff was an elegance. Almost as many women took snuff as men. Common people like seamen chewed; all classes in some degree smoked; but gentlefolk took snuff.

My grandmother, when she wanted to show her ladyhood to the less important who came to see her, took snuff as a part of her status, and only thought of it as a pick-me-up once in a while at other times. At that time my

grandfather took it regularly. Later he gave it up because his boys saw in it an excuse for the pipe. He thought smoking wicked, but not snuff-taking. Divines took snuff; that gave snuff leave to be manners, and manners were next door to morals. Talking of manners, it was customary for men to have two handkerchiefs (that is, when they did have them), a bandana for the snuff and a white one for appearances and polite usage when ladies were about. The snuff my grandmother took was specially prepared for ladies. She let me see her take it, but not her daughters. Also she used to get me to buy it at the chemist's for her. When, in later years, I told one of my aunts that her mother took snuff she nearly exploded:

"Never!" she exclaimed. "Never!" *But she did.*

Those who could afford it kept a Tonquin bean in the snuff-box. A Tonquin bean is a Tonka bean if you want to know.

"Let me see the bean," Miss Curiosity asked. I never saw anything less like what I knew as a bean. It had the appearance of a bit of dried bark. Indeed many did keep a bit of bark with the snuff, but it was cinnamon. Others used mace, caraway-seed, or a clove. In the physical hunger for change of savour on a diet that never varied from one year's end to another, a man would add anything he could get to increase the sensation-value of his hoarded treasure. So too would a woman, but in a lesser degree. Women were not supposed to have the needs of a man.

As in later years roast-beef and plum-pudding became the sign of Sunday, so I have known men long for Sunday because on that day they allowed themselves three pinches of snuff: one at morning, one at noon, and one at night. I spilt some once when a man was showing me his carefully eked-out last bit. He was a Welshman, and it spoke well for his early training that he did not kill me. He lay flat on the earthen floor of his hut and gently blew till he had the scattered grains in a little heap; then with a dried gum-leaf he lifted it—about as much as would lie on sixpence. I only realize now what I did to that man. Had it been any day but Sunday the floor would have been dusty; as it was Sunday it had been swept and mopped, and was sweet and clean.

Of that treasure the poor man had allowed me a tiny sniff. "Don't sneeze!" he cried in agony. "Don't sneeze, or you will lose it!" He said "loss it," his English being poor. I was only too anxious to "loss it," for that was in the year 1871, and I had no nose for snuff, no matter what sort of an inquiring mind I might have.

My father only took snuff as a courtesy to those who offered it to him. He preferred his pipe and thought snuff a dirty habit.

So did Mrs Jenkins, widow of that Captain Jenkins* who took up Buckingbong, Nangus, and—was it Gundagai?—and whose daughter-in-law had that gentle lunatic, Cresswell, examined for the identification marks of Sir Roger Tichborne. She, the daughter-in-law, told me Cresswell had every mark—seventeen in all, or something like that. This Mrs Jenkins (Mrs Johnny in her young years) died in 1932, aged a hundred and three years old. I mention it as it tells how near and yet how far off the partly forgotten things of memory may be.

That she thought snuff-taking a dirty habit did not prevent the elder Mrs Jenkins following the custom. She sat in her great mahogany horse-hair-covered easy chair, dressed in black silk, her collar of "real lace" (and, as she told my mother, she always saw that *it was* real), at her breast a huge cameo brooch, when it was not one with fringe, and with fringed ear-rings to match. With these she wore a long gold watch-chain round her neck, lace cap with lappets on her head, and her hair in loops at her ears like the young Queen Victoria. And, like the young Queen Victoria did then, she took snuff.

"It is a dirty habit," she told my mother. "But I always wash my handkerchiefs after it, because I could not ask another woman to do it."

I liked Mrs Jenkins, she always gave me a biscuit as if I were grown up; but I did not like the captain. The captain had a worse temper, I think, than even Carlo Mariana, that black-a-visaged, witty-tongued, generous old Garibaldian at Young, and of whom, with his brother Camilla, not merely a book but a whole shelf could be written. They too took snuff. Now the grandchildren and the great-grandchildren of all of these stand where they once stood; and where they pioneered a wild and savage land there are towns. Even their old snuff-boxes are gone. As for the Scottish mull, lidded, and made from the small end of a horn, I doubt if anyone reading this has even seen one, let alone owned one. Still we do keep the past with us, and now and then use the saying, "Up to snuff." So are words shown to be more enduring than things, and in their expression the ghosts of the snuff-taking still walk, still tap their mulls and snuff-boxes.

But besides snuff, and "nailrod" for smoking and chewing, there was opium. Quite a good deal was used in a diffused way. It came in as a result of the opium war against China under Gordon. I have not the figures, but it will be remembered that the great owning and

*See note at end of chapter.

exporting London interests, wanting a market for their Indian product, forced opium on China. As it was at the same time much used in England, English people brought the custom here. The Chinese who came to Australia became the usual source of supply, for China, having been forced to take more than she wanted, was glad of Australia as an outlet. Among our early but not earliest self-governing Acts, here in Australia, were those regulating the importation of opium and the restriction of its distribution. But in the seventies, and even later, it was still carried by hawkers, white and Chinese. As travel was difficult and journeys long, they came round about once in three months. Money being scarce, only small quantities could be bought; so, for the poorer settlers and travellers, supplies had to be used with care.

Addicts, however, among decent people were rare. But once a poor man became an addict he would go into the Chinese quarter in the nearest town. These quarters, it will be remembered, were in every town till Henry Parkes, I think, legislated for their abolition, partly by law, partly by instructions to town councils and the police. The well-to-do people, of course, still got their opium, using it at home, as similar people nowadays get their cocaine. The fact that every town had its Chinese quarter, no matter how far out or small the town, shows how widely spread the opium habit was, as there were not enough working Chinese in them even to pay the rents, let alone live and buy opium.

But it was not only those who visited these evil places who were addicts. I remember addicts among the station owners. Apart from these, the ordinary person took opium as a sedative, pretty much as we take aspirin nowadays. Old nurses always had a supply of it, which they themselves took regularly, and gave, after childbirth, to make the patient sleep. I well remember many who retired at a certain hour every day to have their sedative pipe.

Others who were addicted to it in a mild way were shepherds. More than once, as a small child, I have rolled it for a sick shepherd. Once it was for a man in his watch-box beside the sheep-fold, the sheep wanting water, and he too ill to get out and bring them back if let out to go to water. He said he was nearly mad with anxiety as they could not be let out because the dingoes would have got to them if loose and unwatched, and if they stayed in longer they would have died of thirst. I think his trouble was a haemorrhage. Another time, when I was about six, as a special favour I was allowed "a draw." I remember the horrible taste to this day—and that is over sixty years ago. It is like the memory of the mixed smell of the Chinese quarters—a compound of dead cats, fowl-houses in the backyards, unwashed bodies, and opium. The smell of the opium was the bed in which all the other odours rested. There by day, throughout Australia, one saw the most appalling human wrecks, and there after dark went the flower of the country... Let us change the subject.

It is Easter. I am a child again in the big old kitchen at Brooklyn. My grandmother sits in her rocking-chair at the side of the deep-spaced fire-place; behind her is the cavern in the wall that is the brick baking-oven. There a whole sheep could be roasted, three sucking-pigs, and half a barrow load of potatoes and pumpkins; while wild fowl, ducks, and chickens disappeared into its vastness, and were lost in the far corners at the back where the heat was less. The bread that was baked in it made a mountain, and the pies, cakes, and buns were hills. Its use was for harvest, Easter, and Christmas: that is, in the first and middle years; after that it was a cool place for butter. Later on it was pulled down and the hole in the wall through which the spaddle slid the loaves for the baking, and a rake drew them out when done, was bricked up. Whitewash had covered the front for half a lifetime; a white-lead paint in the after years. I thought of it today when I bought a squab for baking, and wished I had a vine-leaf to cover its breast.

Flavours are bought in books and bottles nowadays; then, they grew in the family garden, and were collected in the family mind. And the long absent family mind, gathered for the yearly reunions, always brought home new ideas and tried them out along with the old. Once when something had to be cooked in a special way, I was sent out with a hatchet (and it was a hatchet, not a tomahawk) to get splinters of pine to flavour it, to see if it would be the same as juniper. Like little spears the splinters were thrust here and there into the flesh. But when the meat was cut the flavour was not found. The years had devoured it; the miles between had eaten it; the wood of a new land had not discovered it. Disappointment sat on every face, even on mine, too young to know all about it, but not too young to dream and follow the lure of expectation.

Besides the use of vine-leaves, in baking poultry and other meats, vine-leaves were sometimes tied round cabbages, that were boiled with peppercorns in vinegar and water, along with lard or bacon bones. Sometimes it was the spathes or swaddling-leaves of young corn-cobs were used. I have known a cry for a leaf of the sweet brier that we never had at Brooklyn lest it become a pest (as indeed by law it was afterwards proclaimed); and I have been sent post-haste up to

"... all grew in the garden and gave their flavourings for the kitchen ..."

the orchards for a cherry-leaf, a fig-leaf, or the leaf of some special peach-tree. Mint, parsley, cloves, sweet-basil, marjoram, common and lemon-scented thyme, shallots, garlic, rosemary, all grew in the garden and all gave their flavourings for the kitchen.

And the house as well as the kitchen had its dowry. For the bedrooms there was the lemon-scented tree verbena, which we called "verbenya" as the Spaniards did; and there was lavender, with balm for pomades for skin and hair, and elderberry for sunburn. Up by the barns and cow-yards there were nettles for the blood, horehound for coughs and colds, and dock for poultices. But dock was used like horehound and nettles, for beer; sometimes it was wrapped round tough meat with the idea of making it tender. In the thick, unfelled bush above the horse-and-cattle yards were native hop, "sarsparilla," the bottle-brush flower of the wild honeysuckle, together with geebungs, wild cherry, eucalyptus, wattle, kurrajong, and pine. The wild hop made yeast; the "sarsparilla" made naughty little boys good by clearing their "over-crowded" blood; the bottle-brush soaked in soft water yielded syrup for sore throats and colds; the wattle-bark the aborigines had taught us to make into a tan lotion for unbroken burns and scalds; the eucalyptus (also native teaching) made vapour in pits, or in bed, for chills and pains; the pine, too, was inhaled, and sometimes went as a flavouring into the home-made treacle beer. The caution about pine was that you had to know how little of it to use, or you spoiled your brew.

Into the big kitchen with its cedar tables black with age, all these came; and what was not simmered in the great cauldron, or brewed in a three-legged pot, went into the brick oven; there to soak, there to steep, or there to slowly dry.

The secrets of nearly a century of gathering went out with that fire-place—that oven.

Note: Captain Jenkins sold his commission soon after it was bought for him and took up medicine. Consequently he is better known to history as Dr Jenkins.

The old proud women

When the Wagga Wagga Gold Cup was a hundred guineas, and the cash prize that went with it another thousand—when Melbourne saw Flemington fast coming on to the level of a suburban racecourse because of what the Wagga Wagga Racing Club—no, wasn't it then the Wagga Wagga Jockey Club?—was doing, the Race Ball was the great social feature of the year. So much was this so, that it was then the circus came, the three-card men flocked in, and the joy-makers of every kind for men, women, and children camped, lodged, and slept out all over and all round the town. Among these, hawkers were as numerous as other groups. Just as parliamentarians today find business a reason for Melbourne or Sydney at Cup time, so hawkers for the same reason flocked to Wagga Wagga. From Hay and Ivanhoe, from Booligal and Bourke, from Young and Forbes and Parkes, to say nothing of Deniliquin, Cootamundra, and Albury (which for the period of the races were no more than suburbs of the old cattle town) people came in droves.

But the division of the classes was as marked as the division between night and day. So definite was this division, that in order to keep the grandees and the commonage apart at the ball, a chalk-line was drawn across the floor beyond which "the lower classes" might not go. This had to be because not everyone then had evening-dress—indeed very few men had; and without the line, especially when drink began to tell, how *could* you know who was who? No thought of trespass came to anybody's mind, till, with the multiplication of selectors, business increased the trade population, and enabled people in general to buy tickets. This meant a packed floor at one end of the hall, where two-thirds of the population milled in one-third of the total space, while a comparatively small number danced delicately in the comfort of the other two-thirds. I might say here that when the races first started the ball was practically a squatters' private dance, where home-made frocks, and home-made cake, were chief features. It was the phenomenal rise to importance of the Jockey Club that changed this and brought about a charge first for members and their friends only; then a general issue of tickets which admitted the public, but, as said, under restriction.

A second cause of disaffection came later when, after the "silver tails" (which they were so bitterly and derisively called by the *hoi polloi*) had gone into supper at twelve, a greatly daring and perspiring couple from the so-called lower orders stepped over the chalk-line, and, in the eyes of every longing person below that line, danced a whole waltz. This couple dilated on the difference between the planed and waxed floor at the top end and that thought good enough for the secondary ticket-holders. For them no nail heads were driven down, no wax expended, no loose boards tightened, no cracks closed up with battening!

The next year, to prevent such a profane thing happening again, a rope was stretched across between parties. But the rope only lasted two years; it was cut, and the horrifying spectacle was witnessed of ordinary trades people dancing right in among the squatters, and their wives and daughters. That was a thing not to be borne, and the Race Ball as a special social function declined to nothing. The Masons were invoked, and after that it was at the Masonic Ball that the debutantes came out.

But before this there had been another and more offending cause of bitterness between the two parties. For some time after the introduction of tickets, the station-families still provided the supper, and they did it generously for everyone. But a day, or rather, a night came when the first sitting of supper people ate up all the turkeys, all the jellies, all the special cakes, all the fruit, and all the best lollies.

"... danced a whole waltz."

There was nothing left but corned beef, bread, and the drumsticks of hacked-about, breastless skeletons of poultry and wild fowl. After that a caterer was demanded by the body of ticket-holders, and a requisition set forth that everybody should be served alike.

Anyone who knows the Riverina and the heat of its half-the-year summer will realize at what a cost of trouble the original cooking for the ball was done, and the food kept sweet and firm. Jellies had to be made by main force, that is, with as much isinglass and as little water as possible. There was no ice to be had, and no ice-chests then! The sweets, brought twenty or thirty miles by buggy, would be wrapped in wet cloths and carried in the moulds in which they were made. Then they were ranged along the walls of the supper-room, down on the floor, to keep as cool as possible; and even then they fell. But one year my father brought out coarse salt and ammonia for Mrs John Stinson, and that year her jellies were a triumph. They stood when everyone else's ran. It was talked about for the rest of the year.

But there was never a greater supper prepared, no matter where, than that made by Mrs Dallas when the banks foreclosed and she had to leave the home to which she had come as a bride. "I thought I would never have to leave it," she had said. But she left it with a high head, and the affection and admiration of everyone who knew her.

This supper wasn't a supper; it was a three days' feast to which the stations for fifty miles round came. Twenty guns went out duck, plover, and wild turkey shooting; in addition, Mrs Dallas had every killing-fowl on the place prepared for the pot or the oven. Potatoes were dug, cabbages cut, peas and beans shelled; and a host of friendly women made pies and cakes, puddings and jellies. They even made sweets, the then limit of skill and art being plain and almond toffee. The smell of baked meats, the lilt of fiddles, the singing of old songs, the toasting of pretty women, the healths of men, went on for three full days and nights with a fullness that made a record even in that day of hospitable entertaining.

On the fourth morning when the last whole bird was eaten and the remains of the feast distributed to poorer neighbours living round, when only what the law might righteously demand was left in house or garden, then twenty-six buggies and a host of riders, "men and side-saddles," massed at the front door and escorted this well-loved woman with her husband and children from the home that had been theirs, almost as princes, to the place where they were to live on a manager's salary. It was said of Mrs Dallas in the years that followed that no one ever heard her refer to their changed position, or ever complain. Gallantly she had reigned as a queen in the days of her wealth, gallantly she bore herself when wealth went.

My grief was that my brother, not I, had been taken. But our wagonette was packed to the wheels with grown people and my brother rode a pony.

"Couldn't I ride?" I begged.

"No. You cannot," was the reply. "But if you promise to be a good girl and not to cry, we will bring you home some cake and blanc-mange, the wing of a turkey, and the leg of a duck."

When the family came home, my father had the buggy-whip in his left hand; he could not use his bow arm, he had fiddled for so many dances. And my share of the wing of a turkey and the leg of a duck and some cake and blanc-mange were two sticky, black lollies thick with fuzz in my brother's pocket.

I wasn't Mrs Dallas. I went round to the back of the house and I cried, and I cried.

When baby had a red morocco trunk

The furniture of the period with which these recollections deal was very mixed when there was anything that could be called furniture. Along with split-slab stools and bark-topped tables, one would find the age-old heirloom, the inlaid lacquer table, the writing-desk and the chest of drawers that had come by inheritance, or had been given to a child or a faithful servant as a wedding present. And alongside the tin plate and horn-handled fork on the slab table one would see a silver castor, or a beautiful old cut-glass salt-cellar. Indeed, silver was actually less rare then than now. There were more silversmiths in proportion to the population; there was more care taken of possessions as they were harder to replace, being usually works of art handed down from parent to child; while the silver-mines of the new lands of America had but lately poured out their wealth into a world whose largest total urban population was then not much more than that of a principality of today.

But it is not of silver castors, or ormolu and polished lacquer I would write, but of the little red morocco trunk—the trunk that kept the baby's clothes. Baby's trunk! And there always was a baby. The little trunk never had to change its name, for when one infant began to be old enough to be called by a distinguishing appellation, there was another looking up from the properly made cradle, or from the gin-case that so much oftener did duty for one. When that happened there was another set of little garments in the red morocco trunk.

Rich people had two trunks, a red one for boys and a blue one for girls. We had only a red one; though I do remember that when there were four times a baby between me and the little red morocco trunk, either my Aunt Eliza Pendleton or someone else gave me a blue one. But the blue had not the richness of the red, and I never really loved it. I never sat and looked at it feeling my child's heart warmed and fed with a sense of beauty. There was something in the red of old morocco, in its scent and in its feel, that the children of today can never know. The synthetically stalled hide, the synthetic dyes, the chemical tanning, and the factory can never give what a natural grass in feeding, a home-made dye, a hand-cured and hand-dressed leather can give.

"The furniture of the period . . ."

In any case, the little red morocco trunk with its pattern in shining copper nails has gone, and a tin one has taken its place. No more do we sit on its soft padded, fancifully stitched top, and pull at the rich fringe of twisted wool or real silk that finished off its edges. It is gone with its hand-made brass lock; and, as I have said, a tin one has taken its place.

Its going reminds me that it was immediately followed by the horse-hair trunk. This came in with horse-hair furniture, when mahogany took the place of the oak that had come out in sail. Mahogany showed the increase in shipping, and the beginning of an era of great importation; for it came overseas to the home countries, but the oak had grown in the home forests.

One of my aunts has a hand-made oaken chair coming down through the family for three hundred years. It was old when John Wesley preached. When he used to visit our people in Ireland he loved to sit in it; and, because he liked it above all others, to this day it is called John Wesley's chair. And the same with the bed he used to sleep in. But that has been left with other relatives in Ireland. It, too, was oak and hand-made. But the chair—whenever the minister came to my Uncle Alfred Beattie's house in Kogarah, he sat in John Wesley's chair because it was an honour, and because he was of the faith of Wesley—John Wesley, fore-runner and equal of William Booth. When John Wesley's hymn-book and Booth's drum get together in heaven there will be some wonderful times in that place!

The horse-hair trunk that supplanted the red morocco one, also was beautiful in its way; for it, too, was padded and stitched; it, too, was patterned in brass nails. And they really were brass, not just iron glazed over. They were the real thing, with pure tin in them, soft and velvety to the touch. Silver is fine, gold is splendid, but I know of no metal that has the lovely feeling of tin—I mean tin, not tinned iron. It comes next to the human skin, and to the old-fashioned yolk-of-egg-cured kid glove that fitted so badly, and yet in which the hand always felt so truly a hand to the fingers that touched it.

On hot days, as a child, I used to put my head down on the little red trunk, that had once been mine, to smell the scented leather. The horse-hair trunk gave no such delights. One loved the clean, sweaty smell of a horse; even to the child the smell gave a background of sensations, a field of recollection, or a tale of knights and history. But the horse-hair trunk had no smell. It was rootless. It had no background. It was a receptacle only, not a fellow traveller comforting and companionable on life's journey. Of it, no one ever said of something wanted: "Go and see if it is in Baby's trunk!" That is, never so far as I knew.

Sometimes I hear in memory a child ask for something to be handed—and how children like to hand!—"Where is it, mamma? In Baby's trunk?"

"No. In the horse-hair one."

"Not in Baby's?"

"*No*. Didn't I tell you it is in the horse-hair trunk?"

And such was the effect of horse-hair that you were quite often slapped if you were not smart off the mark on your errand!

Again let recollection wake, and send it travelling old rooms so that it may go on and tell how there were enough old cedar bedsteads burned in Australia fifty years ago to have half stocked the world, let alone Sydney and Melbourne. Now we go to Vaucluse House and pay to see them. My grandmother's best bed (we did not say bedsteads unless buying in a shop) had a top as big as a house, and it was nearly as wide. It was centuries old, and was made when sheets were hand-spun and hand-woven (Did not Queen Elizabeth have only one sheet to her bed? And also but one bath a year, don't forget!) and when sheep were so few that furs or human bodies, in cold climates, made up for our not-yet-come-to-be Australian fullness of blankets. Father and mother and the baby usually slept at the top of these great bedsteads, and the smaller children kept father's feet warm at the foot.

These monumental sleeping places were reached by bed-steps mounting up to them. No one could get into them except by a running jump, otherwise; and two-bottle and four-bottle men were only athletes through the legs of horses. They rode to hounds, but they could not pull their boots off without a boot-jack or a man, so they had to have the steps to get into bed. The steps came with the beds to athletic, though new, Australia.

The canopied top in our bedstead was extraordinarily high, but not *proportionately* high, mark you, or the width of the bed would have had to be double what it was. Because of the ancient cold of the homeland, you slept curtained in, undressed covered in, and in the morning you stood on the bed to partly dress before you descended the steps. When I slept with my grandmother as a little thing, I had always to turn over to the wall while first grandfather, and then grandmother partly dressed before descending the "stairs" to the floor. Then when it was time for me to get up I was always dressed, in part, inside the curtains so that I would not "get a chill" by being taken too suddenly into the open air of outside the curtains—and I was flannel or stout calico night-gowned, from the band buttoned tight round my neck, to my wrists and my heels!

Looking back from conditions at our beaches today, it seems funny to think that I would probably have died of consumption if I had been dressed too suddenly outside the bed curtains. Bone-pointing is not confined to coloured skins. Death comes, by psychological aid, to all peoples and in all times—even to all beds!

This great "best bed" went (whether sold or burned I do not remember) because it was too big for the rooms at Brooklyn when that became my people's home. The great fluted columns, the heavy scroll and leaf carving, the brass rims and fittings, the legs like billiard-table legs, the rich colouring, the brilliant polish all went, and the "little stairs" with them. Then the second-best bed, which had been " 'the girls' bed," became the best. It, too, was pillared and canopied cedar; it too, was curtained and entered reverentially by a step ladder; but it had two steps instead of three, and was lighter and smaller.

A day came when the legs were shortened so that it could be got into without mounting, another day came when the pillars at the foot were cut down and a half-tester canopy of iron made for the two tall posts left at the head. Then one day, before I went to South America to join the New Australia colony there, my mother gave me for a rolling-pin the round scrolled piece that had decorated the top of the carved head-board. The old bedstead had gone to the rubbish heap.

My grandmother's bedstead from then on was iron and brass and enamel. Perhaps some day collectors will be looking even for these.

One of the reasons for the change from wood to iron was that the house-vermin left behind in the Old Country and unknown altogether in Australia till brought here, increased horribly with immigration. The weekly bed-scalding had to become the rule of good housekeeping. It was absent in bad. The result was, that the first thing after a train journey, a night in an unknown hotel or a visit to Sydney, when you got home you went through your clothes and your baggage. If you had an outhouse that did not matter, you made your inspection there, if not, you took a candle out into the backyard before you went to bed, and did it that way. Yet in spite of the country woman's care, vermin crept into the cleanest housekeeper's bed, and incessant care could not prevent it. When I first came to Sydney there were bugs in every house, and in old places they were in the walls and the floors. When the city ordinance came that they were to be cleaned out, there were articles in the daily papers telling how, at the excoriating fluids ordered, the vermin ran out of floors and walls, and even from furniture, in streams. London had little on Sydney in this way at that time, and Buenos Aires, New York, and Montreal, had no more.

So from the United States of America we got the iron bedstead—"the American bed," as it was called—and the lovely old cedar ones went to the "knacker." It was sad, but at the time it was necessary.

But life was not all; besides hoods and bonnets and bedsteads there were the coffins that life needed for the dead, because people died then as now. Where a wooden one was impossible, a sheet of bark or a possum-rug was used. Even when settlement began to gather there were always trees left standing unstripped of the bark, and near enough the steading to be used if the need arose.

"I will take the bark off that tree," said my father to my mother once, and I did not know why he shaped the sheet so carefully when he had measured off and cut it down. I did not know till long afterwards that it was for a neighbour's child.

Once, I remember, he was very indignant because a family, in burying some father or grandfather, had allowed the coffin to be screwed or nailed instead of being morticed and pegged. Rust would eat the metal, the boards would fall apart at the joints, and the bones lie at last without protection.

"What respect was there in that?" asked the man of a time when

the dead still lived. Held that every grain of dust that had been part of the body would count at the resurrection, how that dust would lie most certainly mattered. People still believed in the Might of the Lord, even though they also made a point of keeping their powder dry; so they saw to their coffins when they could.

There was no greater slur amongst well-brought-up people than want of respect for the dead. In anything like that, shame inhabited. You might thrash a child or a woman to death, but you conformed to every tenderness for the dead body. The husband who hated you had honour in burial; the wife you killed by cruelty and neglect had a good funeral; the child whose life was one continued fear of reproach and a blow, had a neighbour-woman sent for to sit up all night with the little body as it straightened. And there she would sew the shroud as she sat.

Without thimbles, or with but one between them, the mother—the sister if the mother were dead—and the neighbour-woman would sew. One stitch at a time, top-sewing, felling, hemming, ruffling. And so often the ruffles were of unbleached calico. My mother, who had a genius for the needle, used to manage a partial bias-cut when she had to help a neighbour, so that the frills would not be so solid and heavy, but would have a ripple in them. A full bias could seldom be allowed, it would cut into too much stuff.

When the grave was dug, if it were for woman or child, it would be lined with grass, bushes, or ferns if possible. Often the ferns were just bracken, but it meant a kindliness in the grave. There was a time when we were sent a mile, just three young children, to a chock-and-log fence on a rocky hillside to gather the few small ferns that the fence had kept the stock from eating. It was either for a woman who died in childbirth or for a baby too early dead, and the bunch was no bigger than a breast-knot of violets today. But there were so few ferns in Riverina just then that it meant an extra tenderness for the dead, and at a time when so many died with no one at hand to help, or to wait for the end and then dig the grave.

When capes were gentlemen's wear

When capes were gentlemen's wear most girls and women wore black-and-white shepherd's plaid, or Rob-Roy woollen frocks, when they did not wear alpaca, merino, cashmere, wincey or homespun, with grenadine or tarlatan for balls and parties. The plaid materials were strapped with velvet; sometimes the strapping was of silk or woollen braid. In any case the trimming was pointed or mitred at the top, and, if money allowed, the point of the mitre had either a tiny pearl or a bright brass anchor-button. The red plaid was strapped, too, but because red was a dark colour the effect was not as good as in the case of the black and white check. To remedy this a piece of the material itself was cut on the bias and more buttons applied—three in a triangle at the top and one at the bottom, or one at the top and two at the bottom. Sometimes, when very small buttons were used, they were set in groups up the sides of the strapping, three touching, lapping or triangulated, with a space; then three more in the same manner of grouping.

Occasionally, luxury added a tiny black silk tassel, sewn under the button at the top of the strap, and another tassel half-way down. This went with the silk tassels on the prunella or lasting boots—as indeed did the pearl buttons. But no dress ever had such tiny buttons as the boots had! Once in a while (I may as well say this here) lasting boots, being of mohair, were white or cream. Besides cream lasting, there were cream cashmere boots. Little girls wore these as well as grown-up women. The cashmere, like the prunella, were truly Queen Victorian; but prunella was the most Victorian of all.

I once had a pair of purple prunella boots three sizes too large for me; and how I hated the flapping things. They were fours and I took small ones. But I had to wear them. "They were a present!" and for children there was no escape from a present, no matter what an affliction it might be.

It was in these years, too, that "deep mourning" was worn for two years by a widow. Indeed, if she were not "a light woman," black was her lot till the end of her days. Only a man could release her from black; she could wear colours if she remarried. But if she re-married before three (or was it five?) years had passed, she was damned. She must surely have been "carrying on" before her husband's death!

Of course, if she were a very poor woman with a large family she could do as she liked. She did not even have to get married—at least, not till the second family was coming to be as large as the first. And I will say this for the times: once she was married she was as respectable as anyone else. The legal right to "his name" blotted out his sin and hers. After all, woman only existed in and through man, socially and legally. It was the day of the man. The woman's day had not dawned. The child's day had not been thought of. The nerves of the man vented themselves on woman and child; and the child suffered the beatings of both parents.

To come to later times. When the Carringtons and the Jerseys reigned at Sydney Government House we wore blouses and skirts. The blouse, called *bloose* if you were anybody at all, went inside the skirt and came well down over the hips. Indeed it came half-way to the knees at times. Over the skirt-band we wore a belt. About this time shirt-blouses came in. First they were cut plain with a shirt-sleeve and cuff, and with a box-pleat, real or simulated, down the front; the buttonholes were in the centre of the pleat so that buttons looked neither to the right nor the left.

After a time we stiffly starched not only the cuffs and collars but the fronts of the blouses as well; the very daring wore "made fronts" just like a man's white shirt. But so strict were still the conventions as to what a woman might wear, that, when I once inadvertently made one of my "waists" to button from left to right instead of from right to left as a woman's should, it was looked upon as a reprehensible oddity, if not actually a misdemeanour. It was almost an indication that one would be so altogether an outrager as to go without stays. To go without stays was to be outside the pale altogether. They were "stays" then, not "corsets." It was only the Americans who said corsets; and it just showed how silly they were!

I have often wondered why we wore those long-skirted blouses. Because at that time we wore flannel next the skin, a long chemise, stays, a calico or woollen slip-bodice, a small flannel petticoat, and if not a quilted black one then a plain coloured, and above all these a white one heavily flounced. All had gores to widen them. Skirts ranged from two plain widths with four gores, to seven and fourteen gores and no plain widths. Besides the skirted things we wore a double allowance of others; and even here whatever could be frilled was frilled. No wonder spinning and weaving made England rich!

As everyone rode, the riding-habits women wore must not be

forgotten. They were of holland for summer, and cloth for all weathers. The earliest I knew were very wide and spread fan-like on the side of the horse. With these the crinoline could be worn, provided one knew how to fix it. To do it, the right side of the steels were gathered up in the hand and tied up close to the waist, the rest falling as a loop close over the pommel-knee, and slack over the stirrup-leg. It was not elegant; but the rider was spared the humiliation of asking her escort to carry it, or of taking it herself as an uncovered bundle shaped like a figure eight on the off-side of the saddle. In this case it had to be tied in the middle (which made the eight) or it would flop and frighten the horse.

When the crinoline diminished and at last disappeared, the full-skirted habit went with it, and a long thing like a bolster-case with a gusset for the pommel came in. Girls still had no legs, so the hem was weighted with shot or lead to keep it from flapping as one trotted, and from riding up as one galloped. From the off-side, the more of it seen under the horse's belly the more elegant. Later on, to ensure a long drop for this, the outer side of the habit was cut with more length than the saddle side, a loop inside on the seam holding it to the foot of the rider. For walking, there was a hook at the waist and another loop half-way down the skirt to catch it up with—but not too high, lest more than the ankle show.

When a day came that women were told by doctors that they would be wise to ride astride, the commotion caused, the horror and arguments that ensued, shook the heavens. That a girl should ride in "britches" and puttees, as now, was a thing no earthly mind dreamed of. The Lady Godiva herself would have been shamed at the thought of it. So divided skirts were used, with a sort of apron effect back and front. When you were in the saddle you had to look skirted no matter from what angle you were seen. This, of course, was in the latest eighties and all the nineties.

A woman who showed her ankle any higher than the ankle-bone was a bad mounter, and a man who had to put her on her horse always "kept custody" of his eyes; that is he looked away lest he should see her leg. To see a woman's leg in such case was as much an offence against a man's honour as against a woman's modesty. Still that did not prevent the unmarried birth-rate being as high or higher than today. It was all merely a matter of taboos. But with what delicacy a man put out his hand for a lady's foot, and with what an honouring air he lifted her to the saddle! It is nice in these casual but much more honest days to remember it.

While on the subject of riding, it is also to be recorded that as a sign of personal honouring a young man held the stirrup for an elder man, both in mounting and dismounting. I have often heard my father call one of the growing boys, our own or others, to come and hold the stirrup for some elder man. It was done oftener in mounting than in dismounting, as a horse was less reisty for the latter, being glad of a rest. An old man's dignity had to be preserved, and preserved for him by the young. Young men could dismount and leave the stirrup at the perpendicular. "His stirrup never moved after his foot left it," would be said of a good rider. But older men, heavy in the joints from years of early toil, had not the spring of youth. Many a man was laughed at (behind his back) because, as he landed on his other foot, his stirrup foot shot out towards the horse's neck, and he had to drag it back and literally extricate himself from the iron before he stood fully dismounted. Such a one was as much laughed at as those who (boys or men) had to go to a stump to get on a horse.

Young people rode a lot, for there was no gas-box then, and "rubbing stirrups" was its own indication.

"I saw Joe Barnes rubbin' stirrups with Lily Sanderson," said Joe's aunt, or Lily's uncle. Then after a while, when they fell out, it was remarked:

"Them two's stopped rubbin' stirrups."

In the end Joe married a Miss Furner.

To return to our *moutons*, which is dress; at this time, apart from the beautifully made French boots, only the old English shape was used in the country. This was alike for men and women, being broad-soled and with square toes, the material being lighter for women than for men, though a man's riding-boots were almost as light as a woman's. For hard wear there was a bar across the toe. For women and children this was of copper; for men it was of iron or steel. When boots came in from the United States they were either Spanish in shape or French. These were more expensive than Australian-made or English, whether the latter were imported or cut here on old English lasts. The wood in these old lasts was beautiful. Possibly most that I saw were hand-made; they were certainly hand-finished. I have seen some that had belonged to the grandfathers of the men who were then using them. They had come from an England that was largely barefoot, to an Australia that was still quite unashamedly barefoot. That is apart from the very well-to-do people. Indeed, squatters' children often went barefoot in the house. Boots were heavy and cost money. Stockings being an item (though they lasted longer, they were fewer than now), mothers found bare feet for the children an advantage as it saved time, backache, and material in darning.

As to the Spanish last, the boot made on it modified the English square toe into a narrow oblong, both sides of the tread being alike. This is the shape that was still ordinarily used in Spanish-America when we were there, and which is sometimes shown here, in a modified right and left by our best and most expensive makers. Heels to these might be fairly high or low.

The French boot, copied or imported, had what was then considered a tall heel. For women it was much like the Cuban heel of today, but for men it was much higher. When they could afford expensive light boots men wore peg-shaped heels. The higher and narrower the heel "the more genteel." The French boots had the shaped sole, and were not interchangeable as were the Spanish or the wide English. The advantage of the last two, in a day when boots were boots, was that as heel and toe wore they could be crossed over, foot to foot, and used equally on both sides, there being no need to consider rights and lefts.

When in course of time, and increase of hides as cattle multiplied and the neater shape with marked rights and lefts took possession, men cursed them, for in the haste of a daylight rising the wrong boot went on the wrong foot.

"I was in misery all day!" was a common expression from men who had been in a hurry to catch the coach, get a passing lift, or ride post-haste thirty miles to be in time for the midday cattle or sheep sale at the yards—then always in the middle of the town.

"I had to wait till the sale was over before I could put my boots on my right feet!" such a one would say, as convention forbade the change of any form of raiment in the presence of others. Sometimes the sufferer might be a juror, as my father was once in like circumstances. Under the eye of the judge, under the unwonted stress of being a juror and of listening, not to ordinary talk but to evidence, a man did not dare to think of his feet. Miseries had to be borne till the day ended.

Consequently it became the duty of wife or daughter to put the boots under the bed at night, and in the right position to be ready for father in the morning. Sons had to look after their own. Women were not thought of. Good mothers did teach the children, and, as community beds were the household rule, there was always a row of little boots in pairs under the front of the children's big bed.

When the round toe displaced the square for ordinary wear, the foot-police still had to wear the old shape with the great broad square toes;

"The troopers, as they are still, were the aristocrats and the dandies . . ."

so that, in the mud or dust of the unmade streets and wheel-rutted roads, you always knew where "the Peeler" was going, where he had been, or where he might be expected. A North Wagga Wagga "Peeler," out after sly grog sellers, once put on someone else's boots and caught the whole lot. Even respectable fathers reprobated him. They said it was a shabby trick. A commentary which, upon thought, shows how really honest people were!

Actually it was contended that the arrests were illegal as the constable had not on his policeman's boots. People said he was not in his uniform, and was then only partly a policeman. The plea was not as strange as might at first appear, because in a later period, an arrest by a policeman who had only one glove on was judged as illegal, and the man could not be held. In that case, whether Mr Crummy in South Wagga Wagga, or Mr Comans in North, it was pleaded that need of haste in arresting the man was a reason for proceeding with only one glove on, and that it was with the gloved hand he had taken the offender. The plea was of no use, the unfortunate policeman (I remember now it was Mr Crummy—and to think that Crummy is a variation of Cromwell!) was censured for not being in full rig.

This sort of thing happening in more places than Wagga Wagga, the Department or the Government made it an instruction that one glove on, or both gloves held in the hand would be enough, the gloves being needed as the sign of the presence of the king His Majesty.

But if you had seen the great white cotton bags miscalled gloves—things you could see a mile off—you would have pitied the police. These gloves had to be big so that they took no time to put on. In a scuffle they had to be watched or they would come off; then the arrested party would point to the bare hand, and, of course, he never had any trouble in finding a witness to agree with him. Also as most of the arrests were of farmers on sale day, teamsters, or other neighbours out on the loose in language or behaviour, it was not so hard for "the Bench" to have regard for an offender who was also a good churchman all the rest of the week—even if the church was a barn when there was one empty, or a kitchen when the barn was full. So the police got it both ways.

I wish I had one half the stories of those days that my father had, for he had the histories of the whole period, tales reaching from Goulburn to Hay. He had the faculty of catching a point, and he had the historical sense in a greater degree than any of his children have. I remember when he had old friends come to stay and they would talk all night, how I, sitting on his or someone else's knee as a child, would nearly cry with misery because I could not stay awake to hear them, it was so interesting. He had a way of making history seem history, even if it were only a bullock-wagon that he spoke of. He made things take their place in memory that otherwise would have been forgotten or seen as mere passing events. It is through him that I remember so much that is recorded here.

The troopers, as they are still, were the aristocrats and the dandies of the Force. Their feet were the riders' feet, unsplayed by walking in wide, flat-heeled boots. They were narrow and highly arched by the pressure on the stirrup, for the foot went right through when riding at ease. Otherwise they rode toe up, heel down (as I was taught to ride) with the stirrup pushed a little forward to give an easy angle for the leg and the knee. Their boots were long and high heeled, with a small, neat, square-cornered toe. They used to shine them till you could see your face in them; and would ask anywhere they stopped for polishing brushes. Indeed some, extra dandy, carried a brush with them, together with a small bottle of blacking and a rag tied on a stick. The blacking-bottle was of stone like some ink-bottles today. When there was no blacking to be had, it was a case of spit and rub the brush on the kettle, the camp-oven, or, best of all, on a meat-pot that had not become too greasy in boiling water. (Pots were only washed on the inside. "The black preserved the iron." Which was probably true when you consider the logs used on the cooking-fires.) It was a trooper who showed my mother how to add vinegar, and sugar or honey to pot-black, and so make a new blacking for the brush.

While troopers wore top-boots, the ordinary Wellington was teamsters' or cattlemen's wear. This had a toe like a doorstep. The leg went nearly straight up and down. "Yankee boots" (and "Yankee Hats") were also worn by teamsters and cattlemen. They had longer and softer tops, wrinkled round the ankle, and had high heels and narrow toes.

I saw exactly the same kind of boot still in use in Patagonia, when we lived there; it was worn by teamsters and sheep-riders. This was the manufactured boot. But on the pampa the *Gaucho* made his own. This was a *potro* boot, shaped from the whole unslit skin of the hind-leg of a colt (*potro*). To make it the hide was cut high up round the thigh of the animal, and again at the fetlock, and then it was turned down and pulled off like a rabbit-skin is peeled off for market. The hide came away clean and without any adhering fat, as it was done immediately after shooting the animal for the purpose. The inner face was like satin. Once off, the small end was drawn up closely with a sinew, or a thin lace, to shape it for the toe of the foot. While

still fresh and soft, the hair was turned in and the whole thing drawn up over the leg to the thigh, where it was hooked, laced or buttoned to the broad revolver-belt or cinch. Great care was taken to see that the skin dried smoothly. It was oiled on the leg and not taken off till it was shaped, and as soft as a glove. After three days it would come off at night.

When finished it was turned, and could be worn fastened to the waist over the hip, fastened at the knee, or it could be dropped. Fastened to the waist it had a few soft graceful wrinkles at the ankle; but dropped, it went down like a pirate's bucket-boot, and rested in concertina wrinkles at the ankle. In Patagonia the hair was left on for warmth, as well as out of regard for the leather.

Potro boots were beautiful when well made; lasted a man's lifetime; and were the desire of every rider of the pampa. Indian and white men alike used them. In good order and well made, they cost three times the price of a colt. The skin of a colt but not of a mare was used. They were hand-polished, no brush being used on them. An exquisite would inlet pieces of dyed leather round the top in a regular pattern, cut a fringe to hang down, make a border and pattern in Indian work, or have great silver dollars, or even tiny silver bells all round the top to jingle and ring as he walked. In Buenos Ayres I once heard the loveliest sound of little bells, and looking round saw two pampa riders coming along in *potro* boots. They had let them down, and walked like men with their feet through two milk dishes. As they moved, they rolled like the old-time seamen of the pigtail and the sailing ship, the ship that was so small that in a storm it had to be balanced by the crew leaning over the side, and yet the proudest moth of a thing that ever sailed the sea.

As to lesser boots, I have known clogs and pattens. But I leave the rest to others; except to say that when we lived at The Old Vineyard, near Wagga Wagga (of which I have written elsewhere), Mrs Baldwin, who lived across from us, had pattens for wet days. Sabots I never saw till I went to Patagonia. In Patagonia I wore heavy cloth-topped wood-soled clogs, lined with wool, and laced high up the leg. Even then I felt the frozen earth under my feet.

But boots were not the only wear to be historically considered. For riding in uniform the troopers wore cords; other men wore moleskin or tweed peg-tops. The peg-top had a little strap that went down under the instep so that the trouser-leg would be kept tight and unwrinkled. My father had both moleskin and peg-tops, with broadcloth and no strap for special wear. His moleskins for riding were white, worn with a scarlet flannel shirt and a wide cabbage-tree or Yankee hat, and a great red silk sash with long fringed ends. As far as I recollect, coats were either the full-skirted frock well waisted-in, or very short, and with pagets at the back. Indoors women wore the laced Swiss bodice, full skirts, and the Garibaldi jacket; for out of doors there were shawls, pelisses, pelerines, tippets, muffs and capes.

But capes were gentlemen's as well as women's wear. The ordinary shop overcoat, a shapeless slack thing with sleeves, and of bad cut and material, had not climbed to quality as it should have done, so it remained poor man's wear. The foot-police wore its horrible twin. The troopers' cape-in-ordinary came to the hips in walking, and just reached the saddle in riding. It was a full circle of heavy blue cloth with a collar; and I think it was bound with black braid. I have an idea, but am open to correction, that officers had gold braid on the collar, and frogs laced with gold down the front. The foot-police, who were "just ordinary men," wore, as I have indicated, a shapeless mackintosh or oilskin, with sleeves wide enough to stand up in. All their clothing slopped. That of the mounted-men was skin-tight all over, and beautifully cut. I cannot remember if they wore gloves, but they had nice hands; and as I have already said their feet were riders' feet, high arched and with boots high-heeled.

The foot-police were officially called constables. Their feet had no chance to look nice; the narrow high heel was denied them. The cap of the mounted-man was cut of the same cloth and braid as the cape. It had a square peak and a concertina front, the rear being pulled well down to cover the back of the head; and it had small ventilators, one in the top, two at the back. The coat was either tight to the waist, or a waisted jacket. I cannot recall which now.

Later on the cap was changed in shape, the peak being rounded. The old "concertina" folds and the lop-over small Uhlan-crown that had gone with them, were replaced by a broad, padded top, set in a straight-cut band. The troopers hated it. It was neither a mariner's cap, nor an attractive mounted's cap. No man could swagger in it. Cocked sideways it was out of place, worn on the back of the head with the peak tipped up, it "made a man look like a carter," or so they said. At about this time, too, the longer, saddle-covering coat came in. There was great complaint about its weight when wet, and against the heat it engendered in summer alike from man, sun, and horse. Before its use a trooper's cords threw off the rain; and they were so skin-tight they gave little room for absorption. The top-boots protected the lower leg, and the short cape covered the body. This allowed the free circulation of air.

Then there was another point against this new arrangement—the new padded cap and the heavy long coat, when wet added an intolerable weight to man and animal, and this at a time when mobility and riding light were most important, owing to cattle-duffing and bushranging. So the trooper did not welcome the change in outfit. Like the girl of today, whose silk stockings dry on her legs as soon as wet, he preferred the lighter to the heavier things.

One strange thing I did see carried, but whether as an individual matter or as a rule, I do not know. That was an umbrella Mr Baylis had. Mr Baylis was afterwards police magistrate, but at this time he was hunting bushrangers. I well remember his umbrella. It was of thick corded material with heavy whalebone ribs, and a short stout handle. The handle seemed short because just then women used very long jointed handles under a fringed top about the size of a pancake. I rode many a time on the front of the saddle under Mr Baylis's umbrella, my father riding beside him. Sometimes I went to sleep under it . . .

All this was in the years when a man would gamble away not only his money, but his saddle, his bridle and even his horse. And yet in the country, because there was open land, there was no man who begged.

Old customs: old forgotten usages

Among other pretty but forgotten usages was that of the cushion laid on the front doorstep at the birth of a child. It was tied with satin ribbons if you had them; if not you used what you could. If there was nothing better there would be a length of home-made embroidery, or a piece of crochet-lace tied like a ribbon. When my sister was born (she was named after Rose Stinson) my father laid roses on the cushion. She was a girl and therefore a flower. He had gone miles to get them.

When towns grew, and cushions were sometimes stolen, even in daylight, people tied the door-knob, knocker, or front gate, with a ribbon; blue for a boy and white or pink for a girl. I recollect in Wagga Wagga going a message to Richard Heydon's when the lilac was in bloom, and finding a ribbon tied on the gate. How softly I knocked at the door! Once, too, I remember a gate somewhere that said "twins," there being two ribbons.

But though the town and even the country might lose the cushion from the outer doorstep it was still used inside. So much so, that if father or mother or a guest wanted to be private, or to sleep during the day, a cushion made its own law. No one either opened or knocked on any door where it lay.

As birth had its gay colours so death had its crape; its crape-tied door or gate, and its silencing cushion tied with black. Those who had no crape borrowed it; those who had, lent it as a matter of duty, even should they not feel neighbourly in the friendliest sense.

Besides the use of crape, there was another custom, whether Australian or brought from America I do not know, and that was the undertaker's notice of the funeral set out in thick black type with heavy borders, and nailed to trees out on the road along which the outgoing funeral or the incoming public would pass. More than once my father going into town drew off the track to such a one, and reading the date found that someone he knew had died and he had not heard of it.

Once it was for his old friend, that William Pike who discovered Sebastopol, and whose children were Louis, Ferdinand, Elvira, and

Diana. His niece, Florida, is married to my uncle, W. H. Beattie—one of the uncles who kept the later Australian spelling of the name, though in his young manhood he had insisted on the original Beatty used by the family after it left Scotland to follow King James. I mention this, as in my books I have sometimes used one form of the name and sometimes the other.

Funeral notifications on trees were really needed, so few people were able to read, or took a newspaper. Besides, the local paper only came out once a week; death came when it liked. The notices, run off and put up along the road, or where two roads joined, attracted attention even if the passer-by could not read. He could describe what he saw, or he could recognize a name when he could not make out a sentence. Few people were strangers to each other; horses were plentiful; everyone you met stopped for a yarn and was told the news. As for those who lived off the road, whoever had most time turned in to their places and let them know. It was counted unneighbourly not to do that. Miles had actually begun to be measured, but time still went without a clock for most people. Families too were like time—unmeasured; and there was always some lad or lass to be told to saddle up, and tell the friends.

A funeral was, in a way, a greater festival than an ordinary dance. The baked meats and the drinks were just as plentiful, and people got to funerals who never went to a dance. You needed light boots for a party, but not for a burying, and so many had but one pair—and bluchers at that. Though I have seen young people dance without boots, because they had never been able to buy them, people had the pride, and liked to appear fit if they could.

Another custom which died out was that of a bell rung at a funeral. A hand-bell, sometimes it was rung by one of the elders in the procession from the church or cemetery gate to the grave; sometimes the sexton or the grave-digger rang it inside the cemetery. Bells being scarce, even a bullock-bell would be used if there were none better to be found. One of my uncles, as a youth, was once asked to "do the bell" because, rain having threatened, all the men were at the harvest. The funeral consisted only of a few women and the minister. He rang so blatantly (I think he objected both to the job and to the deceased) that he was never asked to ring it again. Any sort of bell was used, as I have said, but fitness was asked if it could be considered at all. Once, for a baby, it was a small silver hand-bell we had that was used. Another time, in Wagga Wagga, either Mr Nixon's or Mr Mair's dinner-bell was lent.

And that reminds me that a whole chapter could be written on the bells (and the "bellusses") of the day. Bells have given place to press-buttons; and you never see a bellows now, big or little. The big one has gone with the horse and smithy. As for the little one, who wants a "bellus" with a gas stove or a radiator?

About the time of which I write, the Presbyterian Church we attended had family pews. These were well up in the front and extended back about half-way down, or a little more. Behind these were plain open pews, and the same on the aisles. All the early pews were of beautiful old dark cedar, that being one of the then cheap and common timbers of Australia. The family seats were enclosed; you entered by a little door at the outside end next the aisle. This door was fastened by a button or a spring. Now and then someone, distrustful of his fellow worshippers, had a lock and key on that door.

What kind of seats were in the Catholic and Episcopalian Church (as the Church of England was ordinarily called) I did not then know; for it was still the day when one entered the edifice of another creed with a feeling that one was not only in a foreign place, but with a certain amount of anxiety lest the Almighty might visit it upon one for having gone so far from the *real* fold. And this in spite of the fact that all lived neighbourly together out of church. Later I found that other churches had closed pews; for, as the generation grew up, we daringly went adventuring to all the other places of worship. Then in a decade, as it were, all the barriers were down. If people wanted to hear another preacher, listen to another choir, or see what someone else's service was like, they went without fear either before or behind them. (I suppose you know all the terror before that blanches the face, and the terror behind in which the calves of the legs try to get in front as you go along some dark and unfamiliar road.)

Having grandparents who attended the Wesleyan Church, we knew all about that place. But I cannot remember whether that had closed pews or not after they left the forms behind, with which they managed till backed seating could be made. Also I do not recollect whether they draped the seat of a family in mourning as we Presbyterians did. We Presbyterians had black on our private pews for as long as we were in full mourning. This draping was afterwards shortened to a month, as longer had begun to be thought ostentatious. Also it was particularly awkward when the relict in a case I have in mind, a man, got married again before the black period was ended. Individually crape was used, but only the immediate family wore it; the rest of the relatives had black cashmere, bombazine or merino. That was for women. Men wore a black hat-band and a band on the arm.

When the box pews went the full drape went, and a bow of crape at the aisle side of the pew was all that appeared. Then, when strangers came as settlement increased, even that ceased. Before the increase in settlement, congregations consisted almost wholly of families; the single man or the single woman without relatives hardly existed. The back of a church might be thick with young men, but they were the sons of fathers up in front. They were only at the back because they were too big to crowd into the pew in front, along with the eldest daughter and the little ones: eldest daughter next to mother on the inside, father on the outside to give the collection. Once the heavens nearly fell. A woman reached past the man and gave it. She deserved burning! She had made little of a man! No woman, with the proper feeling of a *wife*, would ever have *dreamed* of doing such a thing!

Reverting to a custom in relation to bells, there used to be a preliminary part of the Presbyterian Sunday service completed before the minister came into the pulpit. While he prepared himself, and donned his gown and Geneva bands, the congregation sung an opening psalm; then came the second bell. Before reading and books were common this psalm was read verse by verse, and sung as read, till in a few Sundays everyone knew the words. The pride of the old Scots was always that "they knew it without having to learn it," that is, they knew it aforetime, before they left Scotland.

The minister entered as the psalm ended, decorum and reverence like a nimbus about him. But occasionally there was scandal. The Rev. Mr Falconer was once seen to come in as if in a hurry; and once he was observed patting his bands straight as he issued from the vestry door. Such things could not be allowed, and he was "spoken to" about it.

Both at my Wesleyan and my Presbyterian people's homes the word Sabbath was the regular usage. Indeed I think that except for the Episcopalian Church Sabbath was universal. Once, trying to be smart during a stay at Brooklyn, I said Sunday. The gently grave reproof of my grandmother will never leave me. Sunday, she said, was pagan. The pagans worshipped the sun. The seventh day was the Sabbath. God named it so when He rested. Therefore it must always be the Sabbath.

And yet for all that strictness we were allowed to believe that a day with the Lord was as a thousand years—perhaps a million—a million being still the world's most incredible number. The word billion certainly was known, together with all the further progressions of numbers, but only as a book word. We used such numbers in school and in dictionaries, but they dwelt not in the world of fact. True, they

belonged to the permitted, unlimited imagination of the mathematician. And certainly to the unpermitted imagination of the unbeliever; for unbelievers spoke openly of evolution, and evolution was a thing that according to their wicked say-so demanded billions of years. But where was there room for billions of years in the two thousand years of the Old Testament, and the less than two thousand of the New?

It seems strange that I remember when the Presbyterian Church in Wagga Wagga got its first fixed bell—one set up on a post in the yard. You will observe that the word is "yard," not "grounds" as now; a thing that marks "the sea-change of time" in regard to language, which after all lives as humanity does—and that is as much by the death of the old and weak as by the newly come.

But what Meldrums, Nixons, Fergusons, Melvins, Mackenzies, Forsyths, and Mairs, if there are any of those old families left, will remember, as I, that hard-sounding, clacking new bell! Prior to its use and the long consideration of expense connected with its purchase and erection (I think it cost thirty shillings: "thirty pieces of silver" my father said, and some of the other church elders with him), we had been rung in by a hand-bell, which for all I know now, might have been the Manse dinner-bell. The verger or elder in charge would stand at the porch door and ring. Presently he would turn and look into the building to see if everyone was there. If a single face were absent he would go out again down the steps, and ring commandingly, possibly to suggest that the Almighty was waiting. If still the missing came not, he would walk round the edifice, ringing as he went, in case anyone was late taking out the horses, these and vehicles having their set places for tying up.

And, let me say it at once, woe betide the Macdonald—or whoever it was—who took the Mackenzie or any other guid Scot's accustomed post or panel! One Sunday it was my father who was overlong in taking the horses out of the old wagonette we had. And worse: he was found talking; actually holding a conversation with a McNickle or somebody, while the minister waited. He was reported, and had to appear before the elders at the next session.

It was a somewhat similar case to that of my grandfather Beattie's reprimand from Rev. Mr Carruthers (brother to Sir Hector) at the Wesleyan Church. This was over his singing. He had a beautiful voice of great range, and he loved to loose it out to the full, "praising God in the congregation of the people." For this Mr Carruthers officially and from the pulpit accused him of "vanity" and of "showing off."

These were the actual words. Yet I never knew grandfather to let his voice go to the full when singing alone. That, he would have indeed regarded as vanity. At home in the house, in the fields or on the roads, he always sang *sotto voce* unless there were others to sing with him.

Besides the bells I have mentioned, the two principal Wagga Wagga stores, Love and Roberts's, and Forsyth's (both in Fitzmaurice Street), rang a bell on Saturdays for their Farmers' Produce sales. This, however, had no special tradition or dignity behind it, and was just a horse-bell or a bullock-bell. No; I am wrong. George Forsyth had a bell with a handle. Probably the bell that was used for the church. Sales at the old Pound Yards in Traill Street had a bullock-bell for cattle, and a horse-bell for horses. Each was rung as the stock it represented was cried. So if you were yarning up the street you knew when to come running. Later years brought a sheep-bell. As to pigs—they squealed, and you heard them. Sometimes there were goats in those old yards, and sometimes one of them had a bell on his neck; the goat-bell was round, and smaller than the sheep-bell, but of course was not a sales bell.

Then besides their use in church and at funerals, at sales and "town crying," there were quite a number of bells used in the houses of the squatters and other well-to-do people. The breakfast-bell was small, as everyone was at hand; the dinner-bell was larger as it had to bring people in from outside distances.

It was also the rising-bell, if one was used. And, how distinct usages and bells were, is shown by the fact that once John Stinson of Kindra, in a fit of anger because E—— and T—— were slow in getting up, took the dinner-bell and rang it to show how incensed he was. The whole family was shocked; with Mrs Stinson, as house-mother, on her dignity as a result. "Father" had trespassed against the domestic usages, and he was let know it.

"Instead of using the dinner-bell he could have knocked on their doors," Mrs Stinson said. But father was too angry to knock. However, he knew better than to do it again. After that he knocked.

Then there was the bell for the parlour or drawing-room. It was the size of the afternoon tea-bell—often really the tea-bell. A pretty and somewhat ornamented hand-bell, it stood, polished and speckless, on a mat of its own, or on the family Bible on the parlour table. Now and then it had a ribbon-bow on the handle. Sometimes, however, there was a small spring-bell, fastened above the parlour door under the veranda, and pulled by a worsted cord and tassels.

"... the procession from the church
or cemetery gate ..."

My father made and mounted one such for Kindra, using an old clock-spring for the purpose. The first in the district, it was an object of great curiosity and interest, especially to the children who came. This was on old Kindra, when, to the original home of four slab rooms, built when the land was first taken up, he added five sawn rooms, took the bark off the old roof, and shingled the lot from end to end. One of the five rooms he built was the old hospitable dining-room in which dances for the whole of the surrounding stations so often took place.

Besides the bells for meals, every lady of consequence had her own personal bell; and family obedience was such that whose-ever duty it was to answer it for the day flew at the sound of it. Usually it was a small silver bell, sounding like a chorus of silver thimbles. It sat on the table when the lady sewed. As "Mother" was the clock and time-keeper of the activities of the house (for many a squatter, and many a son, only learned to read the dial long after he owned the watch—we still called a clock "the dial") she needed that bell. Her mind was ever on the partitioning of time, the hours of roasting and boiling, of big baby's sleep and little baby's food: and there were always babies then. So, ceaselessly, her mind ran in never-ending current while her fingers worked. Usually the eldest daughter worked the sewing-machine; when riches grew, importation increased, and loading allowed of its purchase.

Loading is a confined word now. Then, the expression covered the team, the teamster, the roads, the time of the year, the condition of the roads, and the problem of when all would arrive. The team itself was almost shadowy in the face of its adjuncts. Its arrival was the wonder fact of existence. No king's coronation, however apparelled, ever equalled it.

Usually, as I said, the eldest daughter worked the sewing-machine. Obedience and elasticity of mind were the part of youth; dominance and set ways belonged to parents. The old kept to routine. It was the young who adventured into new ways and usages. Johnny, home from school, might impudently or inadvertently ring the dinner-bell instead of the breakfast-bell, "Father" only did it in a rage and with savage intent. Two things more; one that a bullock-bell was generally used in kitchens; and, two, that it was a mark of special privilege, and showed her as admitted to the company of the great grown-up, when the eldest daughter was allowed, once in a while as she worked, the use of "Mother's bell." That bell meant authority, and bitter was the thought of the second-eldest who had to run at its sound because sister, only a year older, was given the right (let be however temporary) to use it.

A boy never answered it. He called the girls to do that, no matter how near to his mother he might be when the bell rang. Boys were men, and men belonged to out-of-doors. They did not even take messages unless it were to the killing-yard, or somewhere on horseback.

The boys' kingdom was limited to the outside bell; the horse-bell, the bullock-bell, and later to the sheep-bell. And of these each man and each boy knew his own even a mile off, or one amongst a host. But of such bells I have written in *The Tilted Cart* years ago.

When water "sprang"

As settlement in Australia became permanent the shiftless man, still like a nomad, depended on a creek or the nearest squatter's dam, but the provident man put down a well. A man who had a well was fairly comfortable, for good wells had to be deep; the sinking cost time and money; and time and money counted when the land was in the making.

So I can still see Uncle Alfred at the old Brooklyn well in the early morning of the years that are gone. His work was to draw up several bucketfuls, and then tip them back to aerate the depths so that the water for the breakfast tea would be light and sparkling. Sometimes it was my job to taste the water, using a tin dipper or a fine china cup, as delf was useless for the purpose, which was to see if it "sprang" enough. It had to taste like spring water; hence the "sprang." Flat water meant flat tea, and my grandmother had the perception of a tea or a wine taster in relation to food. (My father's mother had died when he was but a little boy, so always I had only one grandmother.)

As an instance of her capacity in this way: in cool weather peas and beans had to be gathered, cabbage cut, and potatoes dug just before cooking, so that you would taste the freshness. If they were a day indoors she would say they were old. In hot weather the vegetables were brought in with the dew on them if there were a dew, and were packed in the darkest and coolest part of the store-room. They were prepared when needed for cooking, so that the heat of the kitchen would not soften them. If the store-room had an earthen floor it was sprinkled to dew-dampness, or the vegetables were laid on a wet bag.

Careful as my grandmother was in the house as her department, equally careful was my grandfather in his outside department. He never criticized her management, but saw that she had what she wanted. She never criticized his; though once in a while I remember she would in a low tone of voice ask Uncle James or Uncle Willie if the burrs were taken out of the cows' tails, combed from the manes and tails of the horses, or picked off the dogs. This was before the Burr Acts.

". . . peas and beans had to be gathered,
cabbage cut and potatoes dug . . ."

Burrs meant a lot in those days. I have seen hundreds of horses so burred that their tails were like clubs and quite useless to their possessors, cows' tails "balled," and were the same. As to dogs, the long-haired dog was done away with and a smoother type bred to take his place, even though all the older ones had their tails "stumped" and, if well-beloved, their coats clipped short. Horses in use had their tails docked and the manes hogged. The habit of docking continued long after the Burr Acts had been enforced, and lasted till special legislation made it a punishable offence. When the burrs were in masses, horses were so grateful for being "deburred" (if I may parallel another word) that the wildest would stand while it was being done, once he knew what it meant. The Brooklyn horses, if I sat on a fence near them, would come and put their heads over the rail or on my knee, literally asking to be done. I used to do their forelocks, manes, and fetlocks. For the fetlocks they would stand as quietly as a dog.

To return to the well. There were the house well and the stock well. The water in the latter was brackish when summer and drought dried up the springs and soakages; but at all times it was steel blue and very cold. Cold, we could drink it, as sometimes we had to do, the other being empty. Consequently everyone who wanted a drink brought up a fresh bucketful, the standing one being emptied out. The result was that there were always flowers round the big well—anemones, ranunculuses, periwinkles, petunias, flag lilies, Love-in-a-Mist, and even German stocks. Seen from the road the spot was a picture.

The last time I saw it strangers had the old hospitable home; the family was scattered, or lying away in little mounded heaps with rosemary at head and foot; the windlass was decayed; the flowers gone, and brambles filled the mouth of the old well from which water always had been drawn even for the birds—their drinking and bathing place being a hollowed-out log.

But, besides the water at the well, my grandfather always left a little stand of wheat in the field for those whom he called "the fowls of the air." This he regarded as a pious duty; because from them, who even as he were God's creatures, man took the earth that had been their home and had given them food. "God made everything for some useful purpose," I used to be told; "and though we may not know what that purpose is it is still there." So it pleased God that His creatures should be cared for out of the increased plenty that man had been enabled through the gift of reason to take from the earth, which, once theirs, had fed its wild children.

Thus I was taught that the earth was the Hand of God in relation to the innocent things of lower creation, and that when man came between these and that Hand it was his place to remember that he had taken, and his part to make a recognizing return. Of wild life only the predatory and the dangerous were to be destroyed without further use being made of them; others were to be killed only to supply a need—and, of course, all *real* needs were God-given. So, for food and shelter one might kill.

There was no analysis and no thought of the manner in which birds, in particular, were useful to man as destroyers of pests and insect plagues; for, apart from kangaroos and emus, there were few in early Australia until increased production made native things a pest, or till alien pests were imported. But it was sufficient for the people to whom I belonged that the birds, and in their places the animals, delighted the eye by form and colours; that they caused one to look beyond one's self in wonder at their beauty and at the miracle of their skill in providing for themselves and their young (without "reason" such provision must be a miracle) and to consider their speed, their ways, their wisdom. In those days of literal Biblical belief wisdom and reason were not one, but two separate things. Man alone had reason.

So at our old family gathering-place the birds fed from whatever grew, and water was left for them at the well. It was as much a household duty to see that the trough was ready for the birds in the morning when they woke, as to bring in the kindling for the kitchen fire.

But besides looking after the trough and seeing that the water "sprang," whenever I stayed at Brooklyn I had other duties; some not nearly as interesting as seeing to the birds and going to the well. One was to help beetle the linen, my part being the kitchen towels.

Beetling belonged to the world's early days of linen, and its universal scarcity of iron. Stout linen was hard and harsh, and in the old countries from which the forefathers came, except for the well-to-do, ironing was a luxury; it took up a grown person's time as well as costing fuel, while the iron itself represented another cost. But children and the old could beetle. Because the linen stared it scraped the face as a towel, was rough to the neck as a pillow slip, and felt harsh to the legs as a sheet or as a bed-tick. So it had to be softened when it could not be bought fine enough to be smooth. To make it soft it had to be beetled.

The custom came to an Australia when cotton was already taking the place of the hand-spun materials that had been brought from home. But tea-towels and handkerchiefs were still of flax, however

". . . as one bred to the use of fine and delicate things."

much sheets and underwear might have sunk to the mixtures or even to cotton itself. So I had to do the towels to make them soft and absorbent, because the sun drying left them staring and stiff. To beetle, you must know, was to beat; and the beetle was either a mallet made for the purpose, or a blackfellow's waddy picked up and brought home. Whatever was operated on was first folded as if for putting away, then laid on a block or a bench and hammered, the folds being turned over as the material became "kind." There was a song that went with it. (Being Irish there would be!) But I had to sing a hymn, or say a verse out of the Bible as I worked, in order to keep the rhythm. But we sang the old Catch "Draw the sheet, Fold the sheet, Turn the linen over," when we pulled the sheets. These were folded and pulled between two people, diagonally corner to corner so that they would lie smoothly and hang evenly on the bed when they came off the line or the grass, or from the top of the rose hedges, or the scented bushes. Sheet-drying on top of the rose hedges was not always allowed. When it did happen the clear hot sun drew the scent into the fibre; then how sweet, how bright and clear, and how light they were.

When the kitchen towels had been done enough they were put away to be brought out as required, the fine ones for the fine china and the silver, and the coarser ones for the delf and the big dishes. And it was in washing-up that the quality of your breeding showed.

"I knew she was a lady the moment I saw her lift the china!" So she was; but she had "married out of her station" and come to Australia, where she was still a lady, though she had no stockings to her feet; had only a camp-oven and a three-legged pot to cook in; and sat on a slab stool at a bark table for her meals. But the few cups she had she nursed, and anyone seeing her handle them would know she was a lady, because she lifted them up and set them down silently —gently—and with care—as one bred to the use of fine and delicate things. In great houses china was washed-up as carefully as a baby, and sets came down intact, uncracked and unchipped, generation after generation, to be the pride of later times, and the desire of the collector. So I remember with what pride (and I had learned my lesson well) that I would hear my mother call from the next room, "Isn't it time you washed-up?" and I would answer, "I have; and the things are all put away." Not one cup had chinked upon another, not one plate clicked against the next, not one dish bumped in going up on the dresser where it belonged; for noise in movement was "a sign of poor bringing up," and a gentlewoman handled china as a gentlewoman should.

Besides beetling and washing-up there were the woollens that were dried "in a cool shade," so that the hot sun would not make them yellow. Neither wool nor weaving was what it is today, machinery was still somewhat primitive, and the world's markets had not compelled the breeding of the fine-woolled sheep that have set Australia in the fore-front of international standards.

So, as the family flannels slowly dried, it was a daughter's duty to shake and stretch them, and this applied from the baby's merino frock or pelisse (I hope someone remembers that word pelisse!) to father's woollen shirt, and the stout flannel so commonly used instead of a shirt. The shaking sent the air through the material and thus helped to distribute the heat evenly. We did not know this of course; we only did the shaking because we were taught to do it. Ours not to reason why in those days of unfailing obedience; habit commanded almost as effectually as authority. Still it was a good thing when the habit had a real reason, as in this case.

Stretching was different from shaking in its aim. It was done to keep the curl of the wool-fibre from shrinking up like a too much curled ostrich feather. Poor housekeepers just dried flannels, so the father wore felt. Middling ones pulled them, pulling being a sort of half-way house between the best and the worst. But good housekeepers, and surely Solomon in all his glory must have known all about these, every now and then went out, put their arms inside the flannels and stretched and stretched, so that the garments came in dry and soft and fluffy in the clothes basket. Then they looked like white clouds in a blue sky, and smelt as only the sun can make washed things smell. The new knitting and weaving do not allow of this stretching; but the Great War saw the resurrection of the wooden sock-shaped stretcher of the grandmothers and the great-grandmothers.

From the seventies to the war . . . And now another threatens. If it comes will there even be socks left to remember us by?

I go to school

My first reading lesson came when I was about eighteen months old and was out of the old black-letter Bible with its heavy woodcuts—the Cranmer Bible—that had come down generation after generation to my grandfather. It was his great-great-grandfather's Bible. The leaves were loose but all were there, when, taking me on his knee, he started me on "In the Beginning was the Word, and the Word was with God." No alphabet, no syllables, nothing as a foundation to start from; nothing but the black letter, with to my eyes for long afterwards, capitals like miniature cathedrals and as intricate in form. But even then that printing and that skin-like rag paper which the Rev. Richard Sellors years later said was worth £14,000, had its effect on my sense of touch and on sight. About that time, however, grandfather finding a leaf out of place had the book put away.

For years it was kept in the cedar chest-of-drawers, wrapped in red flannel and silk to preserve it; but what became of it in the after time I cannot say. All I know is that none of the descendants have it; for, as I mention elsewhere, except for the grandparents, none of the Beattie family had any of the collector's sense of values. So it is quite possible that one of the aunts burned as rubbish that priceless treasure, which, if my grandfather could have brought himself to sell it, would have made the family fortune. My part in it is that I remember it; that even as a baby I was impressed by it; that I got my first reading lesson (purposely) out of it; and that learning first out of it, I never quite forgot how to read the ancient lettering. I last saw that old Bible about 1879. It was then only brought out at Christmas-time for family prayers when all the children, with their children, were at home. I think the last time otherwise that it was used was when my youngest aunt was married.

When I was about four years or a little older my father began to teach me the modern alphabet and how to read from it. He did this from an ABC book given him by Mrs Mackay when we were building their house at Tooyal in 1870—the year of the earthquake there, when the waters of Lake Tooyal, as it was sometimes called, swept right up to the back of the place in which we lived, and the shake

broke some of Mrs Mackay's crockery, and rocked our house up and down like a doll's castle. We were outside at the time, talking to James, Willie, and Barbara Mackay, and, standing near a fence, we all had to cling to it to avoid being flung down. I remember that while the shake lasted I felt very sick. It was my first experience of an earthquake; for a long time I felt a good deal like as if I had looked into the Day of Judgment.

In talking of it afterwards, my mother said that, as the water flowed out over the earth, so the burning lakes of hell flowed out and swept over sinners. Those were the days when people not only lived with the Bible, but in it. It was the background of all life, what was not in the Bible was hardly recognized as existing; its words and phrases measured everything that might be permitted. Still, even then, Darwin and Haeckel, Russell Wallace and Huxley were beginning to breach the world of fixed things in a dream of evolution, and of a God not bound by time, place, or the confined meaning of an English phrase. One of the Hodinotts lent us, practically in secret, some of the dreadful writings. The word atheist was hurled at them for having such books, while we were warned not to have anything to do with the brothers. But I remember to this day the pictures of saurians and other backboned things as Huxley showed them.

When I had learned my letters and could read "Miss Jane Bond has a nice new doll," Mrs Mackay sent for me to go and sit with her children and learn from their tutor. Under the tutor I began to write and make figures, and to say without knowing why it was so that two and two make four.

"Why do they make it four and not five?" I wanted to know. I was told "They do it because they do."

The end of the lessons came soon, as, the building finished, we moved on. However, my father continued to keep me learning some sort of lessons, and by the time I was six my mother set me to teach my brothers. I taught them as my father had taught me—by analysis and comparison of form: A—like a tent with a stick across; B—like two D's, and so on. I got Hugh right on to Z; but John would not progress. I thought him terribly stupid. John was about three years old. I think we all thought ourselves nearly grown up.

The next lessons I had were at Kindra, where I sat with the John Stinson children under their tutor, Mr Arthur, who afterwards married one of the Wagga Wagga Walshes, one of whom was the first girl in town to take the veil in the Mount Erin Convent—if Mount Erin was then built. Wherever it was we went to see the ceremony. Miss Walshe wore a most beautiful dress and long veil. After she retired from view her hair was cut off and laid on a cushion on the spot where she had stood in the splendour of her last worldly dress. This custom is not now in use; which is why I mention it here.

Finishing at Kindra we went to Brooklyn for a few weeks. There I was sent to Brucedale school under Miss Hughena Daley. The Daleys were related to the Camerons and to Lord Forbes of Cumloden. Afterwards one of the girls married Thomas Bonynge, whose niece is the wife of that peer whom (as Mr Bonynge loved in later years to tell) the Sydney *Bulletin* called Lord Beerthirst. That was when he was here as aide-de-camp at Government House. Mr Bonynge had come to Australia from Fiji; later on he was head master at the Wagga Wagga school when Mr Durie left. He taught us all singing when later on we went there. I was terribly afraid of him as he had a very quick temper, which we put down to the heat of Fiji!

When the family went on trek again I was left behind at Brooklyn to continue my education at the Brucedale school. Here I suddenly learned to write; not merely to make letters and spell words, but to express my own thoughts; and from then on, till I left that school, I spent my dinner hours at the slate in a fury of composition instead of going out to play. I was like something for whom the gates of the world had opened. I had wings. I could not help writing.

When I was about eight years of age the three elder of us were sent to Mr Pentland's Academy (usually called the Grammar School) at North Wagga Wagga. Mr Pentland at once set me to learning Greek, the only girl he thought worthy of the privilege; and as five minutes did me for my other lessons, I was put to teaching the other junior pupils in between whiles. My mother objected to my doing this, but my father wanted the Greek, so I stayed on. Then the river floods came, the school was surrounded by the Murrumbidgee, and part of the place fell down. After that people named Hart lived in what was left of the building. A few years and even that went; only the two great poplars, the elderberry, and the acacias were left to show where a Highlander had taught Greek to young Australians.

Mr Pentland and my father were related and were great friends. My father admired him for his languages, his knowledge of European history, and his love of great poetry. They would talk these—especially the Classics—for hours; and I would sit and listen, drinking it all in, though at the time with little detailed understanding.

Mr Pentland's history is interesting. As far as I remember he was sent down from Edinburgh University for fighting a duel after duelling had been prohibited. His family then procured him a post with "John Company"—the East India Company—in Calcutta.

There he met another cousin of his and my father's, a military doctor who (because there were so few white medical men then in India) was allowed as a special favour to the Company to treat the more important of its servants there. Finding the extra work too much for him he sent for a civilian assistant, a Dr Allison, who was just through at the Edinburgh University. In time his only daughter married Dr Allison, who, as his experience grew, took over the whole of the private practice. In after years, in Australia, Dr Allison's grand-daughter married an owner of the Wagga Wagga *Advertiser*. So history is made and families connected.

Mr Pentland, coming into collision with authority in India, was next sent to Tasmania, I think to Governor Latrobe. There, again, his high temper undid him. In an after dinner altercation he threw his glass of wine in either the governor's or someone else's face. After that his family cut him off, and he took to teaching.

Mrs Pentland had almost as unusual a history as her husband, but in a different way. She was heiress, through her father, to a grant made by George III to an ancestor, General Ross, of all that land upon which most of New York City now stands. Besides that there was an estate valued even then at a million in Jamaica or the Mauritius, or perhaps both. This inheritance came through her mother's brother. It was in sugar, grants and lands, wherever it was. One of her daughters married a son of the Hon. James Gormly of Foxborough Hall, Wagga Wagga, who was interested in land sales. Through his knowledge of land-titles a move was made some years ago to revive the claim to the New York grant. International law, however, prevented it.

In regard to the estate in Jamaica, I remember my father asking Mrs Pentland why she did not prove her title to it. She said money meant nothing to her. She was happy as she was. Why should she worry over a thing that would only mean responsibility and trouble to take care of, when in Australia she was free and could live her own life in her own way. In any case Mr Pentland (who had been Captain Pentland, a commission having been bought for him in his youth) would not go back.

When Mr Pentland's little Grammar School ceased to exist, we were sent across the river to the Wagga Wagga Public School on the sandhill above Gurwood Street, then under the headship of Peter Durie, with Miss Grace Annie Cameron Galloway as mistress of the girls' department. We walked three miles to school, and paid a shilling a week for our education. Then while yet only twelve years old, I went to act as an uncertified pupil-teacher to an uncle by

"We walked three miles to school . . ."

marriage, George Gray, at Cootamundra. Next, I was with him at Bungowannah near Albury; and after that with my uncle, John Beattie, at Yerong Creek. Followed the Girls' and then the Infants' schools at Wagga Wagga; and after these in their order, Beaconsfield, Illabo, Silverton, Neutral Bay, and Stanmore. From Stanmore I went to South America, paying my fare there in the S.S. *Ruapehu*, the last direct mail-boat from New Zealand to Monte Video. But all that belongs to another story.

While I think of it—and I do not know why I remembered it just now—it was while on a visit to Brooklyn that I first saw an old friend of my father, the Rev. William Ridley, B.A. of London, and M.A. of Sydney, and who wrote on the language, songs, traditions and laws of what he always called "The Australian Race," that is, the aboriginals.

As a friend of my father he was welcome at my grandparents' place. In the compilation of his book my father assisted him, for he not only was fluent in Waradjerie, but he had a knowledge of a coast and of a mountain tongue as well, besides having Gaelic as his native tongue. The Gaelic stood him in good stead as a collaborator with Mr Ridley, for, he always said, there was a greater affinity in poetical expression as well as in modulations between Gaelic and the native tongues than between these and English. "English was blunter," he used to say, "and without the very fine shades of sound and meaning needed to translate accurately." So he translated first into Gaelic and from the Gaelic into English. In fact, so much time did he give Mr Ridley, both at our place and at Brooklyn, that my mother, who was more matter of fact than my father, complained that he was wasting time over blacks' gibberish (a usual expression of the time) to the hurt of his own work. But the buildings he put up are pulled down or forgotten; the work he did for Mr Ridley still stands though his name is not on it. He was so accurate that I have known him ride twenty miles to send word to an aboriginal for the correct termination of a pronoun, or for a verb in its modulations. And he would wait till he got it before he returned. The book when completed was published in 1875. I was ten years of age then.

Another whom I saw (but only once, and that too was at Brooklyn) was Mr Blair when he was travelling from Victoria through Riverina with his encyclopaedia, the first written in Australia. He and my grandfather, both being irascible, hasty-tempered men, came to high words because my grandfather said the book was not an encyclopaedia as it did not contain certain things he looked for. Mr Blair insisted that it was an encyclopaedia, saying that no single volume could contain everything, but that subsequent editions, as money came in, would enlarge the scope till everything was included—that is "everything necessary to know." He maintained that, what no one wanted to know "only a want-to-know-all would ask for." Still, he stayed to dinner and went friendly-speeded away.

Here, too, came the Magyar, Mr Broinowski—Count, I think he really was—with his book of Australian birds. I only vaguely remember him as a person, though I recollect that he was tall with a sculptured look, both as to face and figure, and that the cover of his book, to me, was beautiful.

And here also came the first man in our district selling lightning-conductors. Lightning-conductors! Might, magic, mystery! Grandfather bought one; and I used to stand outside the kitchen fireplace when it was set up, to see the lightning run down it. It never did.

In the mind of a child

How we love to watch the leaves falling one at a time, slowly, slowly down from the poplar-trees. So light, so inevitable the fall! So unheralded the break, so silent the drop at the end! And then in a puff of wind comes the swirl at the foot of the tree, and the sound of brittle movement grown continuous! I recollect once when I had been very ill, my father made me a bed where I could look out. I actively remember nothing but the poplar-tree and the yellow leaves falling. I know all else that was there—the acacia, the kurrajongs, the elderberry bush, the roses, the scented verbena, the firm road out the gate, the great gate and the huge box-tree beyond it where I once had a swing, and where in summer the cattle lay. I know all these were there, for I had seen them year in and year out of my still short life; but when I think of that bed, and that sickness, I see only the poplar and the leaves falling. As I saw it then, I shall see it till I die.

In the bush, night has a personality of its own; the end of the day has come, and, conquered by that end, sooner or later you go to bed. Even though you sit on the veranda in summer and listen to the crickets, or though in winter you sit by the fire, these things are nothing; they are but the prelude to the reality; and the reality is bed. In the city there is no night in this sense; there is only a period marked by clocks. You go to bed, but not because night forces you; you go because it is bed-time and you have to get up in the morning. The noises in the city kill night; but in the bush, night, mighty, majestic, invisible yet perceived, holds everything. Its very sounds make it night.

I remember how, a child full of fancy and strange thoughts, I used to watch the chain lightning in a storm and almost see the Hand of God behind it. I called it "God's lasso," and when the thunder rolled and then bounced upon the earth, I regarded it as the chariots in the streets of heaven, each thunder-bounce a jolt. Ruts could only be a few in the streets of the Redeemed, hence the fewness of thunder-bounces. When the sun set in flaming, mighty masses of crimson and gold, it was chariots of fire; and all my heart reached out with longing

". . . the huge box-tree beyond it where once I had a swing . . ."

to be going to heaven in one of them. When the clouds were in tongues of flame, scattered, each flaring upwards, they were the Pentecostal tongues of fire; and when the sky was full of tiny downy snow-white clouds, they were the souls of babies. But whether they were coming to earth, gone to heaven, or just abiding in the sky, I think I never tried to find out. How many a time I watched a single small fluff of cloud in a blue sky, wistfully aching to see the pearl-white wings of an angel emerge from it, carrying a soul to heaven! How real the world of the imagined is to a child.

I often think of the white trunks of the newly stripped pine-trees. They seemed sheeted, somehow, and not like other bare trees. These were usually ash-white, but however they might gleam under the moon (and how they can!) there is always in that ash-white a grey that sheet-white never has. Yet a very old pine log is quite grey, grey as a grey eye, or the grey beard of a man not yet grown white. The box-tree and the gum-tree shine like a white bone by comparison. How beautiful was that white, especially if there was a jetted tongue of charred wood running along the side of the white! The drying of the sap by fire made a sheerness such as sun-drying never could. It was this that Lambert loved in his painting.

I wish I could remember the names my father called the different kinds of pine; but the names he used are all gone except Cypress, Pitch-pine, and Jack-pine. I think there was one he called a sort of spruce because its wood was soft and white; but which was which, or what either was like, I cannot say. Nor do I remember very clearly how they cut as timber or what the wood was like, except that the knots of some were very dark, and the deep graining beautiful. The yellow pine I did not like; but those with the rich, mahogany-coloured, rolling patterns were beautiful. Unfortunately, however, they did not come from the best timber for building. They were hard, heavy, and of unequal densities between centre and surface; and they cracked in the heat with a sound like small pistol-shots. Yet I loved that sound, too. I think I had a feeling and a fellowship with wood.

My father in his day said: "Will you dine with us?" or "Have you dined?" His son said: "Have you had dinner?" His grandson says: "Come in and have a bite!"

Dinner, even if there was only bread on a plate, was formal; today it is informal even though it consists of a roasted ox, and salmon on a salver.

"He was the handsomest man ever wore stirrups!" . . . I wonder does anyone ever "wear stirrups" now, or do they only *have* them? . . .

Talking of "wearing stirrups" reminds one of other things to be recorded. One was the custom of firing off guns for the birth of a child. When there was only my father in the house, and no one else for miles and miles around, he fired; when there was a men's hut full of stockmen they were all rounded up and all fired. In some way men gave honour to the newly born not given now; spoke softly of the mother of the young child as they do not today. An old inherited relic of the universal worship of Madonna and Child perhaps.

Then there was the lamb. It was good luck to see a new born lamb; better still if it faced you. We have driven half-way round a paddock in order to come face to face with a lamb. But the lamb did not always have it all its own way. There was that other use of a young lamb: to put it in the bed of an empty hut to gather the fleas before you put your own blankets down. We have camped out when travelling, rather than face such a hut when we could not find a lamb, young and tender and milk-smelly enough to entice the intruders. The lamb was put in the bed and the yoe allowed to lie by the fire. No sheep was then afraid of man: man and the shepherd were one. But even when a young lamb was available, there were times when we went out under the trees and left the hut to the lamb and yoe. How the shepherds lived in some of these places I do not know. The old men used to say that a dog was born with fleas, so how could they escape them?

But what loneliness in an empty hut or house! No sound of the owner, no eagerness of dogs; cold ashes on the hearth; no dish at the door, no pannikin on the wall; the bed bare to the bark that made it and the poles on which it lay. Death never was lonelier than an empty house or hut, for here indeed was the shell that had once been inhabited; here once the living thing had been that was gone.

And talking of old days and old ways, that time and the overweight of increasing population have put out, reminds me of other things put out for many, or at most only sometimes seen now, such as the beauty of the evening star, remote and lovely in an amber sky,

or white against a palpitating blue. Living where no lamps hid it, almost before I was able to speak properly, I can remember pulling at my father's shoulder and pointing, as, having undressed me for the night while my mother attended to the baby, he held me in his arms, or warmed me at the fire. I wanted to see the star, and he would take me out to see it. He loved beauty, and in his loving taught me to love it too.

People went to bed at dark then. Candles were home-made and a luxury. Even when tallow was easily got wicks were not. Besides, sometimes a light in the night was a danger. There were bushrangers; often far worse, unnamed scoundrels who robbed and murdered in between times, and let the blame of their deeds fall on the hunted black, or the hunted white man. So, because the dark house meant the safe house, people were usually asleep when the moon was in its glory, or the stars a blaze of splendour. But I have known my father wake my mother out of sleep to look at the moon, and lift me out of bed to show it to me.

In this way I remember my first notice of fleecy clouds, one here, one there; and the sense of loss when later on I saw the moon again and the clouds were not there. Thus, I remember that as a rule I did not like the non-reflecting clouds, but that once there was a mackerel sky and that it was all silver. I drowned in its beauty. How old was I? Perhaps two, perhaps nearly three years old. But no city bred two-year-old child looks for the star. It sees only the shut door, or the lamps of the street.

Earlier than that, as we drove home late from town, for the first time to notice it, I saw the moon sailing on above our heads. I reached up hands and wanted it. "You cannot have that," said my father. "That is the moon!" I understood the prohibition but not the word moon, and increased my urgence. "It is too far away; it is in the sky!" he said. Again the words were mere words, because to babes what is visible is within reach.

Was a thing on a shelf or on a peg in the wall? Father reached up and got it. Was it something on the wall-plate or was it a flower on a tree? Height again made no difference. Reach extended to the object desired; there was no limit. I did not then know that an arm mattered, or that sight was not the governor of possession. "Say Moon!" said my father not realizing that my tongue was as short in its reach upon a word as his arm to the sky. Some sound I made and for the moment forgot the moon. Then remembering again tried to find it, and cried because it was hidden by my mother's hat. "Look at the horses! Look what they are doing with their ears!" exclaimed father, and in the moving ears of horses smelling and sensing the nearness of home, I forgot the moon. But I shall never forget how I cried for it, that I might hold it within my arms and feel at my breast its loveliness.

After that I was always shown the new moon when it came in and told how it would grow and become full moon. When I was able to walk outside in shoes (I remember my first shoes that had soles and were not of wool; they were home-made of black silk, with kid-glove soles) I used to go outside to look for the star; as, earlier, I had toddled from chair to stool, and stool to wall, to peer through a crack to see the light of sunset in the sky.

When I was older whatever I read I was; whatever I thought, I felt; and thought began very early with me. When I was about seven or eight I used to think with bleak terror, "*What if nothing ever moved again!*" And I used to try to make the other children feel as I did.

"Eternities and eternities and no movement; and after that eternities and eternities and eternities, *and still no movement!*" I punctuatingly would say. But the others went on catching grasshoppers or hunting birds. A bird in the hand was to them what such a problem was to me.

Youth troubles over eternity; age grasps at a day and is satisfied to have even the day. So another of my childhood's troubles was eternity itself. So also was space. And yet another was the terror of when there would be nothing. The doctrine of the indestructibility of matter, the creativeness of change, had not then reached Australia—at least not as far as children were concerned. So I used to stand with shut eyes, and with my fingers in my ears, trying to compass the silence of creation, when all would be consumed, and the heavens rolled up as a scroll, and there was nothing—nothing—nothing—

When that came to pass there would be no moon, no sun, and no stars; no wind on the face, no rain on the head. And how I loved the wind on my face and the rain on my head! I was like a bird in these things; I lived among them like a bird. But, though I could imagine the sun and the moon and the stars and the round world of geography all gone, I still never thought of a time when there would not be a solid earth, and two feet, mine of course, standing on it. As to space! Think of beyond the moon, space; and beyond the stars, space; and after that still space; with no end and no horizon, no matter how far you went! In spite of that the horizon was to me a concrete line around the earth; sometimes I used to see myself cutting holes in it and peering through into the nothing—into space—into eternity—perhaps even seeing heaven, and God on the great white Throne.

I was fourteen years old before the horizon became an imaginary line, the groans of hell ceased, and the implacability of God went like a mist.

The other night I sat and read to some of my on-coming young girl writers things I had lived amongst in a child's imagination, but of which, in these non-classical days, unless they are set in a textbook, youth has never heard. I refer partly to Marco Polo; but, in this particular reading, to the four who were more or less his contemporaries: Friar John, Friar William, Friar Odoric, and that earlier one, Rabbi Benjamen of Tudela.

Till I spoke it Chinghiz Khan was not even a word to my listeners. And as to the Parositae. . . . But of course you know Parositae, "who, having little stomachs and small mouths eat nothing at all, but seeing flesh they stand over the pot, and receiving the steam or smoke, are therewith nourished. And if they eat anything at all it is very little." And of course you know "the country where were found certain monsters, who in all things resembled the shape of men, saving that their feet were like the feet of an ox, they indeed had men's heads but dogs' faces. These spoke, as it were, two words like men, but at the third they barked like dogs."

And reading to my girls of that strange people which has "but one leg, and one arm growing out of its breast, and which moves by hopping, but when tired takes the foot in the hand and, rolling like a hoop, they are called cyclopedes,"* I wondered if life has the same thrills for the present-day child as it had so long ago. Then we lived in two worlds; one was the world about us, and the other was really the supernatural; though of this a large part was the romantic and the pictorial. Now there is no supernatural for the child; no place is haunted; the dragon is slain; the unicorn is dead. There are no "anthropophagi whose heads do grow beneath their shoulders;" no whales to swallow Jonah; the Cham of Tartary is but a Chinese general; Prester John is a myth; the Land of Tay is merely a portion of China; and Marco Polo himself, the long doubted, is contracted into being actually the possible!

Of course I know that the wings of wonder and the feet of adventure are in one's own mind, and that they do not come to us from outside. But they do need the body of an outside to give them scope, together with the roads and the seas, and the adventures of outside upon which to run, and wherein to sail and to upward soar. A

*See note at end of chapter.

ship without a sea is the saddest sight on earth. In it are all the fixities of sorrow; for in the durability of its timber and in the faithfulness of its form eternities are set, so that the mutations of change are not seen by the beholder. In like manner, it sometimes seems to me that, the dreamer of today is flung on a lee shore, his ship of adventure no longer has for its ports the seas of romance that once existed; its world is contracted.

When I think that, as a child, with these eyes of mine I saw men who had crossed the then uncharted Death Valley of Arizona, and remember how I felt, I am again a child on a boundless sea, a child without the need of a compass; for the will to do, to go, to receive, was all the compass one required. I think of the time I saw a claymore taken off the packhorse and shown, when of all the men there only my father could swing it one-handed; of the first time someone stayed at the house who had a walking-stick with a long fine sword in it; of the pistol with a tiny dagger in the side which was released by an unseen spring; of the ring that held a drop of poison at its heart; and saw them knowing that these things were for close fighting, for places where death stood at men's throats!

Today these possessions are in museums and collections, ticketed and numbered; no child may touch them, and death is far away. But I have seen, and handled, and played with them—under permissive guard of course. And death was always near, but though always in the mind no one thought very much about it. I least of all. I had seen too much of death: too many acres of dead blacks, slain as part of life's necessity, to think that death mattered. At least among men.

When one died of sickness, man, woman or child, that was terrible; while a dead-born child was the saddest of all things, and bitterly to be grieved over. So, too, was a man found shot in the back. But death by ordinary violence—by a fight, a fall from a wagon, the thrust of a bull's horn, a neck broken by a bucking horse, a drowning when swimming a flooded creek—death like that was a part of life. A man faced these things as a matter of course. If he went down by them he did not go without having had a man's chance to make preparation and take the natural precautions of the adventure.

So, too, was it when men met in sudden anger, were hunter and hunted, or had gold to protect. For these conditions existed the belt and the revolvers, the stick with a sword in it, the blade that, shut, seemed only a big pocket-knife, yet by pressure on the right place became a dagger; and for this was the pistol-knife set in the butt or under the barrel, and the ring that injected poison. I forget what the poison was now, but sitting on my father's knee, and hearing the talk of men, I seemed to know then.

And that reminds me that I lived in a world of men when I was little. Women, when they appeared a few times a year, were temporary. Men, even if they only stayed for a day, were permanent. Women although they stayed a week were still impermanent, for they had a home somewhere away, and that was their place of permanence. Men had no such fixed place. The world was theirs, and wherever they were they belonged; the road was their range, a log for the fire was their home. Even my grandmother, who all my life meant so much to me with her recollections, appraisements, charities of outlook, and her stories—even she, in the earliest years, was only a passer-by.

Women were again impermanent because I did not know the things they knew, they had a world into which I did not go, and from which I was sent out to go and play in the yard. They talked of sewing and cooking, and the domestic things this one and that one did. That is they talked of the things of individual life that were only interesting as they happened, like eating your dinner, but which meant nothing afterwards; things that had no futures beyond the people to whom they happened.

Men, by contrast, were permanent because they made the world, a world that disappeared before the individual yet had to be reshaped in him. In men was life's continuity, for with them were the roads that went out back, the mustering of cattle, each mustering an event telling alike of last year and of years to come. Theirs were the yarding and the breaking of horses, which meant riders and work and saddles; and saddles meant endless talk, and talk of a kind that was full of the colour of life; talk that went like a broad river, sweeping in times and places and people as it flowed; talk that reached from Sydney to California,

and that covered travel, endurance, seas, and oceans. It was in such talk I heard of the Death Valley. To this day my neck feels as if it has hackles that rise at the sound of the word.

Death Valley, the Alkali desert, the Massacre in the Wilderness, Fort Dearborn, the Alamo, Fort Wayne—a child, I touched all these in men who had been in these places, or were the sons of those who had suffered in or for them.

I have seen a curl, the curl of a child's hair lying in the hollow of a man's hand, and the man who held it looked from it to the curls on my head. Something was said; because it was beyond me to grasp its full significance I cannot remember its words. But I can reach its meaning now, though the words are not there, nor even the clear tones of the voices. And I feel my father's arm about me, his hand on my head, and I know that he would have seen every black in the country shot before such a curl as that should be taken from my head. Indeed, I know that it was the sight of that curl helped him to endure, in common with all other men of the day, what actually the need of the times compelled.

It was then that men said in fear; "*If once the blacks procure arms...*". So the poor black had to die before arms became his possession; before women had to be shut in a room fearing the firing of a roof, fearing the failure of their men's limited ammunition, and having for their only comfort the knowledge that, when the time came, enough bullets would be saved for each of them and their children; as I knew they would be saved for my mother and me. Those were the old days when, by those who knew them, the blacks were still reckoned as an Australian population of several millions. And millions armed meant power.

Note: Of that fabled people which has but one leg, and one arm growing out of its breast, and which moves by hopping, but when tired takes the foot in the hand and, rolling like a hoop, they are called cyclopedes, one may easily see in them the kangaroo; that is, anyone who has seen kangaroos in numbers, and in their native condition. The little hands held close together do look like one arm growing out of the breast, and the big tail could easily be mistaken for a single leg. In feeding they hop gently, but when speeding they really seem to go like a hoop as the head falls and the hinder end rises. Indeed, it may well be that the kangaroo was parent of the "anthropophagi whose heads do grow beneath their shoulders." Perhaps in some old Chinese monastery, in some Javanese sanctuary, in Venice, or the Vatican itself, we may yet find that Australia lived, and had being in tales and records, long before she was discovered by even the Dutch.

The tall masts of memory

Because I lived in the country first and then in the city, I think of the city as I saw it when a new-comer. So I notice how the coal-holes have gone from the streets along with the top-hats and frock-coats which were worn by those then who cantered morning, noon and night, up and down, into and through its often grassy and sometimes shaded streets. Even the whitened area steps no longer startle the eye or inveigle curiosity to follow them down on hot days into their cool dusk, and in winter shudder at their dank chill. They only exist today in very out-of-date houses, for that part of a building that used to be the basement is now in the bowels of the earth, two and three stories down and only accessible by a lift. The flaring gas-jet and the dim candle are unknown in these new areas, but the cockroach still haunts them, even if the mould no longer forms on their surfaces.

Of the frock-coated, top-hatted riders there was one, a horse auctioneer, who always rode either a snow-white or a jet-black animal. He was not Kiss and not Inglis, but he had a bazaar somewhere near where Tattersall's now is. (He also had a brother, an actor, who died only in these later years.) For the moment I cannot recall his name. Perhaps some reader can. He was an Irishman and had a finer beard than even Dan O'Connor, who in his time, was almost the most picturesque looking man in Sydney. Both men in the young years had long flowing black beards and bright eyes; both men in age whitened like snow. As to the horse bazaars within neighing distance of what is now Martin Place, a life work could be written of them. But they are a man's subject.

There were oak-trees and grass on the footpath in Phillip Street when I first lived in it, and bananas, or rather plantains, flowered in a garden in Elizabeth Street near Foy's present shop! The place was an old cottage, built back from the road; the lawn still showed green when I remember it. Hay-carts passed up and down the main streets, and pigs squealed under nets, as they came up from the Quay. There are no pigs in the streets now; and no householder today finds straw on his doorstep, or chaff on his window-sill. The nose-bag is gone from the heart of the city along with the wool-teams and the rich smell of the hay-and-corn stores.

Even the bushes we used to tie to our door-ways and veranda-posts went—officially forbidden. Once I remember my mother had bushes, brought to town for Christmas, set in tins at the door of No. 5 Bligh Street, and tied to its area rails. That was when we had the downstairs front room where Aggie Kelton had practised "Tarara-boom-de-ay" while we managed with an upstairs room till she vacated hers. In those days Mr Johnson (afterwards Sir Elliot) lived there for a time. His pictures hung on the walls of the dining-room where Miss Dunn smiled on us as her boarders, and made peace between those who quarrelled over I know not what today.

Besides Mr Johnson and his pictures, I remember that we had a Mr Lockhart who counted back to Scott's Lockhart, balladry and all. Along with him was a New Zealander, Alexander Bathgate, who had written a small book of verse of which he gave me a copy; if still in existence, it is wandering around South America where I left most of my then-owned books.

A stranger coming to board, Mr Bathgate eyed him curiously. A little more eyeing and the stranger disappeared. Mr Bathgate afterwards told us that he was a man whom he remembered in New Zealand as serving time for killing his wife. I was glad I had never liked him. Besides these, there was Maynard Calvert, who had lost a leg at Spion Kop, or Rorke's Drift, or somewhere like that in South Africa. He loved books, and often we talked of them. Once it was a man we discussed, a man with a maimed hand:

"I could not bear to let him know I noticed it," I said. "It would be dreadful to show one noticed," I added, with all the emphasis and earnestness of the young.

There followed a silence like stone. Then I remembered that Calvert had lost his leg.

When I was quite a little girl sailormen were still sailormen and not just sailors; a barque was a barky; Cartagena was a shipman's dream, and logwood a cargo of gold. Dyers were still kings of trade and their children rich men's sons and daughters.

The Port of Sydney and the Port of London took hands in the word that named them. Now, greater ports than ever, with the world's millions at their wharfs and quays, no one ever says Port of either of them, except officially. Sydney . . . London . . . There stand the words stripped of the glamour, like stones in the midst of time without a past.

"The Port of Sydney!" Nay it was just "The Port;" for people said, "Do you go to the Port this year?" "*Do you go?*" mark you, not "*Are*

"The sky was pierced to heaven with masts . . ."

you going?" And the answer would be, "Not yet; I shall go at a later period."

"At a later period . . ."

"Ah, well! So long. See you later, old chap!" And the past with its Ports and its barkys, its sailormen with ear-rings and pigtails, its snuff-boxes and quids, is gone like the smoke of last year's fire. Yet I remember the Port of Sydney as full of masts as a Sunday pincushion of pins. The sky was pierced to heaven with masts, with purgatory of sailors' years between them and the earth. Iron ships? Leviathans of the sea? Yes: but the lovely wooden ship was the queen of all ships, and beloved of wind and water. She was the thistle-down of the winds; she gave the butterflies of trade; she was the white rose of the world.

The almanack

"Where is the Almanack? . . ."

There are no Almanacks now, there are only Calendars. And Almanack has dropped the "k."

There was a time when no one went anywhere without consulting the Almanack. But in the present century of made roads and street-lamps, the moon has lost her high throne in the heavens. She has become merely a planet in the sky; a mud-heap torn from the side of the earth and flung into space. But flung so far that, unshaped, she took shape, so that we see her round as an eye, as a crescent at evening, or hump-backed at other times and climbing heaven like a silver beetle.

There are no thrones in the sky today, and, the sky not any longer being heaven, heaven itself is become a wandering planet of the mind, moving now here, now there, now undefinably anywhere at all, and suspected even of non-existence. That is on the part of the mind. But the heart always expects heaven and sometimes in unexpected hours it finds it.

When there were no roads, when miles were of varying length, when earth's dimensions were not marked by paddocks, a journey was a journey; and when you set out you might not get home again. Your horses might bolt; a tree might fall on you; the short-cut by the creek become impossible; still worse, you might get lost. For the bush had no landmarks, and not every man who lived in and by it had that sense of direction which takes bees home, and birds to the nest.

But worst of all there was the dark. By day a lost man might hear in the distance a cantering horse or the far-off sound of a gunshot; then he could cooee and perhaps be heard. Failing this, a tree, a sense of direction, and the sun might bring him out. A flooded creek could send him miles out of his course; but, as long as he clung to the creek, that only meant going up one side, crossing when a place to cross was found, and returning on the other side till he came to the starting point again. Even bolting horses meant little if you had a good whip and strong reins; for a flogged horse, when bolting, loses his courage, so that he soon pulls up. But the dark . . . No man conquers the

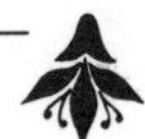

". . . a journey was a journey . . ."

dark, not even the dark of the mind. In it are no roads and no landmarks.

So the moon, and not the sun, was, in case of belatement, a man's first thought before setting out on a journey.

"*When will there be a moon?*" asked the uncles making ready the teams.

"*Bring me the Almanack!*" said my grandfather.

I loved the Almanack! In it were all the world's wonders: the signs of the Zodiac, the first day of spring, and the last day of autumn, Lammas and St Martin's day, the equinoxes and the solstice. The rise of the morning star was there, and the evening star had its setting; the moon was in it, and the tides. Many a time I sat on a log or a stump, anywhere between Narrandera, Forbes, Goulburn, Deniliquin, and Wagga Wagga, a thousand miles as roads then were from the sea, and heard the tides draw out in Devon and Cornwall; come as an eagre up the Bristol Channel; and roar in the Bay of Fundy. I could tell you things then, that, if asked about now, I would say I had never heard of them, and yet then I was only a child and had never been to any school. I was over eight years old when I went regularly to school, and I left it when I was twelve; left it to go as a little girl-usher to an uncle in Cootamundra. There are grey-headed men in that district now, some of whom, it may be, remember me. I taught many then who were years older than myself.

"*Bring me the Almanack!*" said my grandfather...

But my father never said it; for he had a sense of time, and of distance and direction such as few of his own day possessed; and fewer still, in these days of made roads, lamps and clocks, even know existed. Moreover, he knew the stars.

"If I only see one fixed star through a cloud-break I know where I am," he used to say.

"The planets are of no use, they vary in position," he would add when I excitedly pointed to one, for they were all stars to me. He had learned his bush-craft from the aborigines. The first time I ever heard about the true east and true west was one day when he was explaining how the aborigines worked the declination of the sun. To the ordinary white man where the sun rose was east, and where it set was west, no matter how far north or how far south the sun. Not so to the aboriginal. He knew the stars that moved, and the stars that were fixed; and he marked his times of the year by the movement north of the sun. There was no day in which the aboriginal could not tell you just where the sun would set; and what star would rise (and where) hour after hour through the night. His people knew the heavens far better than we did; notwithstanding that we had printed books, and night by night rode or slept under the sky. The stars were as much their book of days as the earth. Now they have lost their ancient lore, as we but for printing machines would have lost ours; and especially had we been hunted and slain as they were.

The dialects of the world have decayed, and the Almanack is gone, the Almanack that was a book! Later it became a printed sheet for the wall. We fastened it to the kitchen slabs with tacks put through bits of cork or thick grass-stems, so that if the wind blew through the cracks the precious paper would not tear. The moon and the tides, the equinoxes, Quarter days, and the feasts and fasts were still marked on margins and inner spaces. Later, the store-keeper sent us one which left out everything but the days and the months; for who, travelling by train, or on good made roads, wanted to know about the moon?

"Bring me the Almanack," said my grandfather; and the last one to hear him say it brought him a Calendar.

The cuckoo

It will be remembered that when the bush was first broken into every little solitary house had its tiny door-yard in front. The backyard only came when there was a back door. For safety's sake, and also for economy of space and time in building, back doors did not appear till some time after beginnings. A house with only one door was a castle; one with two doors was vulnerable; attack could be made on two sides. I refer, here, chiefly to the woman's fear.

"Aren't you afraid?" asked a woman of my mother, when she saw that we had a back door.

"If you had two doors the place would be cooler; there would be a draught!" said my father to a woman in a hut, when the outside day after day at sun-heat was 120 and 130 degrees and over.

The woman answered, "My husband is away all day, and I have only little children." She had no need to say more.

There being no other door at the front of a house than the one, and with the grass dug or cut away from it so that there would be no immediate cover for snakes, that bare place became the centre of house traffic, and the baby's play-ground; often, too, it was the only play-place of the elder children. Small, and regularly swept and sprinkled to keep down the dust, in time it became quite firm and hard. Anything falling or lying upon it was at once visible, whether animate or inanimate; and snakes, being used to the cover of grass, seldom crossed it.

The house in which we lived was new, indeed, only partly finished. It had no veranda and no back door. We had only just moved in, and, filled with the magic of legend and lore, we were delighted when almost at once swallows made a nest under the front shingles.

"Swallows bring good luck!" my father said, and we were told to watch but never to disturb them, or the luck would fly away.

One day, tidied for the afternoon, and sent out to the already cleared door-yard to learn my lessons and mind the baby, I was startled by the sudden dart of a restless bird straight out of the bush to the newly made swallows' nest. My impression was of a driving intent

". . . a tremendous commotion . . ."

and a proposed trespass. As this was always associated with hawks; as the bird's manner rather than its form impressed me; and as the swallows were in commotion (in antagonism rather than alarm I do remember), I called out that a hawk was at the swallows. My mother came out with the broom, and the bird made off. She watched it as it flew, and suddenly she said:

"*That* is not a hawk; it's a *cuckoo*!"

She then informed us that it was the first she had seen since she had lived as a girl with her parents at Mount Gilead on the coast; told us all about cuckoos and their ways; and bid us watch for the bird next day, *as it would come back about the same time, and we would see it lay its egg in the swallows' nest.*

The next day three of us were on watch, and from the same strategic point in the timber out shot the bird again. There was a tremendous commotion of swallows' wings and cries, and of fighting, darting, hovering, and poising cuckoo. But the swallows were victorious; the cuckoo dropped her egg short of the nest and it was smashed. Later we found the day before's egg intact in the grass

where it, too, had fallen in the previous skirmishing attempt.

The third day came, and there was but one swallow on the nest when the cuckoo made her last desperate attack. Before the cock swallow could be called home the stranger had flown at the nest; measured space, time and height; hovered an instant with beating wings; pivoted; turned and shot the egg backwards into the nest. I saw the whole thing. Then the cuckoo-bird flew off and came no more.

Looking back and considering the occurrence I should say that, in order to eject the egg with some degree of security, the cuckoo must have a conscious or an unconscious sense of trajectory, and stronger ejection muscles than other birds whose eggs need only drop. The space crossed by the egg must have been an inch and a half or more; the bird did not at any time touch the nest. There had been space to wheel; in that movement dodge the resisting sitting swallow; retain balance, power, and steerway both for immediate action and for the off-take for the hurried flight that followed. Except for her beating wings, her motion was the opposite of that of a hawk in the hover before his downward thrust or bolt.

We waited for the hatching. First came the swallows, all beak and no noticeable brains. Then unaccountably to us one morning a dead swallow lay beneath the nest; next day another fell, and another after that. Then I saw a frightful object such as I had never seen before. It rose wobbly and looked over the edge of the nest; an evil thing with a great bald head, speculation, inquiry and menace in its appearance. I screamed at the sight of, to me, the unnatural thing, and cried out:

"There's a horrible kind of snake! Come quick! It is in the swallows' nest!"

My mother came and looked at it as it rose up again. "That is the young cuckoo," she said. Later, my father explained how it pushed down in the nest, so that it held the lower place, and then, rising, shouldered out the young swallows. My impression of the cuckoo was of infantile eld, a thing of brain and intent beyond its growth. It was the opposite of the swallow. It was unnatural; it was horrible. These were my instant impressions. Impression definitely precedes thought and perception in childhood, even if only by fractional unperceived instants in after years, and is seldom forgotten when vivid. Even yet I feel the shudder of the young years in the thought of that evil-looking thing.

Looking back I should say that, judging by my mother's certainty as she told us to watch for the cuckoo to lay its egg, there was no doubt in her day as to how it was done. In any case the blacks knew all

about it. The doubt of method arose in later years because birds fled from the white man who destroyed them, moving off at sight of him. So, the later sparsity of bird life lessened the once easy conditions of observation.

Cuckoos feared neither children nor houses in my mother's day, and certainly not in ours.

That the bird laid three eggs, so to speak, and only one in a nest, makes one regard the question of what the effect on feathered life would be if every cuckoo egg were safely deposited and hatched! But apart from this, it is certain that only a limited number of cuckoo eggs can be safely placed, or the birds would be more numerous than they are and observation easier. For I do not doubt that if a hen-cuckoo were dissected, at laying-time, she would be found to contain as many embryo eggs as any other bird of her type and manner of feeding. Then the old European belief, that a cuckoo laid only one egg a year because she could not lay more would go by the board. She drops her full complement as is shown in the case I record, even though two were lost. But one young devil is all that *any* nest would hold, as the stronger of two, if two were hatched, would pitch the other out.

This raises the question of whether or not a cuckoo knows how many eggs she has laid and lost, or if she intentionally drops but one in any nest. Furthermore there is the almost certain fact of intentional memory which regards the days of failure, so that the bird continues to visit the nest chosen till an egg is at last safe, and her sense of duty satisfied.

One other thing: it would be interesting to know if the ejectory muscles of a cuckoo were stronger or different from those of other birds, or if the egg is safely deposited purely by balance and a measuring of distance. However, these are questions for the naturalist, and the subject may be left at that.

Wistaria

Men were elegant in the eighties. The figures and attitudes in the *Young Ladies' Journal* were not all imagination. Men looked like that, stood and leaned like that, and were as sentimental (outwardly) as their attitudes.

Mr Novello (to give him a name not his own) was an elegant. "An elegant" was the word of the day. Tall and slender with wide shoulders, long legs and a slim waist, he was quite different from the thick bluff squatter; the sometimes thicker, bluffer and rougher, selector and farmer. But somehow I did not like him. He glittered too much for my sober young eyes. He had teeth like Mr Carker, extra long, jetty black, Dundreary whiskers; and his eyes were unusually full, shiny, and black. He had a loud laugh; and something about him gave me an impression of uncertainty in the man, a want of sureness that kept him as it were awaiting something unspoken. Yet his position was a good one, and he and Mrs Novello were sought after by everyone. Personally I thought he rattled, and said so; but nobody else did. "What company he is!" cried everyone; and retold his quips and stories far and wide.

But Mrs Novello (to give her also a name not her own) was different. Where he was fashioned, she had an air of distinguished daring. I have seen no one else before or since who had it in quite the same lovely and delicate way. She wore clothes that everyone wanted to imitate because of their inimitable cut, but which no one dared to copy because of their colours. For, in that day of purple merino, black cashmere, and Rob Roy or shepherd's plaid, she wore stripes—yellow and black stripes cut on the bias and set in little flounces. Indeed I think she wore the first striped bias-cut flounces ever seen in Wagga, and she had them, not as a respectable plain one or two at the bottom of the skirt, but as little ones running right up from

"The lovely shadows and the scent of flowers . . ."

hem to waist. So, when she walked she rippled. Crinolines had grown somewhat small when first I saw her, but in her rippling flounces she looked as if she wore none at all. Still, when she went to a ball her hoop was as wide as the widest.

I forget how old I was when I first saw her; perhaps I was eight, perhaps twelve. But there was a beauty of mien and manner and a beauty of character about her, that I never forgot. I do not know now, but I think they lived in an old house on Willans' Hill, and into which they brought pretty things no one had ever seen the like of before, such as fine French lace curtains instead of darned net or crochet, and wax flowers under glass instead of wool or paper ones in alum baskets. Antimacassars were there of course, but there were no pink and green, or blue and yellow daisy-mats. I remember going to spend an afternoon at the house with my mother and Mrs John Stinson, and we had tea on the veranda and wistaria trellised all round us. The lovely shadows and the scent of the flowers are with me still; and the lovely hostess was a part of it all.

Races, race ball, picnics, parties, whatever there was the Novellos were the centre of everything. Women gathered round him; men flocked round her. She was the belle in spite of being married; he only escaped being the beau because he was married. The proudest boast of proud hostesses was that they had had them to dinner or at their parties.

And then fell the heavens. The Novellos suddenly were no more. They had (*whisper it!*) they had never been married! Like a puff of smoke from the pit the real wife appeared; a woman nobody wanted, not even her husband. Who saw her and who did not I do not know. Only was she remembered as a cause of shattering, the shattering of something that had been beautiful. The fragments lay on the doorsteps of a shocked people; and they were still delicate, still lovely even in destruction.

"I always had my suspicions of her!" said a man. And growing more shocked with recollection: "Why," he said, "she was so forward that I once saw her with my own eyes step toward a man who had just been presented to her and she actually held out her hand to shake hands with him. *A man she had never seen before!*"

"I never heard her speak ill of anyone!" said my mother when she heard of it.

All that happened long ago when good Queen Victoria was on the throne.

The man with the top-hat

Out of what distances of space and time the ends of life tie up, the roads meet, the streams of recollection join! I had planned a full afternoon of work, and, as so often happens in my busy life, a knock came to the door. Answering the knock, I found a sensitive and very nervous little old man carrying a bundle of worn exercise-books under his arm.

"I have come to see you because of a sense of duty," he said.

The duty was that his father had written verse, and the son felt that unless he had it printed there lay on him the burden of an undischarged debt of filial obligation.

He had come to ask if I would look at the verse and advise him what to do about it. I invited him in, and, sitting him down, found by questioning that the verse had been written long ago, and that as was usual then the writer had never gone to school. As I looked at the collection I at once saw that the writing was the work of one who was a natural singer; one with nice feeling, but with little else. I had to tell the son that this was not enough for publication, unless one had money to pay for it, and did not have to count on certain loss. Loss did matter, for my petitioner was without personal means.

"It is good of you to relieve my mind," he said when I gave him my opinion. "But I felt obliged to know the truth, and I know that you would not mislead me."

As we talked I inquired his name. He said it was MacD——. I asked of where, and of what branch of the clan. This, too, he told me; for, though the years had somewhat bewildered him, he still had the old Highland feeling and was proud of his name. Gentle, with the gentleness that comes with great strength in the gently bred (and whatever else the clans of Scotland lacked, they had this!), kind, anxious, spiritually minded as well as religious, he told me many things. His father, an old Free Kirk Hielan'man, had been as anti-Papist as Cromwell and his fellow Puritans were when they made it unlawful to keep up Christmas; when, and in addition, they made it a penal offence to eat plum-porridge (now called plum-pudding) because plum-porridge as well as Christmas was Papistry.

"When all were in trouble none could be arrested."

"He was so strictly anti-Catholic," said the son, "that he would not eat a bit of plum-pudding at Christmas-time, not even if he were starving! No, he would not."

And, as he said it, in my heart something stirred, not quite recollection, but as of something shapeless and without form, which, born, would become memory.

"He was a big man," the speaker went on, "and he was always poor, so that when he went travelling he had to carry his swag. But there was one thing that he always did, and that was he always wore a top-hat. No matter what his clothes were like, he never wore anything else on his head. He was known wherever he went as 'the man with the top-hat.' He followed the diggings. He was at Lambing Flat when it was only beginning. And he carried me, an infant, all the way from Sydney on his back, on top of his swag."

While he spoke the shapeless took form, and memory awoke. In the early years I had heard my father tell the story. For when the diggers had come up like ants from their holes, beating their dishes, and crying "*Jo!-Jo!-Jo!*" we were at Lambing Flat. And there my father had pointed out coming across the field the man with the top-hat, with the little boy, some years older than I, even then on his shoulders.

The man with the top-hat ran as others ran; he cried "*Jo!-Jo!-Jo!*" as others; six feet three, with great broad shoulders, a huge frame, and a long black beard, the boy bobbing on his back, the top-hat bobbing, he came head forward like power to the fray.

The troopers were after a digger and the digger had to be rescued, for it was still the day when the law made offences of innocent things and reasonable men had to protect themselves against it. The diggers' battle at Eureka had taken place, but its victory had not yet been of benefit to New South Wales. So it was that honest men had to beat their dishes and cry "*Jo!-Jo!-Jo!*" till, hosted like ants from their holes, came those called to a rescue. When all were in the trouble none could be arrested. A whole field of diggers could not be put in gaol. No gaol would hold them. Thus my father, a born leader, had expounded; and thus was done.

I was at the time so little, that I asked, when silence at last came, to hear again the music of the dishes, with their *ding-ding-ding* and their *drum-drum-drum* (according to whether they were struck by a stick or by the heel of the hand), because it really was music to my ear. When a digger, to please me, beat out a kettledrum tattoo, I was disappointed; because, for one thing, it was only a little sound, and for another only a head or two appeared at the surface of the

surrounding holes. This was not what I looked for. I wanted the volume, I wanted the body, the shouts, the rush of men, the tumult, and then the tremendous silence after the final flurry, as, all over, the men went down the ropes and the ladders once more to their holes.

I have seen many things of moment since then, but few that left such a sense of being in the midst of life-in-the-making as that. It is a great memory. It was a mighty thing to have seen. Half dormant it had lain in the cells of the mind through all the years since. Then, suddenly, here was the son of the man in the high hat—of the man who had run as a giant across the field—sitting in my quiet flat at King's Cross, tremulously telling me of that dimmed and almost forgotten past.

More than that he brought back. He told of how, his mother having died, after he left a Home to go to work, he had been apprenticed to the G——s at their station near Queanbeyan. Bound for a term of three years, getting food, clothes, but no wages in return for work, as the custom then was, there was a day when, bringing in the cows to the yards, he saw "lobbing along a big dark man carrying a swag and wearing a top-hat."

"I was only a boy," added my visitor, "a boy at the most sensitive age of his life. I knew that the other station-hands would laugh and make fun of me because of him; I had not seen him since he had carried me on his swag at Lambing Flat; so I thought I would hide where I was till he went away, as he would go if he did not see me. But when he came to the fence I could not do it. He was my father, no matter what happened.

"He stopped, and, without knowing who I was, asked which was the quickest way off the station, as he had been treated with discourtesy by the people up at the house, and the sooner he left such a place behind, the better pleased he would be. I told him the way to the nearest part of the boundary, and then he asked me my name. 'My name,' I said, 'is Henry MacD——, and you are my father.'"

When my own father told me, a child sitting on his knee, this same story, he said that when MacD—— reached the boundary, as he stepped across it he shook the dust of that station off his feet, and said never would he set foot on it again as long as he lived. And he never did. He would go ten miles out of his way to avoid it, added my father.

I asked my guest if he knew aught about the blacks in the early days; and looking at me he asked a question.

"Do you know anything about the massacre at Myall Creek, on the North Coast?" he said.

And then he went on to tell how one of the proudest names of Sydney today (and equally of that day) was that of a man who had ridden hot-foot all night from a certain place so that he might have an alibi of distance when what he had commanded to be done had been informed of, and, I think for the first time in the case of a massacre, an investigation was ordered. As he spoke I remembered how my father and my grandparents, in telling the story, used to say that this man, being a landowner, had been sent word by the head of the police (a messenger having been ordered out on the fastest horse that could be given him) so that the "gentleman" could get away before the posse, that had to be sent up in response to the complaint, could arrive; and that even then he would not have got far enough away, had not the trooper-in-charge been given secret orders to travel slowly. This the trooper carefully did, his excuse afterwards being that he had to save his horses. No notable landowner might be charged or hanged in those days; magnate and official clung together, however many poor people might be charged, however many convicts could be flogged or executed.

The trooper, becoming suddenly well-off soon after this, gave no account of how he made his rise, but let it be put abroad that he had found a bushranger's hoard—a story no one accepted; for everyone asked how could he keep Crown money, as such would be, if he, as a policeman, found it?

Another story my wistful visitor brought back was that of Jimmy Barron, the one small survivor of the Barron Falls massacre.

The blacks having been rounded up on X—— station, every possible soul was shot or knocked on the head. The stockmen, looking round to see that none had escaped by hiding in a bush or elsewhere, found a little lad where his mother, in a last faithful effort to save him, had thrust him into a hollow log. Up this he had crawled till quite out of sight. Knowing the love of the aboriginals for their children, and that they would trust them to nature where they dare not trust them to the mercy of the white man, besides beating all bushes and scanning all trees, it was customary to tap all logs and judge by the sound if a child was hidden there.

The sound betraying this little fellow, the log was chopped open, and he was lifted out. A stockman drew his revolver to shoot him, though the rule was to save shot and knock children on the head with an axe or a billet of wood. But for once fate intervened. Douglas McCrae said, "No! I'll take him home to my wife."

So the little black boy grew up with the white child, and he was called Barron for the Barron Falls. (My father, speaking of the happening, said that Douglas McCrae was, through some clan marriage, a connection of ours.)

Talk veering, my visitor forgetting the passage of years, and only remembering that I wanted information about the blacks, later on said:

"If you were to see old Wyndham now, *he* could tell you a lot. He lived with the blacks and became a member of the tribe. He could tell you everything about them. He always said they were a finer people than the whites; that they not only had better laws, but that they lived up to them. Once when Mr Wyndham was wanted home on the station to do the wool-classing (he always did it himself) they had to go out to the blacks' country for him. The first time they went they took only one horse. 'How is this?' said Wyndham; 'you have brought only one horse; I do not go without my lubra. Wherever I go she has to go.' So they had to go back and bring another horse. When they got back to the camp with it the pot was on for dinner, and in the pot was a goanna and a possum. . ."

Old tales, old memories echoed and re-echoed in the voice of the teller. Among them there came up the name of my father's kinsman, John Macintosh,* who was one of the early wholesale ironmongers in Sydney. When I first remember about him his home was at Double Bay; "Lindsay" he called it; and set in about twenty acres of land. He told my father that he had so large an area, because he wanted the wild birds about him, the wild flowers, and the native trees. About the house the gardeners could do what they liked in the way of grounds, lawns, and flowers, but beyond these was his sanctuary (which had to be as nature left it) where he could walk at the end of the day and think out his business needs, feeling undisturbed and at leisure and—to use his own words—"on Sunday commune with his Maker."

"Nothing gives me peace like the trees," he told the young man he wanted to take into his business, and who was afterwards my father.

By the gardener's cottage he had a room built and furnished; and

*See note opposite.

". . . when he went travelling . . ."

to that room might come any time he liked "the man with the top-hat." I have heard my father say that when John Macintosh would see MacD —— coming up the front walk he would go to meet him, for the Highlands being a land of singers, and this man writing verse, John Macintosh counted him a bard, and as a bard did him honour.

When I told this to my visitor he gave me into my own hand verse after verse that his father had written to John Macintosh.

Note: Writing to Mr Walter Bethel, because whether of persons or place he is so accurate, I asked him what he remembered of John Macintosh. He replied:

"Dear Mary Gilmore,

"I received your letter as to John Macintosh—the Hon. John Macintosh, M.L.C.—and I might say I knew him without really knowing him. He and the family sociable were familiar to all Sydney when, day in and day out, he drove to town with his boys to the well-known ironmongery store. There were no new-fangled ideas about Macintosh's business. Clearing sales were not a feature known to the Firm, and as a consequence stock piled up, old and new, to such an extent that if you wanted to replace an old thing—one probably out-of-date—and could not get it anywhere in town, you would be sure to find it at Macintosh's."

This I had heard from my father, but I quote Mr Bethel for the pleasure and privilege of having his name here.

Then she turned and rode away

One of the wonderful things that memory shows is how far, how very far we have travelled in thought in this last half-century of ours. Had the world gone as fast in its earlier ages, where now would history have to place us of the later centuries? To what might we not have risen? Sixty years ago there was a ghost behind every bush, a haunt in every shadow and, let it be added, a prayer before every undertaking. Now the ghosts have departed, the haunts have peace, and prayer... Let it go at that.

The elders tell no tales now of an old woman crossing a field, and when you looked again there was only a hare sitting there washing its face. You can be an old woman in perfect safety today; you can keep as many black cats as you like, and no one regards it as a sign of witchcraft; you can say the word gypsy and not shiver. Garlic has become merely a flavouring vegetable, which no one needs in this our children's time to hang round a child's neck, or fasten to a door or window, to keep blood-sucking ghosts away. The werewolf, the incubus and the succubus are all gone. The electric light has banished the haunter; the key in the door has driven away the vampire.

In other words, material possessions and human freedom have brought education, and education has opened the doors of the mind. So, no woman is burnt joyfully as a witch today; no man buried with a stake through his heart, or dug up and reburied somewhere else with spells and a stone on him in order to keep him down. But when I was a child ghosts still walked, and spectres haunted the cross-roads.

In the years of the Diggings in Victoria there came a Portuguese or Spanish woman from the Peninsula to this country—though some said she had come from Hayti, and some said from Martinique. At Bendigo, Beechworth, or Ballarat, she married. Later she travelled with her husband to Wodonga when Wodonga was as much a hive of Chinese as were the wild rushes she had left. Of the Chinese she always had the good word:

"I never had to fear the Chinese," she used to say, "though I lived among them for years and in the lawless times. More than that," she

would add, "when I was in danger from white men the Chinese were my protection."

Working a claim across the Hume, as that part of the Murray was then called in honour of its discoverer, there came a day when her husband said to his windlass-man that it was time to put together the gold they had, and take it for safety to the bank in Albury. He got ready, started for the town, and that was the last seen of him alive. The hills kept the secret, till, in the police search for him after he was reported missing, he was found murdered, and with every stitch of clothing taken from his body. No trace of the slayer was ever found. But some very sinister stories got about, and there were not wanting those who said that a certain person should be made lay hand on the remains to see if they would not bleed. That was only a little over fifty years ago.

But I have run ahead of my story. This foreign woman was a born nurse, no emergency frightened her, violence did not shock her, need called to her. There was at this time no hospital in Albury, and, as far as I recollect hearing, only two doctors. One of these was Dr Harris. A move was made to apply for leave to establish a small hospital. The woman of whom I write, Mrs X——, had been nursing-assistant to Dr Harris, especially in surgical cases—which were, of course, chiefly concerned with setting bones and reducing dislocations. Operative surgery such as we have now was not then dreamed of. If an internal operation had to be faced the patient had the choice of death on the road to Sydney or Melbourne in search of a special doctor (like Dr James or Dr Fitzgerald in Melbourne, or, I think, a young man named MacCormick in Sydney), or, with as much quiet as could be achieved, a man died in bed and with his family around him at home. But besides surgery in general there was childbirth, and its attendant dangers; though instead of dangers one might well be justified in writing horrors. However, that may be left aside.

To the newly approved of hospital Mrs X—— was appointed acting matron-in-charge. This hospital began in a surveyor's tent, as was also the case in Wagga Wagga, where I think I was one of the first patients, though the provision was for men only. Being but a small child I was admitted by either Dr Wren (a collateral or direct descendant of Christopher Wren) or by Dr Large. A trainee there was Miss Gould, afterwards Matron of Sydney Hospital.

Though without a certificated training, but because Dr Harris regarded her as the equal of any trained woman, Mrs X—— remained at the hospital for two or three years. Then, the increase in population creating a demand for larger wards, when they were built

the demand for certification drove the matron out. The whole district, even up to where we lived beyond Wagga Wagga, was in a state of violent upheaval over the case. Men everywhere argued for her retention; women, brought up and trained to worship authority, argued for headquarters (which was Sydney) and certification. The result was a successor who was a comparatively young woman, but one specially trained in hospital methods and operative work.

Mrs X—— left Albury, took up land in the mountains out beyond Gundagai, and there she built her house and brought up her children. Her husband being at this time dead, she had to make the whole of her living in order to pay her way. Therefore, though she farmed a little, she went out nursing. There were no roads then. Wherever one travelled it was on horseback or on foot. So, on her journeys to patients, this woman faced cliffs, rivers, flooded creeks, mountain-steeps and dark valleys in the saddle.

I have said she was from the Peninsula and as such she kept the tradition laid upon Spain and Portugal by the all-conquering Moors—she rode a stallion; even as Spanish and Portuguese South America did when we lived there in the nineties. The stallion had a name which everyone knew, but he answered no voice but hers.* She could do anything with him. He would stand all night where she left him; for she had taught him as South America and the Peninsula still train horses—to stand to the dropped rein. Let anyone approach to tie him up or even to lay a touch on him, and he struck as only a stallion can. In this lay her safety. Once on his back nothing stayed her going.

At a cry from some man, run breathless to her door from the saddle from which he had flung himself, she would pack her kit and off. There were no handy rucksacks then; no cheap saddle-bags. The only bag was a carpet-bag, the only sack a valise. And no woman could go full speed through that rough mountain bush with a carpet-bag at her side, or with a valise lashed across the horn of a side-saddle. Her sideways breadth, together with her habit on the horse's side, made passage through the forest much harder for her than it ever could be for a man. A man crowded by the timber could always lift one foot or the other to the saddle in escape of danger, but not so a woman. A trouser-leg did not flow, but a woman's habit-skirt swung like a billow. A man had strong boots and leggings to save him from the brush; because she had to sit sideways, leggings were impossible for a woman.

*See note at end of chapter.

There being no rucksacks, Mrs X—— packed everything for her patients in her own way, and that was in one of her own strong, specially made calico night-gowns. Everything went into the skirt of this, instruments and all, for she was one of the few untrained nurses allowed to have instruments. Besides these things she often had to add linen for babies who otherwise would have had none, and night-gowns for women who had never owned one.

When she had everything packed in going order—and she always had the essential things waiting ready—the whole lot was rolled up like a sausage as far as the sleeves, and then tied with a cord. After that, with the sleeves crossed, she would fasten the cuffs to each opposite end of the roll to make shoulder loops. Then with the lot slung on her back, and her arms slipped through, she would spring to the saddle, and at full gallop start off for wherever she had to go. She left nothing to chance. Her kit always went with her, whether it was needed or not; her arms were free as she rode, her baggage being behind her presented no surface to bough or brush.

Straight out by a star, lying forward on the stallion's neck, the hem of her habit rolled round her leg and tucked into the stirrup to keep herself from being torn from the saddle by spike or tree, hanging back on the horn going down declivities, flashing through scrubs, clinging to the horse's mane up steeps, leaping logs, rocks and creeks, on, on, on, day or night at a cry went the rider of the stallion. A Latin and a Catholic, yet she fought for every woman. To her the mother came first. Once, I remember, a man wanting an heir begged her to save the child and let the mother go. She turned on him with this saying:

"No. The woman comes first. You can get another child if *she* dies, but your wife cannot come back from the grave!" And I remember how among visitors, or when we would be visiting, men argued for the child

*"No emergency frightened her . . .
need called to her."*

as a possible heir, and my mother for the woman.

Once a man came in such haste that he was almost crying, the need was so urgent. Flinging her things together, full gallop she went, leaving the messenger to follow as fast as he could. She had nearly three miles to ride, and as she came to the house there was only time, as she sprang from the saddle, to call to the men at the shanty or inn door (whichever it was) and tell them on no account to let anyone touch her horse; that it would stand till she came out again, but that it would not tolerate any hand but hers. As she ran to the woman screaming in agony, unconsciously her mind caught the words:

"Don't be a fool! No one is allowed to touch that horse! Didn't she tell you not to touch it?"

But the fool replied. "There never was a horse yet that I could not handle!"

This man walked up to the animal and put his hand on the bridle. The stallion rose and with his hoofs struck him down. Later, when Mrs X—— came out, having saved mother and child, the man lay dead as he had fallen, and a messenger had been sent post-haste for the police.

Because of the slaying, the police ordered the horse to be shot. But so much did the animal's speed and its understanding of its rider mean in that wild place to the women and children of the mountains —so much did it mean to Mrs X—— herself, who had no other horse with its staying power, or trained like it—that a petition was sent round asking that it be spared, at least till after the police or coroner's inquiry. The inquiry showed that the animal was well-known; that the man had been warned by those about him as well as by her not to put his hand on it; and that in spite of everything he had held his own way so that his death was upon his own head.

If I had the power of Emily Bronte what a *Wuthering Heights* I could write of that masterful woman: of the wild galloping through the night, the white gleam of the pack on her back under the moon and the stars; the thud, thud, thud, of the hoofs as she went out hastening on in answer to the cry of life in the fear of death, her mind thrust forward ahead of the speed and the hoofs, alone in the bush, alone in the night! But I have only an ordinary pen, the memory of a child, and the up-gathering of what has lain dormant and almost forgotten in the mind these fifty years. So what is written here is but a fraction of that strange, adventurous life. As to that which follows, it can only show to this matter-of-fact generation the phantom of what then raised people's hair, and was fact to those who told it.

Death was a commonplace of the body, and no one doubted the

body's resurrection in the same and exact form as that in which it had lived. But the soul was different; the soul was immortal, and it was feared. Though the body died and went to dust, that which had inhabited it was an inquiet thing; it clung to the place it had known, and there, had it been troubled, it haunted. If violently torn from the flesh it could never lie down. It could not sleep like the dust that had been its life-covering and home. So in the mountains, little by little a dread grew. Wherever the stallion went, no matter on what errand of mercy, a ghost went with it. There were those who had seen the ghost; it was like a shadow that followed. The witness of evil increasing, there were those who said that, had the stallion been shot at once, the dead whom it had killed might have known peace. As it was, with the animal going about as usual, how could the man it had struck lie still?

So whisper by whisper, man to woman, woman to man, the gossip grew, and people rolled the ball of fear from small things to great. And I, a child, heard how once when she was out, this woman halted unseen above a cliff-edge where down below sounded the laughter of children, and the chink of buckets and billies as they were being filled with water for the house to which they all belonged. Then at some movement of the horse above, suddenly the children stood rigid, recognizing the sound, fearful lest the woman should look down on them, terrified to look up lest they should see the ghost.

She spoke to the stallion and crossed the creek, giving the children time to get home before she went up to the house. Arrived there she knocked on door and window, but neither the mother she had nursed, nor the children she had helped to life answered her. Then she turned and rode away. Her day was done.

Note: The rider of the stallion was Nurse Bennett. She spoke only in Spanish to him so that he would not stop for anyone who spoke English. This was for safety's sake in the rough times recorded. The name of the horse was *El Cid*.

The sister-in-charge

Once, travelling in the country about Yass, and thence on to the Patterson cousins of Berrabangalo near Gunning, we stayed a visit with another connection of my father who was known variously to his friends and family as the McCallion, MacCallum More, and Argyll MacCallum of "Good Hope." His mother was a de Villiers, daughter of the then Chief Justice at the Cape (South Africa); while his father had owned his own ship in the East, well over a hundred years ago. And though I, myself, do not remember them, I mind my father describing wonderful things this sea-captain relative had collected and brought to a land, which, in the country parts was still largely seated on rough stools and living under bark roofs.

While we were at his newly built house he had served us a meal of rice in Chinese fashion. My mother after one attempt at using the chopsticks demanded a spoon. My father by degrees emptied his bowl, and perhaps because I was least self-conscious I got through best of all. Mine were a child's chopsticks, small and flattish, and suited to the size of my hands. When we were leaving, the McCallion gave my father and me the chopsticks we had used. We had them for some years; then in moving they were lost; and now my brother Jack and I are the only ones that remember them.

In the fullness of years the McCallion died. In his lifetime he had loved, as all Highlanders would, the high hill, the wide outlook over plains like a sea, and the smell of sun on rocks. He was six feet three in height, powerful in wind and limb, and a hill-climber. In his will he left instructions that when he died he was to be buried on the top of the peak he had so loved to climb. There, alone with the sun, the wind, and the heavens, with God and the stars above him, he would be one with the unlonely things of eternity, to rest till the Day of Judgment. These words were not in his will, but they embody things he told my father.

During one of the years of the war Dr John Bean—brother to C.E.W. Bean, our war historian: a man the remembrance of whose official reports as war-correspondent at Gallipoli in 1914 wring my heart to

this day—Dr John, I say, was one of a group of people organized to investigate the "materializations" of a then well-known spiritualistic man-medium. The seance took place in two empty downstairs rooms in what I have since learned was the building in Macquarie Street where Dr Arthur had his consulting rooms. The medium was loosely cased up to the neck in a cretonne sack drawn in round his neck, so that arms and all were enclosed. A dog-chain was slackly fastened round his middle. He was set in a chair swung from a tripod of beams so that his feet, though in the bag, were clear of the floor. I kept no record of the investigators; but among them were Professor Lovell, Dr Bean, Dr Arthur, the Sister-in-charge at the Darlinghurst Mental Hospital, Miss Hunsley, and a clergyman or two. I think the law also was represented. The medium, I might state without further ado, did not produce anything that meant *apports*. I was told afterwards that it was my fault. I was too much an unbeliever.

At the old Mental Hospital, Darlinghurst, there was a Sister of whom an Australian writer used to say that she was like a mother to him; and it was a fact, for she was a sympathetic and an understanding woman. Also this writer would tell how that, when at times he was destitute, he would find a stray threepence, get some beer, drink part of it, spill the rest on his clothes, roll in the gutter, and then spar up to the nearest policeman as if raving in drink. On his wild appearance (and the wilder he seemed the better pleased the policeman, in case an inspector was about) he would be arrested and taken for observation to the Reception House. From there he would be sent to the Mental Hospital (both places being in the same grounds) and in half an hour he would be clean, shaved and bathed, and having a cup of tea provided by the Sister-in-charge.

Once, however, he told a number of us, he mistook his policeman, new to the beat, and one who did not know him. "And," to use his own words, "there was a devil of a job to get things fixed"—so that he could be sent to what was like a home to him instead of up before the magistrate. After that, said he, he chose his policeman with greater care.

But how good the force was to this man only he and his friends know. A less understanding body of men would have broken his heart.

There is a charming villa in Darley Road opposite to Queen's Park, which I first saw when we came back to Australia from Patagonia and Paraguay. It was just the sort of place one would like for one's own

". . . the high hill, the wide outlook . . ."

home. Later, we went to my husband's family at Strathdownie, near Casterton in Victoria, and took charge of the old people till they no longer needed anyone's care. It was while in Casterton that I wrote to Mr Lamond, the editor of the *Worker*, and said that women were just as important in the Labour Movement as men, and that he should have a page in the paper for them. He wrote back and said:

"We have tried several people and they have all been failures. Send what you think should be a Women's Page."

I sent it, and continued the work from then on for three years in Casterton, and after that in Sydney—twenty-three years in all.

Casterton is on the western road that runs to where Mount Gambier stands up like a blue thumb in the sky. That is the road along which Tom Cawker, owner of the original coach-line, drove the young Duke of Clarence and his brother the then Duke of York; drove Dolores; drove Melba; and drove a later Duke of York (or was it the Prince of Wales?), who told him that his father, the King of England, had charged him with a remembering message to him—Mr Cawker.

Returning from Victoria to Sydney we again saw the cottage I had so much admired. Inquiring about it I was told that a very charming old lady and her daughters lived there; that the family had bought the place and added to it as a home for their mother. It stood on a high terraced front of green lawns and embankments, two trees shading the front, with a glass house, arbour, and flagged courtyard at the back.

Time passed; the family moved elsewhere; and the place was to let. My sister, seeing it and liking it, went to the agent and rented it, living in it for some years. Then one day as I was describing it to a woman I knew, she looked at me with surprise:

"Why," she said, "that was *our* house. We bought it for our mother."

As we talked I found she was the generously kind Sister at the Darlinghurst Mental Hospital; the Sister who had sat beside me at the spiritualistic seance and investigation; the daughter of the McCallion, and by Scottish reckoning my cousin within the Clan. And so again the threads of life had tied up.

"The advertiser"

There was the case of the "advertiser" Mr M——.

So that no one may locate the place in which this thing happened, let me say it was near Saturn, and we were building on Z—— Station. It was after shearing, and everywhere the sheep that had been sold, or that had to be moved, were travelling. They went light after shearing, and not only stood the heat better but they could do longer stretches; or so it was thought then.

As I was going a message from our place to the other house where the station family lived, an "advertiser" rode up. Later these men had another name. Then they were called "advertisers," because they rode ahead of the sheep (either twenty-four hours or two days), to say that the travellers were coming. This was to give the run-owners time to withdraw their own then fenceless flocks from the route, if surveyed, or for those on the road to get permission to cross the run if there were no surveyed route. In the unfenced states of the newly settled country sheep boxed and then had to be sorted out. Before tar-branding was ordered for travelling sheep many a flock of travellers left a station larger than it had been when it came in. Those were the palmy days of droving. Tar-brands, contracts, penalties, and provisions as to time a delivery would take—these when they came in were the things that made droving a hardship; like everything else that was not land owning, and by which a man had to live.

While grass and water were easily available, untarred travellers were as carefully kept from boxing as the squatters' sheep were. But as stock increased, when farther and farther out squatters' and free-selectors' fences ran, and yet grass and water had to be obtained if the land was to be conquered by the oncoming wave of the land-hungry, boxing was the salvation of the drover; and all sorts of ruses and shifts were resorted to by men in charge in order to bring it about. With a big lot of travellers it meant at least two or three days at the drafting-yards, and as the animals were mixed the squatter could not starve the stranger's sheep without starving his own.

So holes would be cut in fences, horses taught to break through, in which case there would be only horse-tracks to be seen, and any good horse would be expected to break through a fence for food or water. Flock leaders, and rams if the season suited, would be made a lure. Old ewes and wethers, having more brains than rams, would be made the scouts of the army—the eyes and noses (for water) of the intelligence staff. It was either the Sparrow Brothers or an earlier lot, and one of the most successful outfits on the road, who kept the same old ewe as a part of their convoy till she was too old for travelling. She was then pensioned off. She went out on the track on foot, but always came back on the cart after delivery of the sheep was taken so that she would be rested for the next journey.

To the squatters, boxing was the last curse put upon man. But to the drover it meant not only grass and water while drafting went on, it meant rest and comfort to man and beast, with often a dance and a pretty girl to talk to. The men's dogs might fight the station dogs, but they fed with the station dogs. No one would refuse a dog meat! The run-owner might boil over with rage because of the mixing of sheep; but the hands of both sides worked together, told news, swapped yarns, heard of work, and talked of friends and old neighbours in places left long before; for the drover was a second mailman for news.

There was another thing, too. A poor man, through boxing, if the season favoured it, could get the benefit, more or less, of course, of the richer man's better bred rams. All sorts of things were schemed for, hoped for, known and combated, that with ordered roads, railway trucks and regularized stock reserves and routes, are never even thought of now. And if I have brought some of them to mind again, no matter how imperfectly or with what allowance must be asked for error, I shall not have written in vain. Harvest will be drawn from the record.

As I said, I was a little girl going a message between the two houses when an advertiser rode up. An advertiser was always known as far as you could see him. He had a different look somehow. Whether it was his calling, his type, or his clothes I do not know. But with a people who could tell you every bullock in a mile off, every sheep in a flock, every horse-track if you saw only a part of it, this perception was not singular.

In any case this man was expected. The sheep to which he was advertiser were known to be coming on. Later it was remembered that Mr X——, owner of Z——, had stayed home that morning, and had not as usual gone out on the run with his men. As the oncoming rider neared the homestead, Mr X—— was seen to step up to the

"They went light after shearing . . . and stood the heat better . . ."

clock in the dining-room, pause a moment, and then come out.

The sheep-man was dressed in a silk coat that flagged out behind him as he rode; he wore a broad hat with a cotton pugaree, had spurs, and an exceptionally long beard that, carefully combed, polished and oiled, came nearly down to his waist. He was fairish, very blue-eyed, and voluble. He gave his name and handed out his written notice. Not long before this it had been enacted that unless a notice was written it was not a notice. This was very hard on men who had no schooling, as was so often the case then. Not being able to write their slips they were dependent on others, who were not always kind to them, but worded them as a mischievous whim chose. (All the stories of the improper I might say do not belong to the A.I.F.; some of them were born of sheep-men long, long before the war.)

Till this enactment notices only needed to be oral. But as too many oral notices had said there were only two hundred sheep where there were five hundred, and so on, regulation had intervened. The paper had to be in proper form and accurate in particulars. Once a notice was given and accepted it prevented impounding and claims for damages, the accepted flock not then being a trespasser.

Mr X—— looked at the slip as he held it in his hand after taking it from the advertiser:

"This notice is too late," he said. "You should have been here before now. I am not going to accept it."

The advertiser explained that a gate had been moved from what had been the road; that the delay had occurred because he had had to go right round a paddock to the far side before he could make an entrance to the road running to the homestead. As a matter of fact the gate had been moved on purpose, in order to compel him and the flock to go round, the length of detour forcing the drovers to camp before entering the better grassed area. As the sheep would have to get on the hoof in the early morning, they would be through the place before evening; grass and water would be saved, and there would be no need of night-watching to prevent boxing. As to the squatters themselves, the rule was that one obliged the other; but for the poor free-selector there was no mercy. They would all have been shot like dingoes and the blacks, if the squatters had had their way. Drovers on long tracks were equally hated.

Without further glance at the paper in his hand Mr X—— held it back toward the advertiser, who refused it. Mr X—— insisted. The advertiser said the day did not end till the set of sun. Mr X—— declared that the legal time was as measured by the clock—not by the sun. The advertiser said the drovers would be ruined and the sheep

". . . many a flock of travellers . . ."

dead if they could not come through. Mr X—— said that if every drover in the country was ruined, and every hoof of travelling stock dead, it would not make him lift a rail or open a gate to let one of them through.

"Then," said the advertiser, "we will only have to come through whether you like it or not. The notice is delivered, and you cannot say that it is not. How do I know," he added savagely, "that you have not altered your clock, and put your watch on?"

He pulled out his own watch. There was nearly an hour's difference. Actually the station time *had* been put on. I saw Mr X—— do it with his watch; my father had seen him at the clock. White with rage at being found out, he flung the chit on the ground, and shouted:

"If you do not get off my ground at once, I will put the dogs on you!"

"If you do, I will have the law on you."

"There is no law here but mine. I am the owner of this place. And when the dogs have done with you there will not be one bone upon another left of you!"

Then he set the dogs on the man—the dogs he had trained on the blacks. They flew at the rider's legs; he lifted them from the snapping jaws to the horse's back. Then they leaped at the horse, biting at buttock and flank. The horse tried to bolt, but the dogs were too quick. He bucked, tripped in trying to kick, and rider and horse fell. The advertiser put his arms over his face to save his eyes, and doubled up his knees to cover his abdomen. Mr X—— looked on with no more

feeling than if he had been looking at a blackfellow. The man's screams brought my father running.

"Call off your dogs," my father shouted. "Call off your dogs!" Mr X—— stood with cold eyes.

Unarmed, my father picked up a stick and went for the dogs. The stick broke in his hands. But he had strong boots and the muscles of a gladiator. Fearing for his beloved dogs Mr X—— called them off.

The advertiser got up, helped by father. The horse was caught. His owner, broken-ribbed from his fall, torn and sobbing, rode off.

Thus was the land in the early days maintained to the squatters.

Years after, when I was at Goulburn in the nineteen-twenties, there came a small film company to the town to shoot a scenario made on the Rev. Father Hartigan's book, *Around the Boree Log*. I became acquainted with the camera company; and knowing the locality and its history, I was able to be of some use in regard to locations.

One night I had gone from my hotel to see some of the principals at theirs. They were sitting on the balcony, and, with them, Miss——, the second lead, whose father (she told me) was the first man to produce limelight effects on the stage in Sydney. It was a pantomime in which they were used. John Farrell took me to see it, and wrote it up with great éclat in the *Daily Telegraph*. I mention this as it is history, though not connected with my story.

As we sat talking at the hotel there came out on the balcony a very straight, very old man. He had the clear complexion that often goes with great age; also he had very blue eyes, a thick head of white hair, and a long snowy beard that reached nearly to his waist. As I looked at him I was aware of a puzzled feeling that he should be so short. I felt that he should somehow be taller—not that he was disproportioned. I just felt that he was unexpectedly short. He and one of the company falling into conversation, and the one being so old (he was then over eighty) and the other in search of local colour, he was brought over to be introduced to me, as I also was known to be interested in histories of places and people of an older period than my own. The moment his name was mentioned I knew why I thought he should have seemed tall; for at once, as if from a child's height, I saw the vision of a man writhing on the ground, screaming in agony, dogs at him, and my father running. The old man was the "advertiser."

The story of a trek

At Goulburn in the days of the Highland settlement there was a family of MacEacharns (there were also Duracks and MacDonalds; but of them another time). One of the same family was William MacEacharn, who for years was stock inspector at Tumut, and either he or his son was one of our earliest Australian tennis champions. The singer MacEacharn I have been told was also of this family, and so was Sir Malcolm of Goathlands in Victoria. Another of the connection was the famous blacksmith, John MacEacharn, of Albury. This man, who did not know his own strength, nor indeed the full range of his tremendous voice, stood nearly six feet four in height, and was so well built that one was not aware how outstandingly tall he was till he walked about among other men. He had a little wife, the top of whose head reached (as he loved to say), "as high as his heart." She could walk under his outstretched arm with ease.

This MacEacharn lived in what must have been almost the first built cottage in Albury, as its floors were all below its different doorsteps. It was the mode when Australia had no boarded floors, and one walked on clay practically in the raw. For it was not till a pair of pit-sawyers came to a town, or till growing wealth made it possible to send away to some far-off sawmill for timber, that floors were made of either slabs or boards. The rule in such places was for the joists to be put on the old tramped clay floor, as the walls being up, they could not be mortised into the ground-plate. The result was that you had to step over the ground-plate in every doorway. At the back veranda of this cottage there grew what must have been one of the oldest grape-vines on the Murray; for, in spite of dry rot having set in, its stem was still as thick as a woman's waist when I saw it towards the end of 1914; and it was then heavily fruited.

Of this John MacEacharn it was told that in one of the great river inundations he saved the lives of fifteen or twenty people both by swimming out to them, and by pulling across the current to where they were surrounded. Finally, his specialty was following funerals. He let no man go lonely to the grave. The homeless, the wanderer, the solitary, all had one man to walk behind them to their last resting-place.

"Life is lonely enough for such when lived, without letting them go lonely when dead," he said to me when giving me his reasons for this custom of his.

Somewhere in the early sixties, or perhaps the fifties, population increasing in the young colony of New South Wales, and the Goulburn MacEacharns wanting more land than they could get in Argyle, they decided to look for the new country that the Hentys were just then talking so much about in western Victoria—grassy lands with what my father, describing them, called "savannas," rivers for water, and with timber for fencing.

So, two of these MacEacharns, John and William, with possibly a third one, started to have a look at the new country. With packhorses and spares, horses having become plentiful and cheap in Australia by this time, they set out as men set out for El Dorado—facing the uncharted and the unknown, and without knowledge of how long the journey would be, either in distance or in time. They went through what was afterwards known as Riverina, evidently in a drought; for, though they saw beautiful country there was no water away from the two great rivers; consequently they lost most of their horses and had to drop most of their camp gear. After months of travel, in rags, with packs on their backs, but one horse left, and travelling by the sun as they went, they came to western Victoria.

In later years I was told by my husband's people that when they had but the one horse left, each brother took it in turn to ride ahead as track-breaker and to watch for hostile blacks, the other following the horse-tracks. When the first rider had gone his allotted distance he either waited for the other to come up with him, or hung up the horse (if the way was open country) and proceeded on foot. And so they travelled till they came to an end of journeying; for they had arrived at the fertile lands of which they had heard—where the Wannon moves to the Glenelg, and the Glenelg runs down to the sea.

I suppose there was a Lands Office in Melbourne then, for it was before my husband's father went into the West. And he went there about the time that the station-owners took up selections in the names of their working-bullocks in order to prevent small settlers getting a foothold. He told me some of the bullocks' names used, and also the case of that bullocky who stuck to the land his polers owned, defying the squatter to turn him out, saying he had as much right to the land as a bullock had. As the whole transaction had been illegal he had the whiphand and could not be turned out. I was told in later years that his descendants still lived on a part of that land.

". . . no boarded floors . . ."

Wherever the Lands Office was the MacEacharns made application for territory; had it allotted them; called the place Strathdownie; and returned for their flocks and herds at Goulburn. John MacEacharn had gone away an engaged man. On his return the young couple got married; the family packed up, and with teams, baggage, sheep and cattle, they all set out for the new home. Mrs John had a favourite mare, and was a notable horsewoman. She rode all the way, and was the first Australian woman to make such a long overland journey, and for long the first to make it in the saddle.

In telling this part of the story my father said that she set out a bride, and arrived at her destination with a six months' old baby in her arms, as the convoy was over eighteen months on the road. They had two shearings and two lambings; and there was not only wool for knitting socks, but wool to sell on arrival, or wherever it could be sold. But they would never have done so well had it not been for the blacks, who helped them through flooded rivers and creeks; told them where crossings could be made; brought back stock that wandered; attended Mrs John when the baby was born; and looked after the child as the mother rode again on the journey.

In our beginnings the black woman was always the stand-by of the woman of the interior. I remember two of the most trusted nurses in Wagga Wagga, who told my mother that what made them so successful was that they had learned from the blacks. Indeed one said she had to teach the doctor, as he had come to the town a surgeon, but not an *accoucheur*.

The MacEacharns divided their land into two parts, Strathdownie East and Strathdownie West, and there they brought up their families.

In about 1902 (perhaps 1904) my husband's father, who had never been known to make a mistake in a business deal during his earlier years, lost his keenness, and fell upon evil days; so we went to Victoria to look after him and his affairs. And there, as I have indicated, I again heard part of the story of the MacEacharns.

But besides the verbal, there is a written account of work and holdings that has a wider value than that of a mere family chronicle, and which I have condensed from the Mount Gambier *Border Watch*. According to this original the family arrived in Australia from Scotland in the 1830s, William taking a position as overseer to Mr John MacPherson, of Monara Station (New South Wales). After this he went to another MacPherson holding (The Lodden) till it was sold to Mr L. McKinnon, of the *Argus*. Next came Springbank, still another MacPherson property at Casterton, and which for a time was managed by a Mr Pugh, who was brother-in-law to Mr William Gilmore, Sen., of Burnside, Strathdownie. From Springbank Mr MacEacharn went to a fourth MacPherson place; this was Nerrin Nerrin, where he remained till 1851. It was while he was at Springbank that Mr MacEacharn was speared by the blacks, in the attack receiving twenty-three spear wounds. Almost insensible, he reached and mounted his horse, and was attended by his hut-keeper till a doctor could be sent for. Only his sound constitution saved his life. After this the family conjunction of his father, brothers, and brothers-in-law held Heathfield, East and West Strathdownie, and Kangaroo station. It was Mr W. MacEacharn who gave permission to a Mr McKinley to build the first hotel in Casterton. This was the Glenelg Inn; and it was through his influence, together with that of his neighbours, Messrs McCallum, W. and L. McIntosh, D. M. and D. McKinnon, W. and J. Robinson and others, that the first Presbyterian minister, the Rev. D. McCalman, was settled in the district. In concluding its account of Mr MacEacharn, the *Border Watch* says: "One by one are the old pioneers leaving the scenes of their many trials and troubles. Some of them prospered, and others like the deceased gentleman had to endure trials to the end, but he at least died with his faith unshaken."

While staying at my father-in-law's place, because he and my father had been young together, John MacEacharn used sometimes to come to see me; afterwards I stayed a visit at his son's place. There I was haunted by a familiar look as of a half memory—a likeness that I could not account for in the younger man's face. Then, one day, John MacEacharn told me that his wife was that Margaret Mackenzie who had ridden from Goulburn to Strathdownie. Her father was nephew to Sir John Mackenzie, and had come out from Scotland to take a position with the Peel River Company, which at that time owned most of the fertile Liverpool Plains on the northern Tableland. Now towns stand, and newspapers are printed, where the Peel River shepherds slept in watch-boxes by dingo-proof folds, and beside stockades for calves and breeding cattle, and shot down the blacks on sight.

Margaret's brother was Murdoch Mackenzie of Malebo, at Wagga Wagga. Distantly related, he married back to my father's first cousin, Christina Cameron. She, by the way, had the only full flock of white peacocks ever bred in Riverina. There were about twenty of them. I will never forget their dazzling look of silver as they turned in the sun. Ordinary peacock's feathers being thought unlucky, she had bred the white ones thinking to escape "the curse." When she died, the girls said the curse still carried; so they killed every bird, and bred no more.

Murdoch Mackenzie's daughter Margaret, called for her aunt Mrs MacEacharn, was the greatest woman stockrider Malebo ever saw. At sixteen years of age, hills, rocks, logs, mad cows, charging scrub bulls, meant nothing to her. She could crack a stock-whip like a man, and half the time rode bare-back—her side-saddle being most of the time lent to me, then just learning to ride. Malebo was wild country in those days; I still remember the blacks corroboreeing on the top of

the Bald Hill. The sound of the singing, of the bull-roarers and native drums, carried on the night air to Brooklyn though it was miles away.

In after years one of Murdoch Mackenzie's sons married his cousin, May Cameron, who was my father's favourite niece. And his son brought into Wagga Wagga the largest wagon-load of wheat ever taken with bullocks over Hampden Bridge, the bridge across the Murrumbidgee at the north entrance to the town. Being a record I mention it.

Perhaps now it will be seen why, when I went to Strathdownie, I found a familiar look—a Mackenzie look—in a face I had never seen before.

". . . they would never have done so well had it not been for the blacks . . ."

Sevastopol

Away back in the seventies, when the world of this still new land hummed with the rumours of reef and alluvial wash and outcrop, William Pike discovered a show near Junee. This was the Pike who married a Meurant. To them four children were born: Ferdinand, Louis, Elvira, and Diana. William Pike had a bronze medal from the Crimean War; also he was noted for his strength. It was so enormous that it was said he could take a young bull by the horns and break its neck. At a branding he threw all the steers he handled without need of a rope. I record this to place him identifyingly in his historical relation to this country, and to his times.

In the beginning his find was called Pike's Reef. Then reports of the good show spreading, a small rush set in; so a store, a blacksmith's shop and farriery, and a post office were started. When the time came to choose an official name (which still stands) Mr Pike in remembrance of the Crimea and his soldiering years chose Sevastópol. The accent of the word being on the first "o" the syllables divide as follows: Sev-as-tó-pol, the accented "o" being long as in "gold." However, postal authorities and surveyors made it Sebastopol, and put the accent on the "a" syllable. Being a child, it puzzled me that the apparently wrong name represented the right place, which was Sevastopol to those who originally knew it. While it lasted, it was an extremely rich find—apparently a pothole, and one of our noteworthy ones.

Just lately a visitor newly returned to Australia from a tour of Russia came to see me. As we talked of what she had seen, and where she had gone, she said, "And among the interesting places I went to was Sevastópol." And as I heard her pronounce the word as a Russian would, over the war, over Patagonia, over the Argentine, and Paraguay, over what long ago was to me the adventure of Broken Hill and Silverton, over girlhood and womanhood, the years leapt back to childhood and to a man whose hand in one clasp could have broken all my bones, yet who nursed me like a woman: a man named William Pike who found a reef, and in the seventies named it Sevastópol.

This man, during the campaign of the Crimea, dragged, carried, and placed a gun where no one else could or would go, with the result that either some point attacked was taken, or the Russians beaten off and his regiment saved. I think it was the latter. His stories of the suffering of the soldiers, of their starvation as well as wounds, were appalling. The young died like flies, frozen as well as starved; the elder men stole what they could and survived; a fire was like the face of God. He talked of Florence Nightingale (who was not beautiful) as though all beauty dwelt with her. Only to be touched by her hand was heaven. Dead men were happy because she had looked at them...

The column to which William Pike belonged had been led by its officers into such a position that it could neither retreat nor advance,

"... an extremely rich find ..."

and yet the men were held where, when they chose to do so, the Russians could pick them off at their leisure without an effective shot being returned. Consequently death was certain for every one unless they surrendered.

But William Pike, as a strong man would, looked for a way of escape. Studying the cliff-face leading up to the fortifications above the troops, and which Russian and English alike regarded as unscalable—so much so that the Russians did not keep a guard there—he saw far away up some shrubs and a jut of rock; and as he looked he noted that the jut was out of range of all guns. As he further studied it he observed small crevices and broken cracks here and there on the rock-face leading up to it. And as he looked he realized that if a gun could be got up there it would not only be itself covered, but would command the Russian sector that cut off retreat.

When Pike spoke of what he found and thought might be done, he was told that only a fool would think of anything so impossible. Humbly he pleaded and asked to be allowed to see what he could do. At last, by persistence one officer came over on his side, and in desperation he was given the leave he asked for. He studied the cliff-face; with his eye he measured and memorized spaces and distances, for his climb had to be by night in order not to be seen. First he went up alone, clinging here, clinging there, cutting a foothold or a handhold as he hung, in order to see what was on the jut in the way of rock and cover. Then when he had investigated, and reported possibilities, when all was ready, and the strong men he had chosen to haul had done their part and could lift no farther, he harnessed himself to the gun allotted, and slowly forged himself into the only position in which he could hold it and advance. Inch by inch he reached with his unbound arms for a crevice here, a crack there, till with one terrible effort he attained his goal. For a while he could not move; then he sent down the rope with which he had secured the gun to his body. With those who came up on it, when the starving men below had already begun to eat their horses, defeat was turned to victory.

Pike received a pension of tenpence a day, and a bronze medal.

And here in 1933, by a visitor from Russia, are the ends linked up, the Crimea, Sevastópol, Australia, William Pike and a child his great arms had nursed. So I have put his name and his deed here as a remembrance, not only of him, but through him of others like him who may still live in some other person's ungathered, half-obliterated recollections.

They had their culture

No book of recollections concerned with the period dealt with here would be complete without some reference to aboriginal life, either as it was endured during the squatting-period of massacre and persecution, or as it had been lived by the natives in their natural state—when they were free to be themselves in their own way and under their own inherited circumstances. Knowledge of these conditions was gained in two ways. One was by learning what those who had really known the blacks and had their confidence had to tell; the other was by such personal experience as came in one's own way, and by hearing, not isolated "talks," but general and universal discussions about them, and which in period of time ranged from that of grandparents, and those of their age, down to one's own contemporaries. I had both of these, and my own personal recollections as well.

But more than this I had my father to explain, from the background of his own intellectual culture and perceiving mind, the meaning and relationship of things seen and told, which to others meant no more than isolated acts, superstition, or ignorance; and which were never related by them to their own ignorance and superstitions, because even in regard to their accepted beliefs and credulities they had neither an ancient linking-up culture as a background, nor a modern education as an elucidating test.

This is why, till latterly, I have always seemed to hold such a different opinion, and tell so opposite a story of the poor black people, from others. But while others had their tales from the persecutors, I had mine from the side of the persecuted—indeed often through my own eyes, in the dead I saw.

But of that I hope to write another book to follow this. All that I desire to do now is to set down in writing a little of what I have for years been telling people verbally in an effort to influence ignorance, and awaken an interest for unofficial, untrammelled, friendly research. Indeed, I have talked of this wherever I could get a sympathetic hearer, or like the Ancient Mariner, had even forced a hearing. But as I look back I think: "Within the last decade, what a change!" I have no difficulty now in getting attention.

Here I would say that (apart from the Rev. William Ridley in the seventies) the one man who wrote with outstanding understanding of the aboriginal as a man, and as a man like other men, was the late Dr Basedow. It may seem foolish to tell it, but when I read his book the pent-up feeling of a lifetime of pity broke forth in tears.

If, in the pages that follow there seems a desire to drive belief on people, it is evidence of the years of unavailingly trying to make this country see that the aborigines as a nation were as naturally intellectual as we ourselves; that the seeming differences lay in the differences of education and in environment. Greece educated Europe, Europe educated us, we killed the black without giving him the education that made us different from him. Worse than this, we who expected him to understand us made no attempt to understand him. Instead we used him and then we broke him. With this preface I enter my subject.

There are and always have been those who stress, as though it were a sign of a low mental capacity on the part of the aborigines, that they spoke different dialects or languages, and could not always fully understand one another when they met. But Italians, French, and Spaniards are the same when *they* meet. Yet they are of one root-race and one root-language, diverted and made different only by distance and by some centuries of time.

That the aborigines had diverse languages at least shows in some degree their antiquity in Australia; as, however much their dialects varied, racially they themselves did not. Unchanged they carried their characteristic appearance from Cape York to Cape Otway. As to their different languages, I doubt if, take them by and large, they varied much more than those of the very limited areas of the shires and counties of England (even without the addition of Scotland, Wales and Ireland) till an enforced standard of school education made the English dialects one language. And this was a people settled for centuries under one government in one small country. The aboriginals, on the other hand, were a nomadic people in a whole continent.

It may be urged that the varieties of speech in England were the result of conquest by foreign peoples. The variations among the aboriginals were not due to foreign conquest. They were the changes wrought by endless ages of time on a homogeneous people. This as I have already said goes to prove their antiquity; and, let me add, their antiquity is some guide to measure the natural population of this continent when the white man first came here. But while admitting all

". . . then we broke him."

the variants of the original root language, the natives met the difficulty by providing not only for a telegraph of sound (drums) and signs (smoke as well as message-sticks, and marks on trees and earth and shrubs), but also for oral intercourse. They had interpreters, and where needed in case of urgency these were sent out either as runners, or followed runners with message-sticks, to whatever tribe information, warning, or other matters had to be carried.

The interpreters, I have heard my father say, were like the genealogists, chosen in childhood: boys always, and "not old enough to cry for their mothers." That phrase I definitely remember. They were taken a certain distance from their own group to meet those "with whom they were to stay while they learned the second language." When they became friendly and used to those who met them, the lads were taken on and remained with the other tribe till they not only thoroughly spoke the language, but knew it in relation to customs—quite another matter.

When the young interpreters had been away several years they were brought home again. There, because intercourse between tribes was not constant, they kept up the language by talking it among

". . . they were free to be themselves in their own way . . ."

themselves, and any others who by other means had learnt it. The coming of the white man, by scattering the groups and driving them into what literally was exile, broke this down, just as the recital of the genealogies was broken.

Those who had learned the new language, sometimes in its continued use forgot their own, and had to learn it on their return. They were brought home when they had to be prepared for the Bora ceremonies.

A lad who proved linguistically dull in the new environment was sent back again. This was considered a terrible disgrace; he was shameful because he was no good to those to whom he was envoy, and because he misrepresented his own people. I saw one such lad once. He was not exactly sent to Coventry, but very nearly; and to this sensitive people, sensitive in regard to a fall from accepted tribal standard, his state was not to be envied. He wanted for nothing, but special hunting and great adventure that were for the other boys were not for him. His only means of rehabilitation was to do something specially brave or skilful, and he had to do it alone.

Besides their accurate ear—the aboriginals could sound vowel variations impossible to us—the children selected had to be of good appearance and of sound health, as well as quick at learning if they were to be sent abroad. No tribe could be offended by one who was an inferior. For one thing he could not compete with those of his own age amongst whom he was sent, and they would be at strain to be courteous to him—as they must be to one from another sept or clan who lived with them.

While tribes lived separately and had their own laws, regulations, and use of locality, there were some general codes that bound all. So when there were special things to be notified, it was compulsory for every tribe to have word sent them. I remember my father saying that chief among these notifications were: threatened drought, great inundations, possible attack, famine, or a disease; that for centuries whenever the white man's sails were seen, no matter on what coast or in what condition, the messages, first by signal and then by runners, immediately went from one side of Australia to the other. They feared the white man more than they feared anything else; at any appearance of a ship with canvas sails, panic struck the whole nation. The white man was ruthless; worse, he brought disease.

Besides matters of great danger, there was the necessity to observe certain laws or usages as common to all, no matter how different in situation the tribes were, or how far removed from each other. The law of famine was one such. If through drought or other cause famine

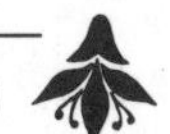

attacked a tribe, they had to be given access to the means of living somewhere else, till their own part of the country could support them again. That was before civilization came and curtailed their means of living and curtailed their locations as well.

To assist in replenishment of areas possums would be caught in the land of plenty, and, when rains came, these were loosed in the trees in places too far for them to travel back from. This was done in order that they might breed in the renewing locality. Possums were the great standby, as they could be carried and transported, and could live in trees, having the dew and the leaves as food and drink, when there was no grass and no water for kangaroos or emus.

In addition to this general famine law, there were those that related to marriage, probably the most complicated in the world; the rites of Bora, and religious taboos of places and objects to be held as private; and there was that rule which suspended battle while either side needed time to provide food for sustenance. Their belief was that a man or a people had a right to food even if an enemy.

Intratribal rule was a matter for the tribe itself; but for that which was general, should there be need to alter, enlarge, or impinge upon it in new ways, envoys were sent, who met, conferred, and, in conference with the heads, decided. These envoys often were the chiefs themselves who had with them their interpreters if they had not themselves been interpreters. The interpreter, who must have ability, was often chosen as chief, as his post was very important. In general, however, he was the outside representative of the tribe, as the chief was the ruler.

No accredited envoy or herald was ever attacked even though he had to go through hostile country. As a messenger he was always fed and assisted on his way.

Native sanctuaries

That native races all over the world conserved wild fruits and animals in the same way as our aborigines did, is a fact that few writers have troubled to note. In Australia, in America (North and South), the invader lived, as never before or since, on the teeming life of the forests, the rivers, and the air of the country. It was nature's prolific breeding, he would have said had he been asked. Indeed, unreasoning creature that he was, he did say it. He never realized that less than fifty years later, with a population much more sparse than that of either the Indian or the aboriginal he displaced, fish were no longer caught in profusion, and meats had to be taken from the farm and the home-paddock. I am reminded and confirmed in this by Edna Ferber's book *American Beauty* where, on page sixty, she says in reference to her own country:

> *Undoubtedly they (the new settlers) all knew many aspects of hardship but there was about their manner of living in this brief period of Connecticut's history a kind of splendour and lavishness that were not to be met again. They were, for the most part, a well-to-do group in the beginning. In every household there were bins of cornmeal, rye, buckwheat, and wheat flour. Festoons of dried apples hung in the attics and kitchens; and herbs for flavouring and for medicine. There were partridges in the woods, pheasants in the brush. In the poultry yards were chickens, turkeys, geese, and ducks. The turbulent Housatonic River was so crowded with shad that one could all but scoop them up by the handfuls.*

That, with other names for birds, fish and animals (the last omitted by Miss Ferber), might have been said of Australia. When I first remember the bush you shot for possum without leaving the camp-fire; when I first recollect the Murrumbidgee you caught your fish in the reeds, or muddied the water at the edge to make them rise, and took them, not with a hook or gaff, but by the hand. Even later, you only set your line when you put the billy on, and the fire was not yet burned down enough for roasting on the coals or in the ashes. At that time, often a freshwater lobster lifted from the Murrumbidgee was supper enough for father, mother, and two of us children.

A few years later when I asked my father why we could not get fish as formerly he said, "When the blacks went the fish went:" meaning that the habit of preserving the wild was destitute in the ordinary white settler. Yet at that time the white population on the rivers was only a fraction of what the black had been. When my father-in-law first took up Burnside, his place on the Victorian Glenelg, he told me that any time he could go down the brink from the house to the river with a kerosene-tin and a landing-net, and half an hour later bring home two freshwater lobsters for the evening meal. He did not bring more than two, as usually these filled the kerosene-tin. Sometimes, smaller ones being lighter eating, he would put back the big two and bring home three smaller ones.

When I was there forty years later, you might fish for days, and bring home only yabbies. Indeed, in many of our rivers in all States the big freshwater lobster, wanting the selective breeding care of the native, practically disappeared.

Beside the fish, where there were deep valleys, running water and much timber, the natives invariably set aside some parts to remain as breeding-places or animal sanctuaries. Where there were plains by a river, a part was left undisturbed for birds that nested on the ground. They did the same thing with lagoons, rivers, and billabongs for water-birds and fish. There once was a great sanctuary for emus at Eunonyhareenyha, near Wagga Wagga. The name means "The breeding-place of the emus"—the emu's sanctuary. The one-time fish-traps on the Darling, the Murrumbidgee, and the Lachlan all indicated sanctuary; the small fish would escape, or could multiply beyond the rocky maze that formed the trap or balk; the large remained within the fishing area. When on the lower side the fish were plentiful, and the upper part required a rest, keystones were lifted, or put in if they had been lifted, and sanctuary was moved over the barrier.

Pregan Pregan Lagoon at North Wagga Wagga was a sanctuary for pelicans, swans and cranes; and the land between it and the Murrumbidgee was a curlew sanctuary. I have forgotten what that was called, though I remember that my father gave it the name he had from the blacks. At Ganmain and Deepwater there were alternately swan and duck sanctuaries. The law of sanctuary in regard to large or wide breeding-grounds, such as Ganmain and Deepwater, where once there were miles and miles of swamps (as also down near Deniliquin), was that each year a part of the area could be hunted or fished, but not the same part two seasons in succession.

"When the blacks went the fish went."

When I first remember Pregan Pregan (pronounced Prahgan Prahgan, and sometimes called Parkan Praygan) it was simply covered with pelicans, teal, duck, cranes, and swans; but being specially a pelican sanctuary, these birds predominated. When I first went to the Wagga Wagga school, as we trudged in from Brucedale Road, where I had remembered clouds of them there were seventy only, then forty, then twenty, then four, and then there were no pelicans at all. The swans went till there were but two; the ducks came only at night—the few that survived. Only once in a while were there swans or ducks on Pregan Pregan in the daytime when I went to school under Peter Durie and Miss Galloway.

On the Lachlan, near Ben Hall's old place, there was another sanctuary for emus, and Cargelligo was set aside for birds and fish. The great plain round what was called "the Basin," was for the land birds and the kangaroo. When Cargelligo was fished, stalked or trapped in freedom, it was allowed on one side only. The same when Lake Cowal was full and was its substitute. About these places I only know what I was told when I was there about 1877. But the places about Wagga Wagga are different. I remember when the blacks were there; and when my father used to explain the sanctuaries to strangers and visitors. At first, even the white man observed the breeding-season at Eunonyhareenyha and refrained from shooting in the season. My father, the Presbyterian minister (Mr Falconer), Mr Mair, Mr Forsyth (of Forsyth's Store) and others influenced public opinion against shooting, and especially against hunting with dogs when the birds were nesting.

Then, the town growing, and land-settlement increasing, there was objection made that one of the sweetest spots for grazing should be set aside for birds, when selectors could farm and make homes there. So in the end the semi-reserved part was thrown open and taken up at once. But even before selection took the land, the growth of the town sent people out Sunday after Sunday shooting.

Dogs were not allowed to go with them, by order of the newly formed Town Council—or perhaps of the police magistrate, Mr Thompson. This, too, was due in part to my father.

In a census of emus, which he took about that time, there were but three hundred left on Eunonyhareenyha. But in two years, instead of an increase, there were only a hundred. My father went to Jim Hawkins, then manager, to see if they could not be preserved. Mr Hawkins (or was it Mr Rand?) had notices put up that neither dogs nor shooting would be allowed on the station. Unluckily the eggs were forgotten; so next year when we drove out to see them there were only about half a dozen flocks of young birds to be found in the whole area. The nests had been raided everywhere.

My father had a great longing for the conservation of the wild. He had advocated taking over a part of Eunonyhareenyha as a Grand Chase, to be held as such in perpetuity for the people. Of part of Ganmain and Deepwater, and of Gobbagumbalin he also spoke, but his heart was in Eunonyhareenyha. Many a talk he had with Mr Hawkins about it, and I really believe that had it lain with the latter alone, and had the town asked for it, there was a time when he would have arranged with his principals to set aside or give a special area, at least for a time if not in perpetuity.

But he was not the owner, the land was not freehold; free selection rolled like a tide over places near water and towns, so that only what could be financially held of the station was retained by the lessees. Like a steam-roller man swept down everything his own will had not planned or decreed. No sanctuary was proclaimed, so the wild went—as it went in England, in France, in China, and everywhere else where machinery and a written code came with a conqueror.

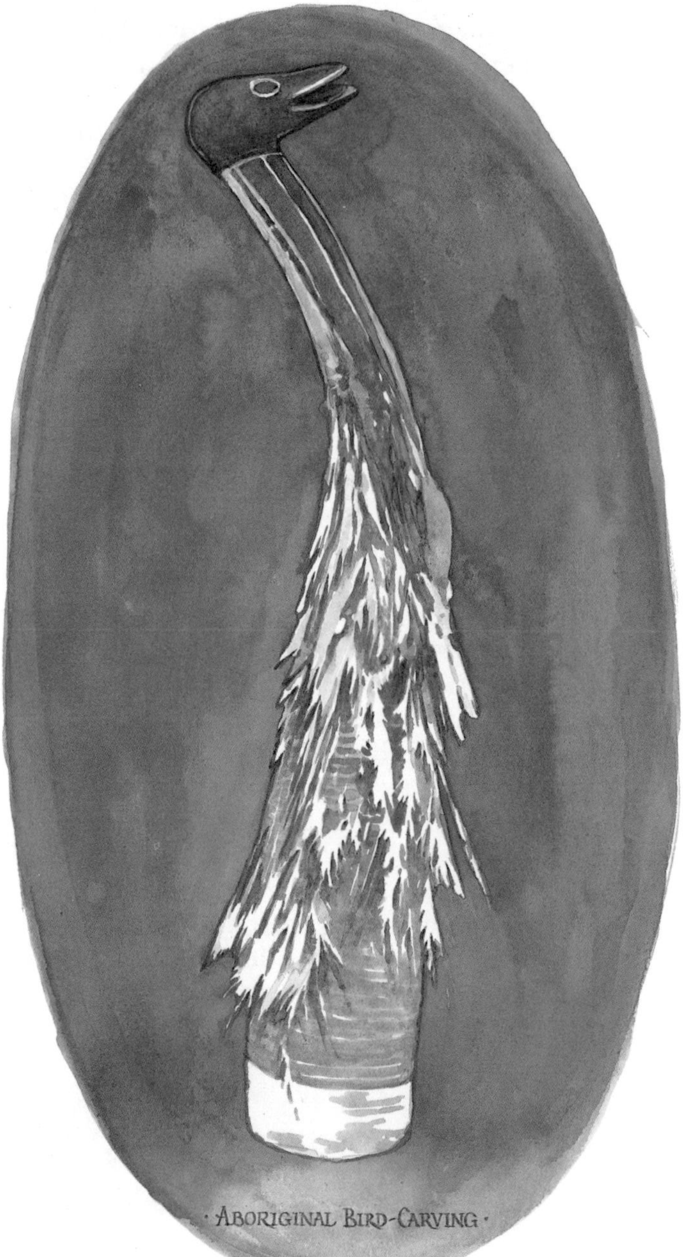

· ABORIGINAL BIRD-CARVING ·

". . . the patience with which the black worked in his own native art . . ."

The ungathered script

My son writes in a letter lately received: "I have just seen a splendidly carved whip-handle. It is gidgee, worked to represent plaiting, and in a part of it is a leaf. It is done by a black stockman with a pocket-knife and a bit of broken glass. The accurancy of the appearance, and the spacing of each represented strand, is a tribute to his eyesight. You would swear each strand came in turn from under the others. I will try to get four others for table-legs if I can. . ."

Some of the old ceremonial spears, handed down for generations, and not used in war or hunting, were beautifully carved from end to end. European perspective and design being unknown to the blacks, the work followed native conventions; and as with the early historied nations, Babylon, Egyptian, Hebrew and others, the design was symbolical rather than, as with the later Greek, merely for purposes of beauty—beauty as accepted. If one may digress, it is curious to note that the cult of beauty in art, by too closely keeping the canon of line and composition, in our time has become a defeated thing. For now life itself is beauty, whether beautiful in old ways or not. So Epstein lives; today, I venture to say, Art's greatest master. The painters reach out toward his world on canvas. The cubists and futurists took the hammer and broke the old; the reconstructing masters brought to the fore a new dimension—they added expression to muscle, and set humanity in planes behind area and surface. In the unsymmetrical they gave movement to detail, where aforetime it had only existed in the massed composition as a whole.

As to aboriginal art: when the conqueror came, with a new convention, native genius loosed itself in European designs on whip-handles, boxes, and walking-sticks. The plait and leaf in combination is one of my earliest recollections. Sometimes the design was a quandong and leaf. The rope also was used; yet another pattern but not so common, was the snake; sometimes it was lizards.

In Sydney, today, there is a beautiful example of the snake. It is a walking-stick given to my uncle, the late Charles White (a writer on Australian aboriginal and other historical subjects), whose father,

John Caspar White* bought the *Bathurst Free Press* nearly a hundred years ago. The carving—now in the possession of his daughter at Mosman—was done with a piece of broken glass. Climbing the polished stick are a number of small wriggling snakes, set at such distances, and at such angles, that I defy anyone to see them and not shrink, they are so alive and full of movement. If you turn the stick at all they appear to be actually climbing. Another stick was made for him, with a pocket-knife, by Jimmie Governor. This was a full-grown snake, in black wood, standing on its tail and with the head bent for a top. My aunt, on account of the Governors, objected to it and it was given away. But the other is still in possession of my cousin. I am hoping she will one day give it to the Art Gallery or to Vaucluse House, the work is so typical of the aboriginal, and so good in itself.

As a child I had all sorts of things carved for me to play with; polished balls, little boxes, and flat and round pieces of shaped wood. Some had plaits, some basket weaves, some mixed patterns. I was too small at the time to take care of them. They were made chiefly from the boree. In the indifference of the day to anything aboriginal—a day when we split up polished spears and other weapons to light kitchen fires and boil water in a hurry—they were all lost.

Other things the aboriginals used to carve for us were quandong-stones, covering them with the plait and the basket weave. When they had pocket-knives they would make these into tiny lockets with a hinge and a catch, and a closing that was almost invisible. Some had a flange instead of a hinge, and only opened when turned in a certain way. Inside would be another, and sometimes a third one. These, of course, were not of remote aboriginal origin, as they were only possible after knives and glass came to the country.

When I think of the patience with which the black worked in his own native art, I wonder that no one has written a popular monograph on this alone. Whatever has been written has been for the scientists, not for the people who are killing off the blacks, or who as travellers go unseeingly past them. Yet these same travellers are the very ones who could do most for science, if they were shown that collection was possible and meant something not only to Australia but to the world in general.

For example, take the *churingas* alone—those sacred things made of wood or flint—and then consider the tiny holes and markings made for the design, bored with a minute splinter of stone, or burned in with a match-like spark of wood. With our poker-work machines,

*See note at end of chapter.

"Every line and every mark . . ."

cutting-tools and electric needles, we think the work poor, But I have never seen a white man with the same primitive material do better. Indeed, I have never seen him to do it at all!

And there is another point. We have contemptuously said of these people that they have no written language. But what do we know of the meanings in the markings of the *churingas*? And how many have we interpreted? I have asked for the official interpretation of even one at the Sydney Museum and received nothing. Yet every line and every mark has its meaning. What again have we written of the patternings in blues, reds, whites and browns that decorated the old properly shaped native-made possum-rugs, told a story, and made the skins identifiable wherever found? Are our *churingas*, our dendroglyphs, even these rugs, a less esoteric record than the Inca, the Egyptian, or the Indian markings on stone?

We have learned nothing and we have conserved nothing compared with what we might have had. Unhindered we let the most ignorant settler, and the most brutal stockman, shoot, starve, burn, poison, break, and destroy the most living record of an ancient world that the later centuries have known.

Where men write, memory is not stored; but where men do not write memories are full. Lore is not less lore, history is not less history, because it is verbal and not written. We emptied out the storied fullness we had, and spilled it as blood in the dust. The black man had his *seannachies* even as the Highlander; and his tribal pedigree

was counted out, generation by generation, to a period beyond the Caesars, and, for all we know now, perhaps even beyond the longest Chinese record. Carried in the memories of trained and chosen relators, these records of life lived. We killed the tellers, and the genealogies died with them.

Besides all this, I have pleaded with more than one professor, more than one student of ethnology, for a wider reach and a fuller comparison with other lands and other times in regard to spoken language as well as in regard to glyph and character-sign. And the reply has always been, "But there is no script!" And I answer now as I have answered always: When was ever an Australian native, with his knowledge of his people, and rich in his interpreter's knowledge as so many were—when was ever such a one, or such a score, taken to the Indian Reservations of the United States of America, to talk and investigate there? or to Canada? or to Patagonia? Yet in Patagonia, I, without any scientific training, found similarity in Indian words; found likeness in the manner of shaping skins for *capas* (rugs); found fellowship in the patterns and staining, and even in the way the sewn skins were worn, by Indian and Australian alike.

Surely it is as scientific to see if a given sound in two different languages has the same meaning, as to see if two written forms of that sound are commonly derived or related! But it was never done; never even thought of. Now the North American Indian is civilized and learns *Hiawatha* in English. The Patagonian is a remnant, the Australian a hunted fragment. Yet it was from the verbal that the script arose. The sound is older than the sign, and the single sign older than the multiple. The single sign is the world's dictionary of beginnings. And still I am told "Comparison is impossible because there is no script!"

Compiled by the first Protestant missionary to go to South Patagonia, a Mr Hunziger, I was shown by his son an old book, even then long out of print, that had been made on the Auraucanian tongue as spoken in Patagonia. There being no script parallel to the Spanish, it was phonetically spelt. And even there I found root words that recalled the aboriginal to me. I myself have a similar book, equally rare. It also is a missionary's work; is in four languages, Guarani, Spanish, English, and German. And there I read in the phoentic Guarani (for it, too, had no script) *aca*, head; *ybai*, bad, ugly; *hee*, yes. The aboriginal is *cab* or *cob* for head; bad is *baal*; yes is *y*, *yi*, or *yowi*, with in the last, the long accent on the *i*—and these are but three words picked at random.

This Paraguayan book, I may mention, was officially ordered to

be destroyed, as the government wished Guarani to cease to be the people's language, Spanish being the ruling and official one. It was feared that any book employing both languages, and especially as giving written form to Guarani, would keep the latter in use to the detriment of Spanish in country schools. Consequently the publication is regarded as very rare. Guarani is still spoken, of course, in Paraguay, but in limited country use. The cities and towns all speak Spanish. Even in this book I have mentioned there is a large percentage of words of either Spanish, or Spanish-and-Guarani parentage.

I have made particular reference to this collection because I think the Spaniards were here in Australia long before the British saw the place, and I am of opinion that they left their traces in the aboriginal languages. I have found in glossaries many words distinctly (to me) of Spanish origin, or if not Spanish then Portuguese.

Here again is a neglected field; neglected as much as the other; and yet one that we should have worked while the field was rich.

Note: John Charles White came to Australia from England for his health, which the cold climate had threatened. He landed in South Australia and held the first service in connection with Methodism in that colony. While in South Australia he learned one of the aboriginal dialects; made a glossary of it; and translated for the aboriginals a part of the gospel of St John. Uncle Charles (his son who was married to my mother's sister) told me that his only copies of these were lost at Bathurst when the children were too young to value them. In 1838 or 1839 the family left South Australia for Sydney. From Sydney the journey to Bathurst was made by bullock-team. Mr White's daughter, Polly, was one of the first pair of twins born in South Australia. One of her Sydney recollections was of being present at the function in connection with laying the foundation stone of Macquarie Lighthouse at South Head. She married and became Mrs Tye. When she was nearly ninety she still curled her snow-white hair, walked miles to church, and sewed without glasses. She died in 1933 at ninety-five years of age—almost to the last a woman with a witty tongue. But what recollections were lost in that woman!

How they counted numbers

What follows here really should belong to the book which I hope later to write on the New Australia Movement and Paraguay, and for which I have a volume of our little daily manuscript paper, *Cosme Evening Notes.* I edited this manuscript journal for a year, and the copy I have contains part of my editing. It came to me in a curious way. Harry S. Taylor, in later years owner of the *Murray Pioneer* newspaper, having been called home from Cosme by the death of his father, was so anxious still to hear of the colony that his friend, James Sime (nephew of Mr Walters of *The Times*), said that if he could get a light enough paper for the purpose he would daily copy out *Evening Notes* and send it to him. Mr Sime looking for what he wanted, came to me, and as I had some very good foreign note I gave it to him. Before Mr Taylor died in 1932 he wrote saying he was sending me as a present something that he knew I would value. The gift came: it was the year of the little journal, carefully preserved and bound. Out of the seven years' manuscript record of Cosme, this is the only copy in the world, as all the originals were accidentally burnt when the library and all its records caught fire. To add to the interest for me, half the journal, as I have said, is of my editing.

Besides this fraction of *Evening Notes*, I have this year (1933) been given another record of our sojourn in Paraguay. It was brought me by Mr D. B. Cody, an Argentine now in Australia. It is the small diary of Mr Westwood, one of our ex-New Australia colonists, and though fragmentary, dates from leaving Sydney Heads, in *The Royal Tar*, till in anger and bitterness he left New Australia; and yet to which, in a letter written years after, he refers in terms of affection and regret. And while the copy of *Evening Notes* recalls colony things I had almost forgotten, Mr Westwood's diary adds his personal testimony to one of the apparent evidences which I have recorded of the probable link between South America and Australia in racial origins. This relates to the method of counting small numbers and reckoning great ones; quite a different thing from the similarities of custom and language which I had found between the Auraucanians and the aborigines when we lived in Patagonia. This special evidence lies in the fact that the Guaranis of Paraguay and the Australian natives count in practically the same way.

I might say here that long ago Mr Westwood had come to Cosme specially to see me, as he had heard that I had told how the aboriginals had germinated seed which, if it perished easily, or if it germinated slowly (like wattle seed), had to be hastened, and that through this information the long-lost secret of germinating *mate* seed had been rediscovered.

We had a long and interesting talk about the aborigines, on my side, and the Guaranis in whom he was interested. As we talked I told him how the aborigines counted, and he at once told me the Guaranis counted in the same way. As he was writing for the Buenos Aires papers he made notes of all I told him. Soon after that he left Paraguay and I never saw him again. Now one of his note-books has come to me from Melbourne, where he died only a year before I received it. As he had collected a great deal of matter about the Guaranis and other South American tribes his knowledge would have been invaluable to the student of the aboriginals. I did not know he was in Australia till after his death; and bitterly I regret that want of knowledge.

The aboriginal power to count or compute in his native state was as great as our own. The methods are different, that is all. I have seen partially trained native stockmen give the exact number of cattle in a group or mob up to four or five hundred almost without a moment's hesitation; yet authorities on the black continue to tell us that the aboriginal only counted to ten or thereabouts. My father's description of their method of reckoning was that they used the half-decimal five instead of the decimal ten, and with the addition of hands and feet could make any number required.

In Paraguay I found that the Guarani, as the aboriginal, had five single numbers, named and corresponding with the fingers of one hand. After that they used a compound term as we do. For anything up to five both gave the single name, and after that would hold up, for numbers up to twenty, fingers and toes grouped as required. Beyond that the thumb of the right hand meant one thing in relation to the grouping just given, the thumb of the left another. The great toes varied in the same way. The other fingers and toes, added singly or in cross combination, made endless permutations. In this way our blacks measured the numbers of the stars, using group words for tally totals.

I have not seen the Guaranis count the stars, but as a child I saw the aborigines do it many a time, and the smallest of them could beat

me at it. I used to number by our arithmetical progression, and being small would lose my count and my place in the heavens at about three or four hundred; but the little aboriginal children of the same age still kept on counting group-thousands. And what scorn they felt for my stupidity in not being able to keep up with them even a reasonable part of the way! I have heard my father say that the elders numbered all the stars, plotting the heavens out in fields; and that no matter what star he might point to, they could not only tell him the surrounding number visible to him, but the number that only by having their location pointed out, and focusing for them when told where they were, he could see.

To know and number the stars was a part of the training of the children, and it began in infancy. The heavens were as much the clock and chart of these people as roads, time-pieces, and calendars are ours. But the ordinary white man who counted to a hundred and then notched a stick because otherwise his mind lost the place, could not conceive of a method of reckoning other than his own. So, he said of what he could not grasp, that "the aborigines could not count."

For those who have still old people about them who can remember aboriginal words and the manner of counting, I append here the Guarani as put roughly into Spanish sounds by the Jesuits:

One	*petēine, petei* or *mōno pētei*
Two	*mōcōi*
Three	*mbohapi*
Four	*iriendi*
Five	*ācē-popatei* indicated by one hand
Ten	*ācē-pōmōcōt* both hands
Twenty	*acepo-acepiabe* hands and feet

Some day when there comes a revision of values, it may be that the last word of recognition has not yet been said of the New Australia and Cosme colonies of William Lane, whether as to Paraguay or to Australia.

When I was with the aboriginals on the banks of the Murrumbidgee, at the time of which I have written in *Under the Wilgas*, the chief woman of the tribe, in whose charge I was, tried to teach me to count in the native way. She began as she would with her own children, showing me two fingers, two sticks laid together, two eyes, two ears, two elbows, two feet. She did not show me two thumbs, then, as thumbs had a group meaning and she did not want to confuse me. Later she used tiny sticks, fragments of bark, and little clods of earth. This was to show that through differing shapes or

"... with the aboriginals on the banks of the Murrumbidgee ..."

differing places two remained two; and it was also to make the eye quick in perception. As soon as I grasped two I went to threes.

I was only a few weeks with them, but she had begun to point out and name the stars to me, and what they meant (also to teach me about roots and food). The only star I now remember was Jiemba, "The laughing star." I remembered it because it sounded like my childhood's name, Jeannie, and because I was told it was *my* star, and that I laughed and danced like it.

So accurate was my counting as a result of this group notation, that later on, when between seven and eight years of age, John Stinson, of Kindra, used to take me with him to tally the sheep at the yards, or when there had been boxing with travelling sheep. I counted by threes (I had got no further at the camp, though I remembered the method and later on practised on sheep up to fives). My tally was never questioned. Indeed it was by the blacks' method all the good tally-men of the old days learned. Most counted by twos; a few by three; none by fives, as the mind of the white man, untrained in the higher numbers, inelastic by age, and feeling its only security in the unitary method, feared to leap beyond the easy and the accustomed. To me it seemed easy to miscount by ones—easy to miss a single sheep—impossible to miss three, four or five; though I was surest with three. As a matter of fact I thought it waste of time to say one, two, three, four, when I could say three, six, nine, and so on.

Afterwards when I went to school in Wagga Wagga, the speed with which I did addition sums was noted, and at last Miss Galloway came to my class (I was then in second) and asked how I did it. I did it by breaking the ordinary units into a group-unit. That is to say, in a column of 6, 9, 4, 5, there would be seven threes, and three over. If fives or tens suited better I used fives and tens; these latter being for double columns. Unconsciously I had carried into the school the method of the blacks; to the so-called educated the accuracy and speed of the so-called ignorant.

The black man's mode of counting in groups is in a general way also that applied to tracking. Where the white follows as it were a single line of point to point tracking, the aboriginal is taught to look at an area and to mark the deviation from normal to abnormal in everything—the deviation in that which has been moved as opposed to that in natural position—and all in relation to the surrounding area in which the noting is done. That is to say he makes the abnormal, the track or trace, stand up against its background of normal, while we make the abnormal (the track or trace) the thing to be sought.

Hence we fail as trackers in comparison with the native as we fail in counting the stars, for we do both by the unit—a painful, slow and wasteful way. In other words, the native counts by group and tracks by area, and this gives him a mobility and a range physical or sensory, that is denied us by our method.

". . . to mark the deviation . . ."

White sails and Dampier's disease

Among the things that have greatly interested me, and one that shows the patience and observation of the scientific mind, is Dr Elkin's reasoned discovery that circumcision (and its kindred mutilation in another direction) began and spread irregularly from one certain localized place on the western coast of Australia.

Just as they discussed the occasional nose-piece (which could only be worn by a spearman who had done something remarkable) so the men of my childhood discussed circumcision, and wondered why some places far apart had it, and others adjoining had not. In the midst of it all there came a day when, standing by my father, I heard him talking of it to the chief of whom I think I have already made mention in relation to tribal history. This man told my father that circumcision came through things that had happened a long while before, when there came to Australia the first ship with white sails of which the natives had record. Many times brown mat-sails had come, but never before the white, which were made differently, were large and in many pieces instead of being but one and upright. Moreover, they filled out round in the wind and had not to be moved, as the brown, when direction changed.

When the brown sails came they put in for a short time only, were given hospitality, took food and water, made repairs if needed, and went away again without intrusion or breach of international or tribal usage. It was a case of each nation respecting the rights of the other. When the white sails came, the natives, although filled with wonder at them, gave the visitors the usual hospitality; trespass and hostility being the last thing thought of. This ship was not only different and more stupendous than anything seen before, but it was the first time people were seen wearing hats on their heads and "clothes" on their feet, that is, boots. At first all was well. But seeing that there were young girls who were to be preferred to the community wives allowed strangers as guests (a usage regarded as a courtesy among the aboriginals as once in Great Britain), a raid was made by the white men of the ship.

The tribes resisted, but the white men killed from a distance by fire that preceded a small "closed" thunder—a death unseen that came from sticks that they pointed, and from which burst the flame or lightning that brought the thunder. All that the stricken man himself knew was that there was a blow such as had never been suffered before, so that his bones would be broken inside his flesh, or he would die not knowing he had been struck. It was not till the dead had been examined (and examination did not come at first, but only after many had been killed) that any wound was found. Till the wounds were found the gun-fire was regarded as supernatural magic from the gods.

When it was known to be human work a great army of natives gathered; for, they realized that if they did not destroy the invaders they would go back to their own country, and, telling their people, these would come in numbers, and because of their weapons take possession, never to be driven out again. The end of the affair was disaster. The finest of the warriors were killed because it was their right and their duty to take the brunt of battle. As fast as one lot fell another took its place till there were only helpless old men and lads left. On these the white men levied a tribute of young girls.

". . . the white sails came . . ."

After a time the ship with white sails went away, but not all her crew went with her. A few escaped and stayed with the blacks.

After the vessel had gone it was noticed that a strange illness broke out among the people—something utterly unknown to the Australians. Nothing like it had ever been seen or heard of before. It came from the young girls, and their babies were born dead or had it. All affected children as lived were put to death at once. Investigation showed that no one had the disease who had not been in contact with someone connected with the ship and its crew. Word was sent to the adjacent tribes for a conference, as the thing had to be stopped or there would be no clean births and no tribal continuity left. In conference it was decided that whoever had been in contact with the ship, and those who had been in contact with these again, should be put to death to stamp out the disease.

My father, asking how long ago this was, was told the time in generations. He reckoned it up. "It was Dampier's disease," he said in telling my mother; for the number of generations went back to just about Dampier's time.

I may add here that there was nothing more dreaded among the islands than "Dampier's disease." I heard old seamen speak of it with horror, how that wherever Dampier went death followed him, so that whole islands were left empty. I suppose I was nearly forty years old before I realized that in this connection I always used the name of a generation older than my own, to a generation later than my own, which had another designation altogether for the scourge.

When the natives first discovered the disease to be amongst them they tried to cut it away on its first appearance. It was when they found this to be useless that they decided, as I have said, to put to death all primary and secondary contacts. But what had been tried as a remedy was by some continued as a precaution, and with these became a custom. Whether this custom originated with the seamen who had run away and lived with the blacks, or wholly with the blacks themselves, I cannot say. But I do remember the chief saying that from the time of this invasion of disease the natives kept sentinels to watch the seas in case of other white sails appearing; and that as soon as they were sighted the women and children were sent miles and miles away inland. This was done all round Australia, no matter on what coast such a ship appeared. It had not to be done if the sail were an island one. It was done only when the Christian white man came.

In writing of this matter I may mention that no disease has ever been given to the world by the Australian aboriginal. Australia had an absolutely clean sheet on that score. But the diseases of the world

have been brought to her. This is an historical fact.

Besides having no diseases to give the invader there was no vermin for either house or body. I could play in a black's camp all day and my head would never need to be looked at. But if I played with a neighbour's children or slept in a strange house—then next morning it was: "Come here at once. I want to look at your head!" It was the same with fleas. When you could not go near an old sheep-yard or a shepherd's hut for fleas, you never thought of them when going to a black's fishing or a corroboree—that is not till the later years when the whole country was infested. As to bugs—they only reached us in Riverina when the railways came through and the bush-folk collected them and brought them home from Melbourne or Sydney. In the days of trails only, they were unheard of. I refer to these things because in an account of a captured black, Governor Phillip wrote that he "took lice out of his hair and ate them." He does not say how many days after capture this was, or how long the man had been among the whites, who, as everyone knows, swarmed with *Pediculus capitis* not only in convict ships and convict quarters, but in later immigrant vessels; and this to such an extent that (so old people used to tell me), "looking at heads went on every day and all day." They also used to say that "The ship's captain and officers only came round when they had to, and then only after everywhere had been swabbed clean for them to walk on," and that in their rounds they never allowed themselves or their clothes to touch a bunk or bedding or human being.

Captain Phillip says that the captured black ate the vermin. If he did, he was probably only copying "his betters" by using his teeth on them, a thing I have seen more than one old servant from English homes do. I have seen much the same thing done by the same class of people with fleas, which, when caught, would be popped into the mouth or wet with saliva while held, so that, wet, they could not hop off before being killed. I refer to this to awaken humility and recollection in others.

That the aborigines had no head vermin was, along with other peculiarities, one of the common subjects of discussion by the older stockmen and settlers generally. It used to be believed that white people naturally, that is, spontaneously, bred vermin. One of my father's additional proofs that the aborigines did not have these things was that they had no word for them in any of their dialects. I doubt if any such word will be found in any vocabulary collected during or before the seventies. Later, it may be different.

To end this unsavoury subject, which as a matter of justice had to

be brought up: if I may come to modern times, our soldiers at the war definitely found that delousing (to use the objectionable word) was not a black man's legacy but a European necessity.

Fish balks and traps

How easily knowledge can be lost for want of being valued during the period of its currency, is shown by the aboriginal fish-traps at Brewarrina, and on the Lachlan, and that once were on most of the long rivers elsewhere in Australia—in some cases blasted out or otherwise destroyed (as on the Murrumbidgee) to let the wool barges have way. They are regarded as a "mystery" now, and in some cases are put down by authorities, because there are so few left, as having been made by a people antecedent to the aboriginals of the present day. Yet sixty years ago they were still in full use by the blacks, and white men saw them and watched their application.

The larger fish-traps were for the purpose of fencing back the big fish in the streams of the greater rivers, so that, when on the upper reaches great tribal gatherings took place, there would be plenty of food easily obtainable, and at hand. There was another reason, too, that I have mentioned in notes to *The Wild Swan.* This was that when tribes needed change of diet they were always allowed safe conduct through others' territory to where rivers were preserved or "sanctuaried"—because no one tribe owned the waters. What water produced was free to all.

There were a number of centres in Australia to which the great gatherings were called for consideration of what one can only describe as the international regulation of general laws. As natural population increased new totems had to be chosen, new boundaries made, new animal and river sanctuaries provided for. One of the great meeting centres was on the Clarence; one at Brewarrina; one on the upper Murray, and another near Hay—when it was not held where Wagga Wagga now is. There were others, but these were the ones I heard most of. Where there were river-fed billabongs, stone traps were not in use, as floods filled the lagoons and bends, and the fish remained in them and grew to full size as freshets replenished the waters. For reasons later on apparent, freshets were then more regular in occurrence than they are today.

It was on the long waters of inland rivers that stone traps were made and outcrops utilized. These were keyed so that the size of the fish to go through them could be regulated. The keys in one of the smaller stone traps on the upper Murrumbidgee, and the method of placing them, were shown to my father. They were so set and fitted that they would not be shifted by the current, and not embedded in silt at flood-time. It was said that white men could not fit them unless taught how to do it. My father was a proud man for having been shown; it was a sign of great trust.

My father never saw what is now called Brewarrina; but in that district two of my uncles said they once witnessed what they reckoned were five thousand blacks assembled, and people who were older said that before the massacres began there were even larger gatherings. The tribal groupings and family camps extended along the tributaries of the main stream for miles, but each group was placed within general reach of all the others.

In these gatherings there were the competitive games, the trials of skill, and the long tests of endurance that were a feature of aboriginal life in its natural state. I heard my uncle Henry Beattie say that a man's endurance could beat a horse in length of time, distance, and the average rate travelled, and that he had himself tested a black against his own horse. This was at the Brewarrina, where he and a number of others were allowed to look on at tests. Besides endurance there was climbing with and without notches; climbing highest in the least time; walking a branch; recovering something at the point of a branch where there was no support, so that one had to get above it and hang head down to reach the object, and then get back the way one had come. If one did not do this one was a failure. Another way was from above to spring downward past the object to a lower branch, and catch it in passing.

The river afforded the water tests, such as to remain invisible under water; to rise from an underwater swim in the most unexpected or most hidden place; to catch birds and fish of different sizes and kinds with the hand or the foot and so on. These are only a few of the games or contests.*

"Cat's-cradles" (there were over seventy of them at least) were played round the fire and taught the children. I once knew the flying possum, the possum running up a tree and out on a branch, the kookaburra laughing, and one or two others, the very names of which I have forgotten, as well as the solitary simple one known to white people all over the world. Now I only know two.

For the great gatherings there was a fixed period. Someone said

*See note at end of chapter.

they were something like our census taking. I remember the comparison but that is all.

Small fish-traps or barriers were placed on tributary streams; and it was a public duty with the tribes (just as in regard to public utilities with us) to see that they were neither clogged up nor broken down. As white settlement increased and stock took the place of human beings, my father pointed out again and again that these barriers were being destroyed; that the conservation of fish in the streams depended on them; and that (as the aborigines taught) without them the great fish would devour the smaller varieties and the end would be loss—a loss that the years since have proved fact.

The barriers were destroyed in two ways. One was by pulling out the stones or timber that formed them; the other was by leaving them and making them the site of a dam. For again and again it was remarked that the "instinct" of the black ("instinct" was the word of the day) was in this matter of location for water conservation equal to the highest intelligence of the white; and that "by instinct" a black could do what it would take a surveyor with a theodolite to do. Wherever there was a native fish-trap, that was the one best possible place for the bank of a dam. On the slopes of a watershed, to use the common expression of the day, "no one but a self-opinionated fool ever thought of putting a dam anywhere else." There were such now and then, and the first occasion of flood or drought proved their folly.

On creeks that were not constant, and in little gullies that only ran sometimes, I have seen scores of timber balks or traps. No white man seemed to know how to make them; they were an art known only to the black. Like the bough wurlies they made which kept out ordinary rain where a white man soaked, and which stood without blowing away till some forest fire burned them, they followed a tribally formulated scientific law evolved from centuries of use.

Whether of stone or wood, they were always made and placed with an eye to the slope of the land above them; the run of the water as it came to its height; and the one position best fitted to withstand pressure and yet let unwanted water go by. On seasonally dry creeks the structures were made of boughs, or a sapling or two. Where the water backed out of a fish river and there was not deep storage for long holding (as in a billabong) I have seen six and eight inch saplings used. But on billabongs like the Edwards at Deniliquin, Pregan Pregan and the Wollundry at Wagga Wagga, logs made the barrier.

Speaking of the Wollundry Lagoon (today in the middle of the town of Wagga Wagga), I remember once we caught fish there in a tub. The lagoon was a mass of fish. The same thing occurred again in

about 1879 as far as I can recollect the date. But when the white man killed the black this plenty ended. There were no sanctuaried areas; no close season for breeding; no selection in netting fish; and, as I said before, the seventy pounders ate the smaller fish, and the once plentiful breeding diminished. You could not suddenly put five thousand people down on any river in Australia now and expect them to live, not even for a week.

The last small fish-balk I saw was in about 1880, when driving with my father somewhere near what is now Ardlethan. As we camped to boil the billy we made the fire of long, dead wood lying across the bed of a dry gully. A fire made in a gully was safer than one made above, as it did not catch the wind, and the grass was like tinder that year. As I stood looking down at the dry sapling logs with their interlacing of desiccated twigs, I suddenly saw and picked up some bones, snow white and unlike any I had seen before.

"What a strange backbone for a snake," I said. "I never saw one like *that* before."

"That is not a snake," my father replied, looking up from the fire. "Those are fish-bones."

"But how can they be fish-bones when there is no water here?" I protested.

"This is an old fish-trap that we are burning," answered my father.

And he went on to explain (to me who had temporarily forgotten what I had often seen) that the aboriginals made balks, so that, when flood currents took water back up creeks and gullies, as the water fell the up-taken fish remained impounded behind. As I still poked about among the debris, I found not only more bones, I found bleached scales, and some that were still a little blue. They were such a curiosity to me that they were among what my mother still called my "rubbish" when I went to Paraguay fifteen years later.

Besides holding fish where these had been carried upstream from a junction, the aboriginals would bring fish caught in coolamons, water-filled hollow logs, and in baskets, and put them in places where rains were held. If the water was not replenished by further falls the fish died, as at the balk I have described. But if the water lasted and more rains added to it, the fish lived and there was provision for another day. Old bushmen, travelling, would look for such places. One of my uncles got the surprise of his life, once, going to fill his billy at water in a bend, and finding there a fish big enough to make him a meal. As the blacks took them male and female, it was plain

"It was on the long waters of the inland rivers
that stone traps were made . . ."

Fish Balks and Traps

that this fellow had survived at the expense of his wife. Another time he found a big fish and two smaller ones.

Because people in the past, as well as now, did not relate cause and effect when a dam was made or a tank sunk where there had been a fish barrier, and later on fish were found there, it used to be thought they came as a spontaneous effort of nature—just as eels were thought to develop from horse-hair. The fact was that they came from survivals left there by the blacks in a day when every gully had its tiny balk of brush and wood, and every running stream its barrier of stones and logs. I speak now of fish, not of minnows. The blacks had some explanation about minnows, too, but I cannot recall it.

Only the long rivers needed the traps that today puzzle the scientists—the long slow rivers going through the wide lands where the intertribal conferences assembled, and for which much food, near at hand, was a necessity. The condition of the food-supply in such places decided which was to be chosen for such meetings. It was said that for at least two or three years before such gatherings the waters would be examined for the quantity and size of the fish; and at least a year beforehand the trap, weir or barrier, would be closed by its key stones so that only the small fish could go through. It was the knowledge of what these preliminary examinations meant that led to the timing of some of the worst massacres.

Besides attention to streams, for several years before a gathering in mass, no kangaroos, possums, or wild fowl were hunted or disturbed round the area devoted to the meeting, the duration of which depended on the supplies at hand. My uncles said of the one they saw that the children were endless, and that "the noise they made would deafen you"—as it would solitary men who only saw a single family at a time! In any case, a language not understood always sounds twice as much like noise, and many times more noisy, than one's own. They said that the first week the whole country-side was alive with people, after that they began to drift away, and in three weeks' time there were only isolated scattered families left.

Of my own recollection the largest gathering I ever saw to know their number was a meeting of about three hundred* on the Bland in about 1879. It was only half the number expected, as those from the Lachlan could not get across in time, owing to drought. It was held at Morangarell, the home of my father's cousins, the McGregors. There I saw the last Gundagai chief. The blacks had called the meeting of the localized tribes, expecting and knowing it would be the last they

*See note at end of chapter.

"... the children were endless ..."

would ever hold. Larger bodies I had seen on the Murrumbidgee, but was too young to have any idea of numbers. In my numbers I always reckon the children except where otherwise stated. Most other writers usually refer to adults alone, and often to males only. This is to minimize the number of deaths due to reprisals and massacres.

After the foregoing was written, part of which appeared in the *Sydney Morning Herald* (8th November, 1933), I was asked to talk over the air from the Trades Hall Station (2KY), and chose fish-balks as my subject. As a result of the talk two different women wrote, one through the station, one to me directly, saying they had heard from their fathers of balks such as I had described. Actually it was for the purpose of arousing buried recollections that I chose my subject.

Why more people did not recognize and recollect the small temporary, and yet not so temporary balks, is that, unless it is forced upon them, few people observe, and after observing reason back to common knowledge in the case of common things. In regard to logs across a creek or a river, even today it is taken as a matter of course that "the wind blew them there." Yet it has never struck any one to inquire why ninety per cent of the trees they use as foot-bridges fell just in the right place to cross on, and that they almost invariably lay directly across the run of the current. The wind is not such a continuously good friend to man as that—nor is a river flood. A river flood usually leaves its trees slope-set or endwise when it is strong enough to bring them down; or they lie length on in the bed.

The small sapling balks of which I have written sat head to tail so that the boughs filled the middle of the hollow—and again no one in general read their meaning; or, as usual, put their being there down to wind or flood. Where the logs were felled boughs were interlaced under them so that only small fish could get through. These interlacings I have seen the black carefully renewing. Again it was said only a black knew how to do this.

But I have a greater balk to write of than those on small creeks; this was one of which I saw half put in its place.

People who went to school in Wagga Wagga under Peter Durie and Miss Galloway, may remember the two big logs at the mouth of the Wollundry Lagoon; and the one farther up near where, in later years, Mr Wunsch built a house and made a garden. If they do, they will recollect that the two at the river end blocked the egress there, and that the one quarter of a mile up was one we used as a foot-bridge. They may even remember it when it was a big upstanding green tree, as I do.

Besides those on the Wollundry Lagoon, there were the same log balks directly across Pregan Pregan (or as we called it later, the North Wagga Wagga Lagoon). One of these logs was up near The Sand-ridge and was used there as a foot-bridge. I think there was another on the town side of the old North Wagga Wagga flour mill, which, it will be remembered, first began with sails for the wind. We lived in it while it was a windmill. But about this Pregan Pregan Lagoon I am not quite as clear as I am about the other; for while the Wollundry had only a few slanted logs on its banks, owing to the curvature of the river, the other had not only many on the banks, but a number in the bed as well, so that it was hard to know which was a balk and which not.

I do not remember in just what year it was, but the chief of the tribe at Wagga Wagga in talking to my father, said that, white settlement increasing along the river, it was not only fished in by the settlers, but fished in season and out, so that the breeding-stocks were diminishing as well as the grown fish which the blacks' laws allowed them to take for sustenance. He said that to provide against this depletion the Wollundry Lagoon would have to be closed, whether as a breeding-place, as a reserve of supplies, or what, I cannot recall. But it had to be closed at the river end.

It could not be done that year as the floods were over, and it could only be closed when the water was up high enough to carry a certain sized, and already chosen tree then standing on the bank some distance higher up the stream. The kind of tree, the set of the limbs, the length of trunk, the distance it had to be floated, and the height of the current, all had to be noted, known and considered. My father was so anxious to see the thing done, and he was so much a friend of the blacks, that it was promised that when the time came he would be notified so that he could attend and look on.

As the season turned he drove us all up the Murrumbidgee to see the tree chosen. It was one with very white bark, and slim and almost pendulous branches. That is to say it was not one with a stiff top, but one with flexible terminals. I thought it a very pretty tree because it was so white, and the leaves were long and slender. The blacks had already undermined the roots a little on the river side—just a little, not enough for wind or an insufficient rise to bring it down before its time.

When later on the snow water was reported as flowing in rising spate, word came to my father to be ready. We all went to the place allotted us. There were my father and mother, my grandfather and grandmother, several of the uncles and aunts, Mr Sellors or another Wesleyan minister, and one of the Davises from The Sandridge. There may have been others, but I think not, as only those my father invited were supposed to be present. For one thing the chief had said he did not wish to have the work seen by those who jeered and mocked at the people they were displacing and who were too ignorant to understand knowledge outside their own limit; and for another, my father stipulated that no one must be told, lest, if some jeerer came, anger would rise, spears be thrown, someone might be killed, and a gun-massacre result.

We all stood watching the waters casually, the chief intently. Suddenly, as the moment came, he gave an order. Half a dozen blacks plunged into the stream swimming upward and well out, others ran up the bank and with poles at the base, and hands at the trunk of the prepared tree, pressed it forward as the rising tide washed away the earth still left under the roots. I remember the crash of the tree falling. It floated down toward us, and a dozen more blacks sprang into the water and they also took their places in guiding it. The aim was (if I may use the modern word) to streamline it into place. Every man was alert; no man got in another's way; and each was captain in his own place. The chief went into the water and took the most dangerous place, that of guiding the trunk so that the root end would hit the lagoon bank in the exact place in which it would hold while the top was worked in to the other bank. Not a second could be lost, not an action could cloud another, as there was no recall for these ropeless and engineless people once the tree shot past its mark.

Twice it nearly got away. The second time, my father seeing it (and excitedly shouting directions loudly in aboriginal—as a white man would to this quietly spoken, silently moving race), he flung off his upper clothes as he ran, and, behind a bush to be out of our sight, stripped off his remaining garments and plunged in. Catching a branch that had escaped a youth not strong enough to hold more than part of its top, he bent it till the tree shot where it was wanted and came to rest like a ship at anchor.

Just as a ship is trimmed against the wind to go forward, so these people used the tree-top and the current to do what was wanted. They guided throughout, they did nothing by main force. Anyone who has seen a native take a handful of twigs, and in troubled waters steady and guide a canoe by such small, streamline means, will know how this tree was guided and compelled by its twigs and leaves, now pushed here, now held in curve there, till it had to turn on the current; go where it was wanted and then stay there.

When the work was over my father, telling a boy to bring his clothes, swam up the river to dress. It was growing dusk, and never having seen more than his arms and face unclad, I asked as, at a distance up-stream I saw a white form dart out of the water and run behind a tree, "Who was the white blackfellow?" As a good many men lived among the blacks then, we called them all "white blackfellows." For long enough after this I was teased for calling my father a white blackfellow.

After the floods went and the season changed, the leaves withered and fell from the newly placed tree. Then one day when we came into town, perhaps a year, perhaps more than a year later, as we drove over the round pine logs that formed the first crossing at the Fitzmaurice Street end of the lagoon, I saw stubs standing up slantwise between the logs.

"Look!" I cried, "someone has made a fence to keep the cattle out of the river!"

"No; that is not a fence," my father said; "the blacks put the poles there for the fish."

They stayed till those who had put them there were dust, and the town wanted the logs for firewood.

I mentioned a log at the small end of the Wollundry Lagoon, and that I had known it as a tree standing tall and in full leaf. The roots had been undermined on the side to which it was to fall when the floods would be high enough to bring it down. We all knew the tree, and my father invariably drove a distance off from it as we passed, because (he said) it might fall by reason of its own weight. After it did come down, in about 1874, it was used as a foot-bridge for that end of the lagoon. But this tree was not the only one we avoided because the blacks had undermined it to make it fall where wanted. I remember others, some near Deniliquin, some near Narrandera, and others on the Bland.

The reason the blacks felled this tree was so that the fish in the body of the Wollundry would not in flood-time be swept over this end and then as the water subsided lie stranded on the surrounding flat just about where Peter Street now runs. I have seen the blacks on this flat, as flood waters fell, collecting the stranding fish to put them into the deep holes and the lagoon. When the big tree that I have mentioned came down, the space under it was laced with small branches and rolls of grass. This closing was recognized wherever seen as the blacks' work, as debris left by floods was gapped, irregular and lumpy. There was another thing: what the blacks did remained, for they repaired it; what floods and wind left, quickly diminished with time and was blown away.

I may say as a concluding word that my father was always very proud of the assistance he gave in helping to place that tree balk at the mouth of the lagoon. "I went in just in the nick of time," he used to say. Not only then, but in later years, he always declared that in putting in such balks the blacks had a sense of engineering that no white man in the same untaught conditions had.

Note 1: In the *Sydney Morning Herald* of 15th March, 1934, there is a short account of tests the blacks have to this day for children. It is in the report of an address given by G. A. Francis, former Federal member for Kennedy, who was born and reared in the Gulf country. He said, after being trained, among other things the children are set to do is the task of "finding such things as a small bird's eye which had been buried, or to track frogs that had been released, unseen by the children, on pebbles by a stream."

The training of the very young children is the women's work. I have seen a mother take a small twig, break it till only about three inches of wood and a knot were left, and a toddler of two years taught first to recognize it among others held in the hand, and then to find it when thrown a distance, the child being given only a general idea of the direction in which it had

been thrown. Sometimes it would be a small piece of grass-stem that would be used. Another thing the little ones were taught was to follow a certain ant among its fellows. Being so much amongst them this was one of our own games.

The other examination of men with boomerang, spear, and shield mentioned by Mr Francis, I too have seen, together with much more serious work, such as when a man was tried for his life. I saw a man stood against a tree till one, two, and three spears quivered in the trunk on each side of him. Had he flinched or moved, in any way, the next spear would have gone through his heart. Because he bore the ordeal he went free, courage and self-control counting for so much that they raised a man above his misdemeanour or breach of law. Nemarluc, up in the Northern Territory, would have been counted such a man after his last escape from the police, though he would still have had to undergo his tribal punishment.

Note 2: In a series of articles called "The Pioneers and Patriarchs of the Bland," written by the late Rev. George Grimm, M.A., and sent me by his son Arthur Grimm, mention is made of corroborees on the McGregors' station (Morangarell) of "as many as five hundred blacks at a time." These would be just local gatherings, as there would not be fish enough in the Bland Creek for anything larger, nor would the adjoining station-owners allow unlimited hunting on stocked lands in case of cattle-spearing, as this would lead to reprisals which even friendly owners would not be able to stand against.

The old Bogan and Barwon swamps

Among the sins to be one day repented of in this Australia of ours is the diversion of waters from the great fish and bird sources. For instance, there were the marshes on the upper watershed of the Darling and the Lachlan, of which the Bogan and the Barwon swamps were the most important; the Deepwater and Ganmain marshes on the Murrumbidgee towards Narrandera; Morangarell ("The nesting-place of the waterfowl") on the Bland; Tooyal or as it was originally, Toe-yoe ("The place where the white crane, or spoonbills bred"), which also was on the Murrumbidgee; and one down near Deniliquin. There must have been hundreds of others; but these I knew of, and most of them I saw while still under native law and protection.

Dams on creeks cut off the supply of water from periodic rains, and other diversions diminished the annual floodings and freshening through the overflow and landward spread of the rivers. What this overflow must have been is shown by the fact that, at Wagga Wagga on the flat near where Mr Bayliss lived, the skeleton of a bullock caught in the top of a tree remained for years to show the height of the low-spread waters.

In the eighties the Lachlan had its barges for wool; and, till years later, the Darling had its small "fleet" of passenger and freight launches and steamers. But long before this my father built a "wharf" on the Murrumbidgee at Wagga for the wool fleet of the "Mother of Waters." Slowly the want of the diverted rain and creek-waters put all these fleets off the river trade routes, because of the slow silting of channels undredged by great floods. Now it would take millions of money to make even the Darling river-bed as deep and as clean of snags as it was before damming prevented its annual washout and brought about its shallowing. But besides these there is another river that shows the difference between aboriginal and white management in the conservation of watercourses. That is the Castlereagh. In the words of one who spoke of it only lately there are those who remember it "as a noble stream"—a great and beautiful river. Now I am told that the bed is silted up, with trees growing in the middle of it.

As a matter of fact none of the little old wool-fleets of the Murrumbidgee, the Darling and the Lachlan, could ever have made their beginnings had the rivers not been clear of logs, for they sailed up and down in low water and tied up in floods. Some day I hope there will be a great novel written on the old wool-barges and steamers of the Murrumbidgee, when all that was Wagga Wagga, Hay and Narrandera, used to turn out to see them. I even remember one barge that had a small triangular sail, used when winds were favourable, or when a boiler blew out.

All billabongs, rivers, and marshes were treated as food reserves and supply depots by the natives. The bird whose name was given to a place bred there unmolested. The same with plants and animals. Thus storage never failed. But besides birds and plants there were the fish—yabbies, freshwater lobsters, eels, catfish, cod, and other varieties peculiar to Australia. One I remember was a swamp-fish, flat, with few bones, and an exceedingly white flesh. It came from Deepwater and Ganmain, a reed or swamp fish regarded as a great delicacy.

It is curious to look back and think that in the now almost fishless Riverina, we as children fed largely on fish—creeks, waterholes, marshes and billabongs all had them. "We will camp at such and such a place," my father would say when we were travelling for his sawpits, and later on with his mill. "Then we can have fish for supper." And he would turn out the horses, make a fire, take a rod, a small net on a Y-shaped bough, and sometimes even a dipper or a dish, and (in the last case trampling the water to roil it) come back with fish for tea and breakfast.

The aboriginals trampled the water to muddy it when they wanted to catch small fish by hand. The fish had to rise for air, otherwise they would drown where the water was heavy.

But the great Bogan swamp was a thing of wonder—still is, I am told, even in its attenuated condition. I once described it to John Farrell—described it as I had heard my uncles and others tell of it, and he wrote of it from what I told him, and published the article in the *Daily Telegraph*. I had the cutting for years, till in returning to Australia from South America it was lost.

I have not the words now that I then commanded, for the picture its description made for me has been blurred by life, and dimmed by the passage of years. But the waters were full of fish, leeches and frogs; the mud thick with crayfish and yabbies. Swans, ducks, geese, and pelicans swam in such thousands, that when a gun was fired its echoes died in the sound of the rising birds; and the cries they made

"... the homing of flight and the settling down for rest ..."

". . . the river trade routes . . ."

as they swirling rose, drowned the voice of man calling to fellow man to look up at them in wonder. In this great sanctuary the swimming birds had the waterglades between the lily-pads; the waders (and there were clouds of them as they rolled when disturbed) had the reeds and the sedges; the pewits, magpies, crows, soldier-birds, babblers and the like, had the water-brinks, the grass, and the trees. Eagles sailed continuously in the upper air; the grass was alive with seed eaters;* parrots were moving lawns of colour, and cockatoos were like white fleeces on the trees. Only the wild creature had eaten the grass, only the bird the honey in the tree. The richness of unbroken centuries of an untilled land sapped through everything. Life teemed in the water, life teemed on the earth, life teemed in the air. Life fed upon life in balance; bred, multiplied, and knew no famine.

When evening came the falling dusk was pierced by every bird-cry known in the homing of flight and the settling down for rest; all night long the bull-frog, the reed-frog, the plover, the curlew, the bittern, and the mopoke cried. And day and night there was the scent of the grass, the wafted smell of the flower, the whisper of little local winds rising and falling, and the swish of the reeds; reeds that were matted

*See note opposite.

and hedged higher than a man's head, higher in places than a man's hand could reach up.

Once, when I was about fourteen, travelling with relatives from Lake Cargelligo to Wollongough we had a breakdown—a swingle-bar slipped off behind the unicorn leader, and the pole broke in the tracers' bolt that followed it. So till repaired for next day, we camped on the banks of Lake Cowal. I shall never forget it. The stillness and the sounds of which there were so many, yet each sound solitary and distinguished; the starlight and the night-dusk that lessened not through the hours; the *boom, boom, boom* of the frogs; the horn of the bittern; the cry of the curlew; the whistle of the plover.

When in the morning light I spoke of it to my uncle, James Beattie, he laughed at me. "This is *nothing*," he said. "You should have been with your uncle Henry and me on the Bogan, and seen what we saw *there*!"

Note: As showing what bird-life still is in what are left of our frontier lands, my son wrote me during the late long drought in his part of northern Queensland, that in the second year of its continuance the parrots came in looking for seed and honey, "in flocks three and four miles long, that as they moved rose and fell like waves of the sea, and as they flew were so dense that they hid the trees behind them." And this was after a century of destruction of natural food by stock locally, and the demands of population elsewhere.

*". . . the wagonette cushions for my mother . . .
a rug for us . . ."*

Fire and the planted seed

The other day, reading Zane Grey's *Tales of Lonely Trails*, I came across three reminders, or rather two reminders and a confirmation. On page 103 he says:

> *Most of all spruce branches drooped toward the ground. That explained why they made such excellent shelters from rain. After a hard storm, I had seen the ground dry under a thick foliaged spruce. Many a time I made my bed under one. Elk and deer stand under a spruce during a rain, unless there is thunder and lightning.*

There are funny people who would call the standing away when there is thunder and lightning instinct in elk, deer, or kangaroos, and reason in man. These are the ones who call the same thing instinct in a black and reason in a white; who think it stupid in the black not to be able to read print, but do not think it at all stupid when they themselves do not know what the black reads on message-sticks.

Many a time we found what Zane Grey says equally true of certain of our Australian pine-trees. Old hands looked for a broad-branched pine under which to camp if rain were about, as, unless very heavy, the drops were divided by the feathery foliage and clung to it instead of running into drips and falling. There was a silver-grey pine whose lower spread was very wide and which had a sweeping downward droop. It was scarcer than the black pine, and, because it was larger, it was sought by pit-sawyers, saw-mills and splitters, for house-timber and for fencing. It had quite a different nut from the black pine, the plates forming it being narrower and of greater length than those of other kinds. When ripe these plates opened out widely like an uncurling daisy.

My black Mammy taught us to eat the tiny upright centre which was the seed. Old bushmen, wandering hatters and shepherds, all collected and carried these as a concentrated stand-by for food, they also having learned their use from the natives. The germ of the black pine we did not eat. It had not the same nutty flavour as the other, being coarse and rank in taste. The centre in the one we ate was

about the third of a large grain of wheat, or nearly the size of an oat.

I have often wondered in late years if the big moss-grey pine still exists, or if like some of our birds and animals it has been utterly destroyed. It had a very hard, definitely corrugated bark that like a good wood burnt to a red glow before falling to ash. The ash was very white and was used as whitewash. The bark itself was much sought for the top fire on camp-oven lids, because the heat was intense and steady, and made for a light bread in the baking. It was no good for use under the oven as it was too fierce, and burned the bread before it was baked. I remember Californian diggers talking to us of this pine, and of dual sex in trees, and how to distinguish between the male and the female nuts.

Under the dense old mossy branches of this tree we used to play, the earth being quite dry in rain, the withered summer grass thick and flocculent, and very fine because of the humus, except when the kangaroos made it a dusting- or sleeping-place and thus kept the herbage down. The sunlight at noon never came through there, no matter how hot or how intense; but as the sun westered spots of gold fell on the grass, spears of gold shot down between the limbs; sometimes Jason's golden fleece was spread on the earth or hung from a limb, and in the night the moon peered silver and very white. Sometimes it was a star.

Zane Grey's second reminder came on page 106 of his book, when he says:

> *After a while I gathered that Haught did not hunt deer except on horseback. He explained that cowboys rounded up cattle in this forest in the spring and fall, and deer were not frightened at sound or sight of a horse. Some of the thrill of interest in the forest subsides for me. I did not like to hunt in a country where cattle ranged, no matter how wild they were. Then we came to a forested ridge, bare of grass and smelling of sheep, that robbed the forest of a little more glamour. Mexican sheep-breeders drove their flocks up this far sometimes. Haught says bear, lion, lynx, coyote, and sometimes big, grey wolves, followed the sheep. Deer, however, hated a sheep-run range.*

How the woodsman in that paragraph puts sound before sight in regard to the horse! No townsman could have written that paragraph and packed into it all the unsaid gathering that it holds. In the forest sound comes before sight; in the plains, as in the sky, sight comes before sound. In the dark trees the night-flying bird is heard unseen till he crosses the moon, or a moon-white cloud. The possum is

". . . a broad-branched pine . . ."

mooned on a branch as the result of the sound of a piece of falling bark, dropped because he moved. But by day the kangaroo hides in the shadows, and, unless he betrays himself by a visible movement, he remains unseen.

The kangaroo and the emu, curious as to the new beast come among them, at first used to come up closely to investigate the white man on his horse or the traveller in his wagonette. And the white man who jeered at the black for being afraid of the unfamiliar whipped up and went for his life, and then told people what a narrow escape he had had of being ripped open by a beast with terrible legs and frightful, long nails, or kicked to death by a monstrous bird with feet like a camel.

But we, knowing the wild as children, had no fear; and many a time as the horses stood while my father lit his pipe or looked abroad for pine, the emus came up all around us. Sometimes the first thing I knew was an emu's head poked over my shoulder. The kangaroos, less curious than the birds, merely looked up from their feeding, then

returned to it again. Yet they would be so near that one could smell the warm fur and hear the sound of their eating. Later, cattle, sheep, and the hunter came. Then the sight of man or horse caused panic until the creatures knew the smell, the sight, and the sound of a horse without a rider—and the difference between the wild and the tame.

It was the same with the stock. On the cattle stations, after mustering and branding, the cattle were wild; the hands would be notified not to go riding where they fed, as it would frighten them still more, and looking for security from the invader they would leave good food to go farther out. This was bad alike for cows and calves as it affected the milk. In South America stock-whips are not allowed to be used on the cattle *estancias*, as they disturb and frighten the animals, and make them much less valuable for milk or market.

There was, at the time of which I write, no question of shortage of feed in Australian pastures, the ungrazed richness of centuries still existed in the soil and in the grass. It was a question of water. There being no fences in the thousands of square miles of country, cattle that had been disturbed would go far, and wander waterless for longer than was good for them rather then return to the locality they thought dangerous. Going without water made cattle hardy, but it did not put beef on them; nor did it add to the value of their hides when hides meant more than beef.

But though the sight of man, and the smell of the saddle on a hot day, would send the animals tearing off into the scrub, we children went among them unafraid, and with no more than an inquiring eye turned carelessly on us. But if we had a dog, till they knew it was our dog, it was different. When they knew the dog and that we were of one party and one mind, and that that mind was hunting something which was not cattle, or was mere wood-craft-wandering, they took no notice of us. Now and then there would be the crash of some startled beast fleeing through the timber, as the wind took it the smell of human being and dog, or carried it the sound of barking, or of voices, before it had time to see us. Coming across the same beast later on, if it saw us before it smelt or heard us it would feed on—warily, but without panic.

When to this cattle frontier came the free selector with fences, and lastly and abominably, sheep, how the cattle-men hated them all. And how they despised the servant of sheep! He was a footman, a man who walked where all the world rode. He was a drudge, a creature who carried his belongings on his back when anyone who was a man had a packhorse—perhaps three if his baggage required it, as well as having a spare saddle-horse.

And how the horses hated the sheep! Horses would shy at sheep and bolt from them, as they did later on from camels and motor-cars. These would be stock-horses that could bring in a beast on their own if their riders would let them, that would shoulder a steer, wheel on a plate, and back up against a bull; horses that would stand to the sound of a gun fired over their heads practically between their ears; endure the lasso whirling above them, and suffer the calf slung across the saddle behind or in front of the rider. Such horses would prick ears, snort, rear, and bolt at the sight of sheep when these first followed cattle. One such bolt flung me out of the back of the wagonette where I had stood up in order to look over the front seat between my father and mother to see what sheep were like, these being the first I had ever seen.

"Sit tight, children, there are sheep in front!" the word would come; and as we heard it we would catch hands in the middle, one to each other to hold the smaller ones in, and, grasping the bar at the side, wait for the bolt. I might add that if it did not come we were disappointed. It was one adventure less for the day.

Looking back, I have wondered if there still has to be the special horse paddock, because horses would not feed over sheep-fouled grass, or if they take no notice nowadays, but eat with a universal nose and palate. And in the midst of thinking I hear again a horse-bell and see my father stooping to hobble the mare, for the horse will not wander without her. The dusk is falling, there is the crackle and the smell of fire, the sticks writhing and turning as they burn. A star shines in the blue amber of the western sky, or perhaps there is a thin sliver of a new moon; my mother is getting out the cups, the tin pots and the china mugs, together with the rest of the crockery from the ration-box. The plates rattle; there is a smell of bread and meat; and my father, returning from the horses, gets the wagonette cushions for my mother, spreads a rug for us, and takes a stump or the horse-collar for himself to sit on.

"Sheep are going to be the ruin of this country," he says, as he puts an edge on the knife before carving the meat.

"Deer hated a sheep-run range," said Zane Grey in Arizona.

Mechanical invention killed literary invention in Australia. The fence came too soon for us to have a literature of the frontier written in language evolved by the frontier as its own. Money came too soon as well as too easily, for invention and a world market made money as a cloud, and it only had to rain down on us. The world was filled with markets. So, land was fenced in a day, roads made, schools built,

lawyers' signs put up, libraries opened, while bookshops grew in the second counter put in by silversmiths and jewellers.

Then we brought in an imported literature where we should have been writing our own. Before we had begun to realize it, except in the far north, and the great buttes of the centre, the day of our frontier had gone, and its distinctions and its language with it. Now, a language for that period would have to be invented. That mixture of Scotch, Irish, county-and-shire-English, with its interlarding of aboriginal words, its sprinkling of Californian Spanish and its Red Indian hunting and gold-digging terms (which once was the speech of the land-ward wave inward from the sea — and the city such as the city was even then), it has all gone; and there was no one eager enough to save it. Still the field is there; and some day genius may stride forth and re-create it, and make us a literature wholly our own in expression, and as unmistakably characteristic as African is of Africa, and American of America.

In 1932 I wrote in *Under the Wilgas* of how the aboriginals conserved the wild and made and kept animal and bird sanctuaries. A confirmation I found, by parallel, in Zane Grey's *Tales of Lonely Trails*. On page 106 he says: "The Apaches had once lived in this country, Haught informed us; and it was a habit of theirs to burn the grass and fallen leaves every fall, thus keeping down the underbrush.... Usually, Indians were better conservationists than white men."

That is my third quotation from Zane Grey. But before developing my theme from it I have yet another authority, also American. Miss Sheba Hargreaves in her book *At the Trail's End* tells, on page 317, how the Indians prepared for winter, the winters being icy from snowfall, or from the winds from the snow regions where snow was not a part of the local winter. This preparation was by a fire-encircling *battue* of animals. She goes on to say that the system was by firing and back-firing so that conflagration could be stayed at any time, and only sufficient fire let run to circle and drive the animals to a common centre. Which, of course, was the same method of firing for a food-supply used by our own aboriginals.

Miss Hargreaves goes on to say:

> *When the circle of fire became small enough to make hunting a very simple matter, the best hunters went inside and selected the game needed. They were careful not to injure the animals left for breeding purposes. With the same attention that a breeder of fine stock would*

give to his herd, the best males, the youngest and most vigorous females, were carefully cut out before the rest were taken. In a sense the Indians had bred up the game until their source of meat was assured. One of their bitterest grievances against the settlers was the wantonness with which they destroyed wild life. Deer, bear, and elk were plentiful and easily taken before the coming of the white man.

That is exactly how the aboriginals complained of destruction of wild life to my father, and what they also did as providers. As to fire, it was the natives who taught our first settlers to get bushes and beat out a conflagration. My grandparents used to tell of how new immigrants when they first came to the country, unaccustomed to the danger in the wild country, would start fires and let them run heedless of the result; and then stand panic-stricken at having loosed something they could not control. And they would go on to relate how the natives would run for bushes, put them into the immigrants' hands, and show them how to beat back the flame as it licked up the grass. Indeed it was a constant wonder, when I was little, how easily the blacks would check a fire before it grew too big for close handling, or start a return fire when and where it was safest.

"Send for the blacks!" was the first cry on every settlement when a fire started.

There was a difference between the blacks' methods and the white's. The white man used large bushes and tired himself out with their weight and by heavy blows; the blacks took small bushes and used little and light action. The white expended the energy of panic; the blacks acted in familiarity, as knowing how and what to do. They used arm action only, where the white man used his whole body. Where, as a last resort, the white man lit a roaring and continuous fire-break, the aboriginal set the lubras to make tiny flares, each separate, each put out in turn, and all lit roughly in line. The beaters they used were so small that they hunkered to do the lighting and beating.

The aboriginals said that not only must fire be met by fire, but that it could only be fought while still not too hot to be handled closely; that when it became so hot that it burnt and exhausted men, it had to be met from a distance. They also said that a big fire as a fire-break was as dangerous as a big fire itself, as the wind might change and bring it back on the watchers; that the value of the small flares was that they could be put out at once; that only lanes of grass were left between them, and these, if ignited, could easily be met.

I have seen a whole station in a panic—men, women and children

nearly killing themselves with frantic and wasteful effort; and then a handful of blacks and lubras under their chief come and have the fire confined and checked in no time. Having the confidence of habit they allowed the fire freedom where it seemed least dangerous. In one such fire they concentrated on the sides, letting the centre flame run forward. But far in advance of this ran lubras hunkering down over their half-yard-wide flares. Behind the first row a second line was at work, and behind this a third, each fire opposite the gaps between the forward ones. The advancing tongues of flame having been kept narrow by attention to the sides, the draught was narrow, so a very wide front of little fires was not necessary. When the advance met the little islands of burnt grass it died there; in the lanes between it was beaten out. The chief told my father that unless fire was kept narrow and beaten out before it created a high wind it was no use trying to fight it. Once it created its own such wind it was invincible. It seems strange to think that there was a time when we did not know this, but it is a fact.

At this place the chief spoke bitterly to my father of the white man's carelessness in lighting bushfires, saying that he lit and let them run like a child that loved destruction; that such destruction was wanton; that forest fires spoiled the fine timbers from which weapons were made and bark taken for canoes; that it took years for a forest to come back to itself after being burnt; that fire destroyed birds, bees, seeds, and animals. He was to learn later that fire, miles wide, would be lit to burn him and his.

It was here that I first saw more or less extensive planting of seeds by the lubras. This was done at the direction of the chief, who, when the earth was cool enough to walk upon, went first to one shrub and then to another, testing and examining the burnt capsules, and where these had been destroyed directing the attention of the women to them. The women gathered fresh ones from untouched shrubs, and planted them where the destroyed ones stood.

The use of ammonia was apparently known, for when the seeds were in the scratched but still warm earth, the little boys were requisitioned to damp them.

Grass-seed was gathered, a heavy kind, and I helped in this. When a lot, still in "the ear," had been collected, it was rubbed by hand, and then by a turn of the wrist the bark container into which it had been put was shaken, tipped right and left, and the grain lay clear at one end, with the husks in a little pile at the other. The movement was something like that of a digger with his dish when

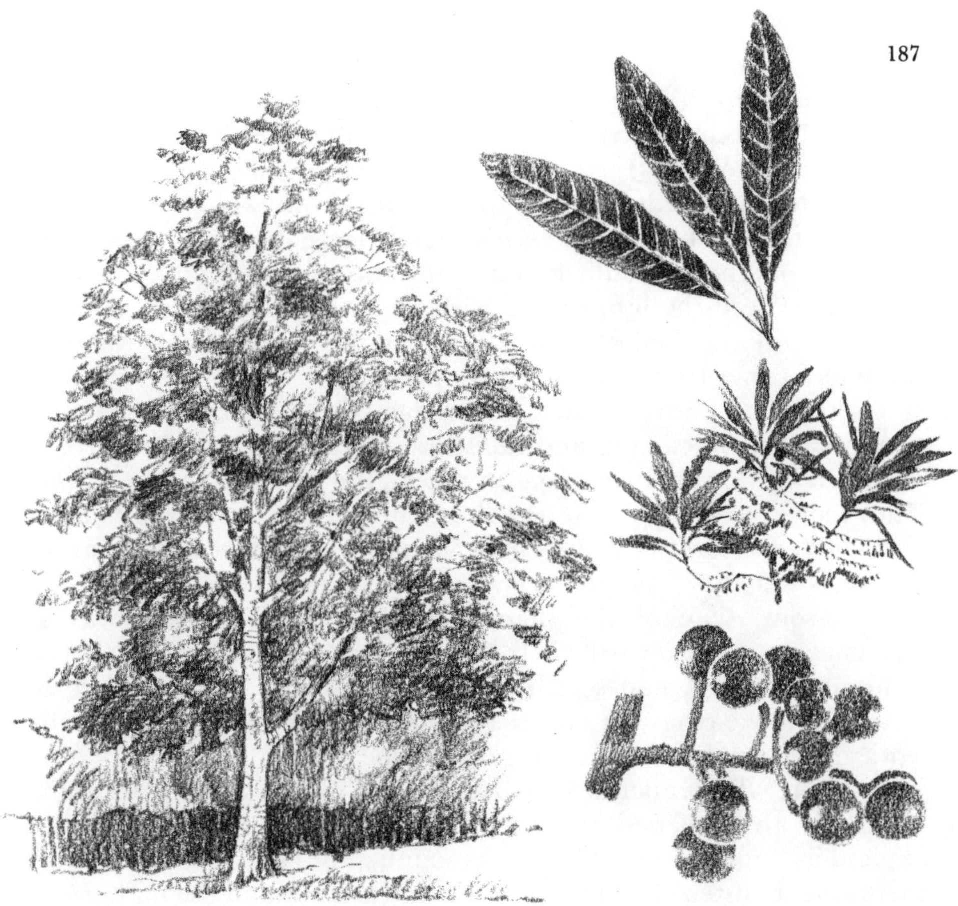

". . . the quandong-tree."

separating the gold; but while his movement was circular, this was first lateral and then from end to end. Yet the movement was all in one piece so to speak—continuous and without break. The separated seed was sorted, the unsound or small rejected and the best planted in the burnt area but very lightly covered. It was not scattered, it was put in in small pinches so that if some failed there would still be enough for a tussock.

How I remember the grass planting so well is that being a child I thought all seed was the kind wanted, and gathered ripe and unripe, and chiefly the sort that rolls on a sickle-shaped terminal. This, I was told, was not what was required, that the wind would plant this; that it was what did not run, and then catch in the earth, that had to be planted by hand.

I had often seen the blacks set individual seeds as well as replace, where the plant grew, those of what they ate. But the former was usually done where they themselves first made a small fire of twigs in order to prepare the earth by heating it. Whenever they gave me the fruit of the ground-berry, as we called it—and they always gave me the best they found—I was invariably asked for the seed, which was immediately planted beneath the growth from which it came. I remember once I had an exceptionally large berry, and without thinking spat the seed out when the pulp was eaten from it. Because it was a large seed the lubra I was with scolded me for waste, hunting the grass till she found it, so that it could be put back where it originally came from and a strong plant grow from it. This alone shows that the natives had a knowledge of their own in regard to conditions of soil, shade, and moisture in relation to seed.

Then there was their usage in the matter of the quandong-tree. They looked to see which of the stones or nuts were male or female, and planted accordingly. But there was more than this. When a grove was in flower they brought branches from another grove to fertilize the blossom. One of the places where I saw this done was at Yarrengerry, then owned by J. Barnes, whose wife was one of the Stinsons. Earlier I had seen it done near what is now Bethungra. Often I saw the twigs left on the ground under trees to show that the work had been done and need not be repeated.

Whether the branches were used merely to fertilize or whether to introduce an unrelated strain, I do not know. I heard my father explain it to my mother, but I was too much interested in the flowers themselves to listen. In any case I was only a child, and the matter was not meant for my ears. In these later years remembering the aboriginal laws in relation to human strains and their matings, I should say it was done for both purposes.

From the top rail of the fence

Easily taken in, I was one who seldom doubted other people. Consequently I sometimes saw things happen, and, told that it was something else which had occurred, have only through the accretions of knowledge gathered by years of experience realized what it was that I actually did see. Sometimes the knowledge came in sudden and tragic ways, as the following account will show.

I referred once to men being killed when riding buck-jumpers. Perhaps, too, I have mentioned that our frontier, wherever it existed, and in whatever part of our world it might be, was a law to itself.

Community law belongs to community life. Law reaches out in single tentacles where space ignores it, and where there is hiding-place and running-room for offenders. But still in little waves, and with every wavelet of encroaching and spreading population, law does move broadly forward. So, after the mounted trooper, to our Australian frontier came "the inquest." Inquests meant a demand for "the production of the body." The production of the body, which I may tell you was regarded as a very annoying demand to early settlement, first entailed no more than acceptable evidence that there had *been* a body. Later it meant that some pernickety magistrate, coroner, or policeman, would demand to see the grave. Today even this is not always enough.

To our frontier, if the law came and demanded an answer about anything, the law was told what was thought sufficient for the law to know. If no demand came nothing was said.

Only the settled man had an address; and almost no one on horseback had any other name than Tom, Brummy, Tambo, Jim the Shearer, Paddy the Horsebreaker, or Boundary Jack (the boundary-rider). Consequently, when all you knew of a man was his horse and his name, and you always knew his horse though you might be doubtful of his name, what was there to do if he were found killed, but just to bury him? If inquiry came you told what happened; if no inquiry came what was there in *any* way that you could do? The world was a haystack and a man but a needle slipped into it—and for a century man kept on slipping. In all this I speak the feeling and the

". . . the stockyard, the horses, the men, the bucking, the fall . . ."

language of the time, and as the men of the day expressed it.

It must also be remembered that the old evil and harsh laws, brought from overseas to be ours, were still in operation; and that people were hanged, where today there would be imprisonment only—and not always a long sentence at that. So the frontier thought:

"Why prepare a noose for a man for what was the accident of temper, of drink, or only a lark?"

To come to my definite subject. What was more a lark than to sit on the top rail of a fence, and watch someone who couldn't ride, trying to sit a horse which even a good rider couldn't sit? And wasn't it the more a joke if the man was young and a boaster? Had the law of the day been more merciful, and its administration not been so much in the hand of hanging and long-sentence judges, it would have been informed of many things left untold; and fewer people would have been buried unknown.

There had ridden up to the station, where my father was then building, a number of men on the way to one of the innumerable and exciting gold strikes beyond Cargelligo (known as Cudgellico then). Among them was a young man of whom all that we ever knew was that he came; that his mates called him Tom; that bets were made about riding a certain horse which so far had thrown everyone; that he had taken the bet; and that ten minutes after he lay limp in the dust with (I know now) a broken neck. Picking me off a fence where I had been sitting to watch the riding, my father rushed me into the house for brandy, and to send out water. There was no brandy for a wonder, and I ran into the girls' room for the eau-de-Cologne—which was never short. No matter what a girl went without she had to have eau-de-Cologne, as men had to have their hair oil or pomade. When I came out again to the yard, from which I had been purposely detained, there was no sign of the man; his mates were gone; and only the stockmen were standing about talking, while the horses, run in for the handling, were stringing out the sliprails.

"*I heard his neck crack!*" said one of the men. I did not know that a cracked neck meant death then. I had heard too many joints crack to think one mattered more than another. So I believed what I was told—that the man had ridden on. No one else, law or anybody, was told any more.

There is a limpness about the suddenly fallen dead that no living frame, however placid or unconscious, ever has. I did not suddenly see it again till nearly fifty years later. Then one hot summer's day at a luncheon of journalists, I heard a commotion in the annexe behind me, and looking round I saw something being carried out.

"What is the matter?" asked Miss McF—— who was next to me.

"Nothing!" I said. "A man has just fainted."

But I knew he was dead, for I saw the look on his face, and that all-comprising body slackness, even of the hair, that I had seen so long before. For a moment, there was possibility of panic. But the president took up the thread of his discourse; cigarettes were again lit up, and the luncheon proceeded as usual. But, for me, at sight of the man carried out, memory suddenly flung open closed gates, and I saw with inner sight and coincidently with that moment of memory, the stockyard, the horses, the men, the bucking, the fall, and the man's body limp in the dust. And so strange a thing is the human being, the shock of that sudden realization of that unsuspected death in the past, shook me at the moment more than the death at hand.

No! . . . There is no such thing as the past; there is only the present. For though we may fold the present away in the drawers of the mind, it is still there. And there, the unrealized waits to stab us with shock, and with the pain of a sudden understanding.

"Oh, if we had only known!" we cry in regret and remorse for our own dead gone beyond recall.

"The man was dead!" we say of the stranger.

When? Actually in years long after the occasion. So in times after the war, that worse frontier than ours, men will suddenly see a face and a look they had not known they had ever seen, and seeing it will sicken of an old memory.

He was a Yarmouth man

He was a Yarmouth man, and he bent at the knees, at the hips, and in the back—not because he was so old, but, first, because of the hardship of his childhood, and, second, because he had grown tall and was a Yarmouth fisherman. He had sat crouched up in a boat so many years, growing years and others, that even when he stood up, an adult man, some of the crouch remained. He had left Yarmouth because the fishing trade for such as he had been ruined by the formation of wealthy companies, the introduction of the newly invented steam trawlers, and the mile-long seines which boats-in-sail could not carry and stand up to in heavy weather, and with which no small trader could compete.

Seines are longer now; tugs and trawlers heavier and larger; but this man's day must have been nearly a hundred years ago. He told how when steam came the small men attacked the big boats and were shot down; he told how desperate men stole across the waters by night to cut the great seines; and of how power called in the law, and the waters were patrolled as by an army and such as he attacked as by an army. Because the small net was doomed, and the hand-sailer and hand-puller with it, many of those who had manned the fleets of little boats left Yarmouth. This one became a seaman, went whaling, and in the end was a harpooner.

On the whaling ships he saw the sea alive with whales; he saw men killed by brutal captains; he saw men forced to stand where the throw of the harpoon took them beyond their balance, and they went overboard with the throw; or by a slew of the boat were sawn in two by the racing rope; and he saw men driven under musket fire too soon near to the whale, so that the thrashing of the great flukes smashed the boats to flinders and the men were drowned with them. Of one boatload he was the only man left alive. After that his nerve went, and he was no more good as a harpooner.

On sea the only law was the captain's will; on land was the press-gang. Between the navy and the whaler, the choice was between hell and the grave; with a hope of some sort of resurrection from the grave when the whaler put into port and men were paid off.

After he left the whaler he was in the slave trade along the coast of Africa, and talked of Barbary corsairs, of piracy and privateering, of cutlasses, pikes, muskets, and the splendour of a pirate captain's clothes. And it was from him that I heard of "galloons" (he had sailed in "galloons," using all the old words forgotten today, but which his forefathers had used). The old man told of slaves battened down; of slaves being thrown overboard to lighten ship; of starvation and floggings by white captains of white men who refused to do their foul work; of men triced up to the mast with no law at sea to appeal to, and no redress on land; and he spoke of dead calms, and rotting seas, putrid food, and weevily biscuit.

Yet, even afar inland in Riverina, he longed for biscuit as he had never loved and longed for bread. So much he loved it, that, whenever he was near enough to a port town, he laid up a supply, keeping it as a stand-by, sparing it as much as he could, and eating it slowly as men spared and took snuff on roads that were then but as the flight of a bird or the twist of a snake's track in the grass; and where to them the only lamp was the North Star they never saw. For in the early breaking-in of Australia men looked for the stars they knew in the north, and were lost till found by the blacks, and taught to steer by the Southern Cross and the Pointers.

He talked so wonderfully to me of ships' biscuit that I pleaded for a bit. He had only one left, he said, and resisted my pleading. But to please the child who had so lived in his life as he told it, there came a day when he unroped and unrolled his swag (dirty grey blankets that smelt of his tobacco, of grease, and of his body) and out of the heart of it he took what looked like a piece of wood, tooth-gnawed at the edges. With a hatchet he broke off a fragment. It was stale with old must, and smelt like the blankets.

"I do not like it," I said with a grimace.

And I do not know which suffered most by the fall of expectation: he hoping that I would like it, or I that I should taste it as he did. He put it away again as a man wraps his dreams.

He had very long hair, which, in the custom of the fisherman of his day, he wore in two long plaits either hanging down under his woollen smock, or coiled round his head. He told me you always knew Yarmouth men by their hair. In the cold of winter nights in the boats, or when the icy gales blew from the North Sea and no one knew when the sun would be warm again, they loosed it out and it was like a shawl on their backs. Men died in their boats of the cold; only the strong survived. Sometimes a man and his boy both died, and the boat bob-bobbed on the water till it was seen from afar and the dead brought home frozen in it. Sometimes the boat sank and the woman on shore waited in vain.

"But why did they go out?" the child would ask.

"Hunger drove them," he would reply.

In a low, almost tuneless voice he would croon over long sea-chanties, unexpurgated and monotonous. Once I asked him the meaning of one. He looked at me, and no matter how I asked for it he never sang it again. It was he who taught me "The Golden Vanitee," which years afterwards I taught to Henry Lawson.

Many tales he told me; stories of the Caribs, of tropical fruits, of negroes and Spanish ladies and mantillas, giving me a black-beaded and fringed mantilla he had carried from one knows not where. He told of the Bahamas; of the Barbadoes; and of a high wind in Jamaica. The shiver and the terror and the romance of these words have been with me ever since. "A high wind in Jamaica" . . . The other day when I saw where someone, who knew not the right word, wrote in our leading daily paper, "High winds in Jamaica," I felt as if I had seen sacrilege or had looked on the dead. Why didn't the writer know the right word?

"This one went whaling . . ."

We called the old man Tom, but he had the Yarmouth name given as a generic to the sea-fishers, and which distinguished them from the despised salters and landsmen. Someone may recall it, for today I have lost it. He was our knock-about man, who cut wood, lit fires, swept the yard, and so on. But in the end he had to be sent away.

Fisherman, harpooner, slaver, pirate—he had lived a life of blood, and his life had shaped him. My father, who had checked him for some neglect, by an intuitive instinct of danger one day, turned suddenly to find him at his back, bent as he might have been for the launch behind the balanced harpoon, in one hand a billy held as a guard, in the other a knife.

"What do you mean?" my father demanded.

"I mean nothing," he answered sullenly.

Yet it was when his swag was rolled for departure that he opened it to give me a taste of his hoarded biscuit.

A strange relic

Words remain with children even if they are not aware of remembering. They sink into the unconscious, and in the after years emerge and are known. But it is well that children hear without understanding, or some would live in great unhappiness.

There was a man who once came to our place, when we were somewhere near where Griffith is now. He was slender and dark; he did not roll on his feet like a stockman nursing his spurs, and bow-legged from the saddle; nor did he walk lurching heavily as did teamsters and fencers, who broke down in the feet from carrying heavy posts and rails. Sitting at our door talking, this strange visitor showed my mother the most pitiful thing man ever showed. It was in the days when surgery was most brutal, and the agony in his voice as he told his story lives with me still.

As he talked of his life he slipped his hand inside his shirt and drew out and showed a sac, soft as velvet, and ivory-coloured from the sweat of where it lay above his heart. The sac had been his young wife's breast. It had been taken off for cancer, and she had died under the knife. In the anguish of her screams as in her struggles she was held down by the students (there being no anaesthetics then), he had put his hands to his ears and run, and run, though she had asked him to stay by her, for she thought that with him there she could endure as she could not without him.

But, though he had run he had to come back and wait for the end that was her death. His brother was one of the surgeons of the Infirmary, and after taking off what was wanted for observation and study, the delicate outer skin of the breast was left. The bereaved man pleaded for it as a part of his wife that he could keep though she lay in the grave. His brother prepared it and gave it to him.

"It is all that I have left," he said, and the tears ran in his voice as they ran on his face. He laid it against his cheek and anguished over it.

"She suffered so under their hands," he said, "the brutal hands of men. I went mad with her screams, and could only wish her dead."

He spoke of the delicacy and purity of her mind and of her modesty.

"No man's hand had ever touched her but mine; no man's eye had ever looked on her whiteness but mine...."

And they stripped her and strapped her down to a table under the hands and eyes of the surgeons and the students. There were no nurses then in the Royal Infirmaries—not as we know them now. The students did what women do in modern hospitals. At that time the matron followed the doctor on his rounds, carrying a wash-basin for his hands, while her probationer came behind her carrying the towel. Men did the rest. Consequently there were thousands of women who died rather than lie exposed to the eyes of strange men, rather than that alien hands should touch them.

He, himself, was a young clergyman not through his finals. In his agony of mind he broke down, and had what was then called brain-fever. When he recovered they sent him to the loneliness of almost unpeopled Australia. In Australia he wandered with his Bible and his grief; and the long roads took him where there were neither books to read, nor people to talk about them.

"I cannot believe in God," he told my mother. "But I can believe in Christ, because He suffered, and was pitiful to women. He pitied even the woman taken in adultery, for He said: 'Let him that is without sin cast the first stone.' ... He was hurt; but He hurt none."

Because he had lost faith, and in that had suffered a second loss, and such a depth of loss as nobody of the light living of today can even imagine, for religion then was a part of the root of life—because of that loss his career as a clergyman was closed to him. And yet, a clergyman was all that he was fitted to be, both by temperament and by training and inheritance.

"It will be buried with me," he said, as he put away his relic.

"How can you ensure that?" my mother asked. "People will not know what it is or what is your wish!"

He told her that his lungs were gone; that he had not long to live; that he knew the symptoms, and that before he became too weak to walk he would go right away into the bush where no one would find him. Then the dust that was her would mix with the dust that was him; and there would be no more separation, no more loneliness, and no more pain.

I was so much a child I thought the robins would cover him. Next day when he was gone I asked would it not be so. My mother replied: "The trees here are evergreen. There will be no leaves."

". . . no more separation, no more loneliness,
no more pain."

The proud men

What chapters and chapters could be written on men who loved their horses! Once the track of every broken-in horse was known; and whether he was broken to saddle or to harness was remembered and talked of.

As to saddles and bridles, and leather traces—today's leather would not stand the strain and long wear and tear of time that the old leather stood. From an earth full of its own nature, from a grass that ate and drank of it, whatever fed on that grass carried durability under and in its hide. A brumby, whether a brumby horse or a brumby beast, could live where the finely bred of modern times would die, and die almost before the fat had gone off it.

Did someone ask if a horse wasn't a beast? A horse might be an animal; he was never a beast. A beast was a beef animal. "*They're killing a beast* . . ." "*Bring in a beast for the killing* . . ." "*There isn't a beast left* . . ." "*He had a fine beast* . . ." But none of them were horses. Not in Australia.

A man's saddle was himself and his horse; he and it and the animal were one when girths were up and the seat made. A man's ease in riding depended on the make of the saddle, and a horse's back was made or marred by its set. Even the exact place where the girths came mattered. Too far forward and they cut, too far back and the wind was affected. A bad saddler had to go to the city to live; the country that loved its horses, soon dried him out; or he had to turn round and become a harness maker. As harness belonged to settlement he had to go where settlement was growing. But a good saddle maker was a king. He lived like Shakespeare—in the hearts of all men.

As an example, there was that Fortescue at Goulburn, who used the first pictured saddle advertisement in Australia. Indeed it was one of the first pictures ever used for a locally manufactured article. "A Fortescue set of harness"—a man was noted who had it. My grandfather's Sunday set, used only on Sundays and special days and visitings, was Fortescue. Fortescue harness never wore shabby; it was good to the end. The sewing was as good as the cut; the cut worthy of the silver mountings; and the silver worthy of the leather; for Fortescue only used the best. However, with increase of population and therefore of vehicles and trade, Fortescue at last left saddles to the younger men and specialized in harness.

Making in Goulburn, he sold in Narrandera and in Hay; was known at Fort Bourke and at Booligal; and his saddles were ridden at Ivanhoe and Mossgiel. Between these places men rode at night by the stars, and by the easting of the sun, and with the shadow of noon by day. There were fewer beaten tracks then than there are kings in Europe today. In those days, too, Rudd's Murrumbidgee saddle with its wide skirt, its broad seat, its high pommel and cantle, and its protective knee-pads, was famous. A man could ride the scrub with untorn knees, and a tired horse could have the girths eased because the great breadth of the saddle kept it from turning.

I used to ride on my father's sideways, of course, long skirt almost to the ground, knee on the pommel. Once, after a ride, as I slipped off I found the girth hanging slack. It had never been buckled up. It was a tribute to my sitting; and, luckily for me, I had ridden a straight road with no sharp turns. Once, when riding, the mare I had did a pin-wheel—and the next thing I knew was that I was standing on the road. But she was that beautiful thing, a good stock horse, and missing my weight on her back had stopped in her own length and was waiting for me. Another time a slack girth slithered me, along with a turned saddle, under the horse's belly. But Rodney had been an old military horse, or a steeplechaser, and he knew he must not tread on what lay under his feet. He was my father's favourite mount. And yet there came a day when we had to shoot him, so that he would not die lingeringly of drought.

For years, when there were no flowers, I made wreaths of grass for his grave. Grass seemed better than nothing. I never thought how appropriate, as I do now. At one station where my father was building we had a whole cemetery in the bottom paddock. It contained horses, dogs, cats, birds, and even a man. Everything there had a name except the man. We did not know who he was, where he came from, or how he died. All we knew was that he was dead—and buried. Then one day I wired two pieces of split paling together, made a cross for a headstone, and wrote on it "*Resurgam.*" Of all words to have chosen how appropriate! For today I know who that nameless man was, though only by inference. His story I have told on another page. Fixed population grows so rapidly that the ridden is no longer a common theme—as a horse to bestride, as one to drive, or merely as one to look at and talk about as one leans over the top rail

"... a good saddle-maker was a king."

of a fence. So there have been occasions when, where streets are, I have heard hobbles called hopples, and vice versa. But, where hopples belong to the town and the trotting course, hobbles belong to the country. The hobbles with straps, a chain and a swivel, came from America; before that we had a chain without a swivel, and a horse had to have brains in order not to be crippled when wearing them. Once let a twist come on the slack of such a chain, and there resulted a condition that tightened the thong of hide or strap on the fetlock till it cut, or a link broke.

The strap taking the place of the hide brought the buckle; but before there came the strap and buckle there was the peg. I loved these pegs. They were always made of hardwood—boree, yarran, myall, hickory, or even wattle. They were acorn-shaped at each end and with an indented band all round the middle; and they were smoothed and polished by use—sometimes by hand as well. A man who had a mare or a horse that he loved, would attend to everything that made for finish in his outfit, or for comfort and artistic decoration for his mount. The unloved packhorse would have hide hobbles and unmatched pegs. It used to be my delight to put in the pegs. Sometimes I put the wrong pegs on the wrong horse. Then there was a scolding for me, and a quick changing.

Though wood was everywhere, I have known men keep the same set of pegs for a year, or more, and boast of it as writers do of long-used fountain-pens today. One man had his pegs for five years. It was so long a time that, almost, he hung his future on them as the ancients pinned victory to the "insides" of a cock.

A horse hobbled for the first time, especially if closely shortened, has to be very wise or he is liable to fall. If there are small stumps or rocks in the grass he will catch, and being in a state of unprepared balance, down he goes unless he has room for a recovery. Accustomed to free feet, his body flexes automatically when not hobbled, but when the feet are bound, and his forward base narrowed as he moves, to have any ease at all he must reason—unless all reason toward accommodation is instinct. Bumping along, both forefeet up in the air at once, this diagonally moving animal does the best he can. As he feeds he forgets for a moment, and goes to step forward, one foot at a time.

And it is here that one learns whether a horse is well or ill hobbled. I have seen a horse lamed by a new-chum who wound long strips of hide through the links and in a continuous coil round the fetlock, and then tied a knot. At every movement the coil tightened till circulation stopped, and the suffering skin dripped blood. I never

heard anything more bitter than my father's condemnation once of one such who had been told to hobble out the horses while we set up camp. That man knew how to hobble a horse properly the next time he was told to do it! . . .

"What are you making, uncle Harry?"

"A wimwam for a goose's bridle! . . ."

But I knew better. I knew they were pegs for hobbles, and that they would be of good boree heart, properly trimmed and polished, because they were for a favourite mare. . . .

There are times when I grow absolutely hungry for the sight and smell of an old-fashioned saddle. What lovely colour there was in the long-used, much-cared-for leather; what delight in the feel of its texture; and as a child with what sensitiveness I "loved" it with hands too small to cover even the narrowest stirrup-tread!

There were plenty of Californian saddles in the country then, and sometimes Mexican saddles, too; the latter high-horned and with a back rest, and both had wide flaps—but in the Mexican there were real *tapaderos*. There was a good deal of silver used both on these imported saddles and on the bridles that matched them. But besides the American or Spanish ones there were the smaller, lighter-coloured, thinner-leathered English saddles, and among them were such as were stamped with roses, sometimes with thistles and shamrocks or ivy leaves, with other patterns in ovals, and in running traceries and lines.

If possible the stirrups matched the saddle pattern. Stirrups were made with the single brace to the thread, or with the double brace; some were plain and narrow; others had the metal leather covered, with a small pad under the arch of the instep. Some had a surface-fret as a design; some a scroll. At three years old I knew the stirrup of every stockman on the station. The men used to mix them just to see me pair them and take them to their owners. And I had favourites among the stirrups as I had among the men, favourites that called to the eye, to the touch, and, in their "clink," to the ear.

The early stockmen as far as Australia was concerned, were the world's aristocrats. To have asked one of them to handle an axe, to cut wood, to take the cart into town for supplies, would have met with a look that would have prevented any repetition of the offence. The stockman was a stockman, not a menial; he took instructions, but he listened to no man's bidding.

"Why did you leave Sanderson's, Bill?"

"He asked me to cut the wood!"

Mark the "the" and realize the enormity. Only a very mean man would ask a stockman to cut house-wood, and no stockman worked long for any man not his equal in manhood. An employer might be richer, he was no better. He might be bigger, taller, more educated or far-travelled; he was only more interesting for this, but no better than the man who mustered the cattle.

". . . the world's aristocrats."

You must not confuse the stockman with the "tailer." The tailer, and, for years the later rouseabout on the sheep-run, were no-account men. They were weaklings; they were menial; and could be asked to cut wood and would do it as a part of their lowly, wretched, and good-for-nothing lot. They were no better than the swan-hoppers. Indeed, they often did the swan-hopping. I had an uncle, who, to help his father, once went tailing. He stood it for three days and then went prospecting. As a prospector he was alone; he had no men's-hut to go to, no meals cooked for him, no talk by the chuck-fire or at the woodheap at mornings and evenings. But he was a man. He wasn't that scorned of scorned things, a tailer.

He never told anyone he had taken on tailing, and sternly he told me I wasn't to tell anyone. I never did, till now. But then he has been dead these twenty years; and only I and one of his last two old brothers left could tell you his name.

As to the swan-hoppers, they were the untouchables. They were the unskilled and the unfit of their day.

Because the wild fowl of this country were so enormously plentiful, because cattle and profit and wealth were to grow in a day in this unknown land, the swans were a nuisance. They filled and fouled the waters; their feathers, as they moulted, massed in the reeds and were blown by the winds through the wide miles of grass; their nests and sleeping-places smelt, even though in their sanctuaried places they enriched the ground to greater productiveness. While there were no cattle there was no offence. When cattle came they became an offence. Cattle snorted away from the reeds they polluted; and feathers, taken in with the grass eaten miles away, made feather-balls, impacted the stomach, and killed the beasts. Cattle were still so few that a beast was a loss to be counted; the loss of a hundred made ruin. So the swan-hoppers came in. Their work was to hop the swans off the nests in the breeding-season, and smash the eggs. It was filthy work; they reeked of the half-hatched and the addled, and their trousers grew stiffer and stiffer, and filthier and filthier, as the yolks and the whites of the smashed eggs set in the material of which they were made.

The old cattle town of Wagga Wagga once had its swan-hoppers on all the stations round about; and the more they stank the prouder they were.

They boasted in stink. Stink was the guarantee of ability and valuable endurance.

But this is not saddles, nor is it the horses that bore the saddles, and which were so much a part of the man himself.

Neither is it that kindred thing, the sound of a rider's foot coming into the house, the jingle of the spurs on his feet, the dry, warm "run" of the stock-whip trailing from his arm. Nor is it that other part of the camper's outfit—the hobbles. Again I hear out of years of distance the sound of hobbles in the night; of hobbles on a horse just turned out to graze; of hobbles, chink, chink, chink on a saddle—going east, going west, going north, the cattle lowing, the goldfields calling...

Dust on the trail

"I seen a dust right over the top-side of the crick, yestiddy."

"Musta bin someone goin' furder out."

"I hadn't time to go and look. But I heard say there was a lotta new land thrun open out by Mumbledool."

And Mumbledool may have been Mossgiel or Ivanhoe, Nariah or Big Mimosa, Merringreen, Menindee, or Lake Cargelligo—for they were all frontier once.

It was then the mighty army of the teams went out; and in lonely places men made friends of bullocks, and bullocks made friends of men, so that loneliness lost something of its alone-ness, and space and solitude found company; and this even though, from the sky, the slender company tracking its way through would seem little more than the specks, that, seen from the earth, were eagles in the altitudes.

As the teams went out they took loading, they took families, and sometimes they took both. At first they made no dust at all as they travelled, for the grass, untrodden through ages, was too thick for dust to rise, except when a disturbance was made in crossing the dry bed of a soak or a watercourse. Afterwards when cattle, first, and then sheep followed, the tracks that once went on top of the grass became roads. So "crossings" turned into beds of pipeclay, red dust, and golden sand in summer, and made lakelets of porridgy mud in winter.

Roads coming, after the rains were over, the misty particles rose from the wheels, mile by mile; day long, week long, year long; while beside the teams plodded the teamsters; a bandana, a square of calico, a piece of worn, napless flannel shirt or anything else one had, hanging down the back of the neck and the spine to mitigate the heat of the sun, or else tied over the mouth to keep the fine choking powder that rose unendingly from the tormented throat and lungs.

There is dust still on the roads, but that was primeval dust; a dust from grass and earth, from flower and tree, that had never known anything but the soft foot, and the soft hand of those who had moved in their own time and way, and when rested, bedded, or settled, had lived at their ease.

". . . misty particles rose . . ."

The land read the dust-cloud risen upon its surface as later men read helio, and today we read the air. Sometimes it was a sudden spot moving in the distance so that it hung like a small low cloud, and then went bellying out like a ship's sails filled with wind. In that case it would be a tilted cart with a trotting or a jogging horse, followed by a cow and a steer or two, and perhaps some calves. Or it might be a cart, and ten or twelve or even twenty sheep. When it was sheep the dust rose, swung, and fell more gradually.

We knew every kind of moving pillar and read each as later people read books and papers. The dust was our news sheet, for every kind of hoof made a differently shaped rise, and every speed a different roll; every variation in hoof-mass raised a greater or less volume, and a greater or less height, hang, and fall again to earth. A long mob of cattle made a long run of dust, a wide one gave a more hesitant drag before the last and finest of the sifting powder fell.

And all these were conditioned in their time and place by the heat of the sun, the wind, the time of the day, and the rate of the hoofs that clicked, beat or plodded on the road. Also, every kind of hoof—sheep, cattle, horses, pigs—all sent out a different odour on the wind, and left a different smell in the dust, till a new wind came along and blew it away again.

In the settling of the land, the tilted cart, whether it was a dray or one of the kind with heavy inelastic springs, and usually with a horse, but sometimes with a bullock in the shafts, see-sawed its way ever forward like a beetle in a tussock or like a wandering ant delayed at night. On the seat the mother sat driving, the baby in her arms or on a folded shawl behind her, and with the next littlest sitting on the floor of the vehicle beside it. Following, the others would come skrimshanking along, barefooted and busy, the father pushing along behind with the stock.

Where there was a spring-cart and a family there would be a hen or two carried on the tilt, perched on the tail-board, or even sitting where the billy and the waterbag hung on the axle. Sometimes there would be a goat, with the kids in with the babies. The kids had to be saved, for one of them would be a billy, and the nanny would fret and lose her milk if he were taken and only the nanny-kid left. When, as the day went on the nanny tired, a halt would be made for a rest, a sup of cold tea or water given her so that the milk would not dry up, and the kids (and perhaps the baby) perish for want of it.

When the piles of dust rose higher than for a cart, it would be a team, mass giving body to the upward flung cloud; and with the team might be a dray with tents, pigs in a bag or loose on the deck, fowls

*"On the seat the mother sat driving,
the baby in her arms . . ."*

in coops, cows in milk, a small mob of mixed cattle, or a flock of sheep up to fifty or even a hundred. This would be a man of money, taking up a smallish station, or adjoining selections in sons' and daughters' names as well as his own, with a good pre-ẹmptive right wherever he could have it allotted to him. There would be chairs and tables with such a man; perhaps even a piano. But the cart had the concertina, and wherever the concertina went there were those who danced, and those who sang.

But the teams—the teams when settlement spread like a tide, when herds and flocks grew even for selectors, and mustering and then shearing made places, that once only the kangaroos and brolgas knew, into milling and feverishly busy centres of population—the teams were the caravans of all the roads. When they gathered in the towns they were like an army ranging for the outward march. Then, every publican and inn-keeper had his yard for the short team, and his paddock for the spares.

Less noisy than the drovers who preceded them, yet only by a little, trade hummed in their gathering. Empty they came from all directions, loaded they set out singly or in groups, east, west, south, north—and the longest trails went west and north where the lonely looked for them and the tales of wonder grew.

The story of the teams has never been properly told. Some day one will rise and tell of them as Homer told of Troy.

The sled

The sled preceded, or at need took the place of dray, cart, or gig; even of that smartest introduction, the American buggy. In shape it was a triangle. Sometimes it was just a forked young tree or a forked branch; but usually it was "made." Two small logs were notched at the top, and bored or mortised at the bottom ends. The notched tops were drawn together and tied, or pegged one above the other. The other ends were splayed out by a cross-piece secured by pegs, or let into the mortises and then pegged. Of all the jolty things to ride in or on, the sled was the joltiest. Its floor was of round sticks, short split slabs, palings, or rough boards. At its best it was of hide put on wet, then allowed to shrink till it was taut and set hard. Even so, your teeth snapped as you rode on it. Still, many a girl going to a dance saved her finery by riding on one. Often it was all there was to hurriedly take a woman to a neighbour's and get her there "in time."

When there was "trouble" the case was desperate. Once, in response to a neighbour's despairing appeal, after talking things over and showing the impossibility of anything else to be used in safety, father went out with his axe, brought in two long slender pines, and made a *travois*. It was the only one of the kind I ever remember seeing. There being no pack-saddle, the ends were fastened like shafts through the stirrup-leathers, on each side of a riding saddle, a trace being run round the horse's chest. There was a spreader half-way down the poles; and either with a rawhide or a possum rug, a sort of pocket-seat was made for the woman who had to be got somewhere, but who could not go on a sled. The man walked beside the horse, the child that could not be left behind, because the mother would not let us keep it for her, was held in the saddle.

. . . I heard that woman say in after years that that *travois* jumped like a kangaroo. But she came home with her baby all the same.

"In the Queen's name"

Free selection and cheap or assisted immigration going hand in hand, frontier life soon began to know change. The wurlie under a tree and the bare bark hut without a fence gave place to a more permanent thing. Instead of a man putting up a new wurlie under another tree as the old one fell to pieces in the summer heat or was blown to smithereens in a storm, or instead of the usual tent-shaped hut of bark, places began to appear with corner posts, walls, and a fireplace. Sometimes the walls were of stubs or logs, sometimes of bark, later on of split slabs. These newer huts were large enough for a partition.

Then (for where there were two rooms there were a woman and children) an enclosure of brush, a sapling rail or two, or even a row of poles standing on end like palings, either fenced the front, made a fowl-yard at the back, or surrounded the whole place. The brush fences stood till the custom of firing the grass to provide green feed in a new growth of herbage made them too dangerous, as such fires, running wild, swept everything before them. Often the brush, where still in being, was set upright like a wall, with a small gate entrance. Outside the gate was the woodheap.

In these days of patent locks and city burglar-proof devices, it seems strange to remember what a sense of security lay in a fence of brush.

In continual alertness men and women lived. A housed human voice was a terrifying thing, with its dominating proprietary call of "*Who's there?*" when an intruding outside sound broke on the silence; for no one slept without the gun or the axe a handbreadth off at the head of the bed. The odds were with the indoors, not with out-of-doors; for a charge of heavy shot from a crack—and every crack gave a loop-hole—covered a widening area as it scattered. But the same kind of charge from outside could only scatter against the walls. Even if a stray pellet or two went through, one shot was nothing unless it hit the eye. But shooting in the night was seldom head or even body high. A lower level was chosen.

"... in the midst of her preoccupation she suddenly has an awareness."

"IN THE QUEEN'S NAME" 

"In the Queen's name I call upon you to answer, or I shall fire!" called my father, one night, the call waking us in the next room.

There was no answer. Twice more the orthodox warning was repeated in the might of the Queen's name, and still no answer came. Then in the direction of the stealthy sound that waked him, my father fired.

A man yelped and ran.

"It was mostly salt, with only a few grains of small shot, and he will carry the marks on his legs for a few days!" grimly said father as he returned to bed. And that was all we ever knew—the stealthy hand on the door, the running feet, and in the morning my little dog Toby dead of a bait at the front gate.

"Evidently he did not know that I was home," my father remarked to my mother, "and thought only you and the children were here."

I was no more than eight years old, but he showed me how to lay the gun across a stool and shoot through a crack. Three times he made me load an old pistol to see that I really knew how it was done and would not forget. I could always load a gun and shoot in greater certainty than my mother.

". . . a more permanent thing . . ."

Frontier life was so solitary—except for its immediate familiar sounds—that man, who, through generation by generation of housing, had grown away from his natural animal habit of alertness even in sleep, went back to it.

Though centuries removed from it, he was only one generation born from it; and not even that, when native to, or long resident in the bush. So, one would wake from a deep dead sleep, not knowing why one waked, but with every sense at spring, and feeling that in the silence something stood—was static in that stillness of movement which was will-forbidden to allow itself to be distinguishable in the stillness. Something was there, undetected by the senses, yet felt, heard, discovered by the subconscious. In other words something—secret, silent, and menacing—was recognized because it was alien; and perhaps actually more so because it was itself on guard, alert, and wary. Even fowls would give an alarm in the night for the same reason. The strange was about; the atmosphere of the known, of the familiar, was intruded upon by something that was not familiar.

"It was the fowls woke me," a tank-sinker's wife said. "They seemed to know, and started cackling on the roost..." Indeed there were people who had their fowls roost in trees as close to the house as possible for this very reason.

The loss of this alertness is due to community life, whether for man, dogs, horses, fowls, or anything else that lives as man, or that man tames and keeps. Yet the mother who nurses her own baby always retains something of it, no matter how much a townswoman she becomes. In her sleep she is alive to every changing breath of her child; in the midst of her preoccupation over the kitchen stove she suddenly has an awareness. "Baby is awake" her heart says; and turning she goes into the bedroom where an interested infant is silently watching a fly on a bed-curtain, or turning his head with seeing eyes looking from one side of the space above him to the other. He has made no sound, no call, no claim. He was simply an intelligence become active where sleep had held the intelligent in dormancy. But the mother knew it.

Solitude is full of such embracing community of spirit; but actual community life is lacking in it. Man delegates the watch to the policeman, and ceases as an individual to keep the inner sentries alert.

I was correcting the initial type-script of this when I had the following letter from my husband, written from our place in northern Queensland. Dated Longford, 4th December, 1932, he says: "A man came last night to the house. Somewhere about twelve or one o'clock,

as my sheep-dog was growling, I knew there was someone about, although it was so dark that I could not see. So I grabbed my rifle first, and then called out, 'Who is there?' But it turned out to be a traveller who had got his car bogged and had walked five miles in the mud (the yearly rains had started) so I gave him a cup of tea and made him a shakedown. In the morning I let him have a horse to ride away and get help, as my own day for lifting and pushing is over. . ."

The bush does not greatly alter, not while it is the frontier. In 1873 my father taught me to load a pistol, in this year of 1932 my husband says: "I grabbed my rifle."

Note: We had the old horse-pistol for years after the period referred to in the text. We called it "Mr Gale's pistol," because it had in part once belonged to him. This was when he and my father had the first mail that was run between Goulburn and Braidwood and Queanbeyan. The contract was either taken out in Mr Gale's name, or else it was he who guaranteed my father to the government, a guarantee being required. The position was dangerous owing to bushrangers and escaped convict-robbers; and responsible because a good deal of gold had to be carried for diggers sending their lots to the stores and to the banks. The date of the contract would be 1864 or 1865. When we went to Riverina the pistol went with us. It was a cap-hammer muzzle loader. Once, in fear of a man camped in front of the house, and who looked insane, it was loaded by my brother Hugh with little stones as our only substitute for a bullet. He was to do the shooting, and was just about seven years old. Fortunately we had no need to use the pistol, as after a while the man went away.

My brother Jack, that John Cameron who was British Consul at Danzig in 1933, in his long ago Bookstall novel *The Spell of the Bush*, based a scene in one of his chapters on this incident.

Fire

How quickly the mind had to act and meet great issues when settlement was sparse! Perhaps it acts as quickly now, but the occasions are different.

There was a woman whose husband either had a selection on the run where my father was building, or else was working for sheep as payment for his labour. This was often done when barter was easier than to obtain currency. Cheques were the usual exchange, of course, till faked signatures came to awaken people to the need not only of recognition of a name, but of hand-writing. The readiness with which cheques, or orders, were once taken as money, shows how little education there was. No man needed to read or write till he owned property and had accounts to deal with.

As all the stations and storekeepers were known (just as a racing man knows racehorses today) and as only these used cheques, for a long time a name was a guarantee of genuineness. But as I said, where a station-owner did not have a good enough banking account, he paid (or part paid) his boundary-riders and stockmen sometimes in stock, and sometimes in land. Whether the man in the present case was a selector or merely a paid man I have forgotten. But, stores being needed for his family, he harnessed the dray to go to town to sell his skins (such as he had) and buy supplies. Men shopped then, not women; and while he would be away the wife and children would be alone.

He was only gone a day of the four that he must be absent, when, as night came, the wife noticed the glare of a bushfire on the horizon behind the house. No help was near; no one who could be called in or given a message was likely to pass, as the hut was just a tiny nest in the midst of miles and miles of grass and forest. Did she know the danger? She did. Did she fall into panic? She did not. A bushwoman, she looked at the glare (it was a thirty mile wide front of fire as it happened), and estimating distance judged that it would be quite safe to go to bed.

The measurement of distance is one of the first things one has to learn in the bush. It is the equivalent of the "How long does it take?"

of the city. Distance has to be realized in relation to direction, in regard to how far one has travelled in order to know where there would be grass or water ahead for camping at night, and also to know whether to press the horses or to travel easy; because to press horses without need was not only folly, but, in bush estimation, a fool's crime.

Horses were cheap, but not only did they not grow on every bush, but wages were low and purchasing power correspondingly limited. The knowledge of distance and place had to lie with the senses in the mind. A man without a horse was lost; he would perish of thirst if left on foot. More than once we have had men with sun-blotched faces, blistered lips and bloodshot eyes, stagger gibbering to the cask, or cry "Water!" as they reeled to the door, because they had misjudged distance, and lost a horse. In any case a waterless horse will wander. So in the bush security is based on perception of distance in line and time; on distance plus direction where there are no landmarks beyond a blazed tree every mile or so, and on what a horse can do in a given period.

When morning came this woman, who knew distance and direction as men knew them, made no hurry for all that the fire was enormous. She dressed the children and got the breakfast as usual. When this was over she took the dog, and the little ones, and went out and rounded up the small handful of sheep that was to be the foundation of their future flock.

She brought the sheep to the hut after having watered them. There she let them rest for half an hour. Then, the dog and the children behind them, and herself on the outside, she drove them round and round, round and round the place. They were so pitifully few, and the grass so strong and thick, that their little hooves trampled but little more than a couple of furrows wide at a time. An hour passed, and she rested them. At noon she let them feed and go to water. Then she began again. All day she kept them resting and going, resting and going, till dark. Six miles a day is sheep travelling at stock rate. Because they were so few, and her one narrow chance depended on them and their endurance, she did not dare to over-drive them. If they began persistently to lie down she would not be able to get them up after a while; and if, at the end their hooves foundered from being too long on them, and later sweated off them, the flock would be ruined and her husband's toil lost.

When dark came she could smell the fire on the isolated puffs of wind. These puffs came from the sudden ballooning of masses of air from the cooler spaces of the forest as opposed to the warmer open areas of grass. Rising to a high altitude as they heated, there they cooled somewhat and fell again, forming air puffs that reached earth miles ahead of the flaming front itself. The sheep were done. The dog had such swollen feet that he whimpered as he licked them, the children were so dead tired they fell and slept where they had stood. Her own boots were worn through, and she went barefoot in the last rounds to ease the tension of the muscles on the ground.

She could do no more than the next thing, thought was dead, but automatically her body did what her mind had earlier set it to do; so she looked at the narrow ring of trodden grass, put the sheep and the children inside the hut, and lit her return fire. Whether it would go forward to meet the on-coming monster now roaring on the wind of its own heat, or whether when started it would flare back across the narrow trodden "break," she did not know. But all that could be done she had done. She nursed the trickle of flame as it began to run, then as it widened forward she went inside, laid the children on the bed, gave the panting dog a drink, and after making a billy of tea, sat by the fire and sewed.

I have forgotten what their name was. But I remember the released wonder, joy and relief in my father's voice, when, though the horses still danced in places from the heat of the earth, the ground was sufficiently cooled for us to get across to see the family, and we

"A man without a horse was lost . . ."

". . . a tiny nest in the midst of miles and miles of grass and forest."

found it safe. Through the burning logs and still falling timber we went, my sharp eyes the first to see that the hut was still standing. It stood with a little ring of trodden earth about it in a sea of ashes, some of the tussocks still smoking and glowing as an air moved, or a tussock-puff rose. The dog's feet had to be dressed and wrapped in oiled rags, and two of the sheep were broken and would never do any good again. But that was all. Even the one solitary hen they owned was saved. We camped by the dried-up waterhole and stayed till the husband came home.

"Because," said my father, "after what she has been through she might suddenly break up and go mad..." The physical strain, alone, had stretched endurance to the limit.

The husband came home nearly frantic. The slow travelling with the dray, after he had heard there was a fire, made every mile seem ten. On the last afternoon he took the horse out of the shafts, packed him with tea, sugar, flour, and a tin of jam, and sometimes riding, sometimes walking, did the last miles home. When he heard the barking of a dog (ours), he said he could hardly breathe for the leap of his heart, and in spite of himself burst into tears.

In that same fire, another man farther on was completely burnt out. He had tried to save his roof with wet blankets, having first burnt his "break," but all he had when we saw him was the one blanket he could tear from the roof as it caught alight; and even that was full of holes.

"And they were new blankets," he said sadly. "I had only just bought them," he added. "Now we will have to do with boughs over bags." As he had only been a few months married the blankets were to have lasted till a family came—till they would be turned over to the children.

Have you ever slept under boughs over bags? I have, two or three times, when owing to knocked-up horses we could not make a destination. The bags were so rough that I asked for boughs under bags. The leaves were soft and like silk, but the ends were sticks, and sticks stuck into one's flesh. In addition the twigs were full of life—beetles, moths, caterpillars, spiders. I have slept under grass and under bracken, too. But you can make a nest of grass or bracken; you cannot do that with boughs. Still, they are very sweet with the stars overhead, and warm as feathers once you are warm.

"Boughs over bags..." I have said somewhere that there is no past; there is only the present. I still see a burnt blanket; hear a man's wistful voice; feel the heartache of a loss made long ago.

By the "Edinburgh Castle"

There was once in the middle years a claim of kinship strong enough to call two of us back to Argyle and the wide family hearthstone. The hearthstone stood wherever relationship, however distant, held to old names. We went by train to Goulburn and thence by coach to the Middle Arm—and such a coach! Its top rocked like a tilt, while its curtains flapped like sails. It rattled, it jerked, it sprang, one joint at a time (it really did seem jointed!) and made a noise wherever a bolt, a mortise, a strap, or a brace held two parts even moderately together. The inside seat was so narrow that one held on to it by the hinder muscles of the body, and stayed one's self from slipping by propping the feet hard in front. The coachman drove by his voice, and he used it so much in driving that he had none for passers-by, many and all friendly though they were. Them he answered by a half movement of the whip held at slope, which was all the use the whip had. He ran his own coach, and was too good a bushman to abuse his horses, especially when roads were bad.

At the Edinburgh Castle, which then had its licence, we pulled up. My brother got off the box-seat—the one comfortable even if exposed spot on the coach—and shaking the sleet from his coat came to the side of the vehicle and pulled open the curtains:

"Will you get down from the coach, and come into the hotel and take a glass of wine?" he asked.

In the form of the question you can mark the period. He neither said, "Have a drop?" "Have a nip?" "Whisky?" nor "A peck?" I looked at the mud between the high wheels and the inn; at the sleety mist about us; and said I would stay where I was. But as I sat looking out, my brother having gone with the coachman to the fire and the bar, the landlady passed up the veranda with the mail-bag, a tiny room at its far end being the post office. A great round tumbling-looking woman, lurching sideways from foot to foot on feet too small for her bulk. At sight of my face she started as if shot.

"Are you Donal Cameron's daughter?" she cried astonished.

"I am. What made you ask?"

"The likeness," she replied. And then she went on—she who had

not seen my father for over twenty-five years: "Ah, but he was the kind one! Many's the poor woman's cattle lost in the ranges he went out and found when she had no one of her own to help her. Wherever he went his name was spoken with a blessing. He was the one had the good name and the open hand for anyone who was ever in trouble."

It was a great thing for me to hear, coming a stranger into my father's country after him being so long away; and I said so.

"Will you not come in and warm you at the fire? It is cold in the coach." Her friendliness looked from her eyes as she said it.

But I was fitted into my place among the baggage of the "inside," the road was a bog; the sleet was falling. I thanked her and said I would stay where I was. But she insisted on a drink, and because I did not take wine, I put that poor woman to the trouble of making tea, as, for my father's sake I had to have something; and it had to be whatever I wanted. I do not know what her name was. But how often in later years I passed the old inn, doorless, windowless, falling to ruin; within it, as a grim jest, a tankard nailed to the faded and dust-covered bar, and wished I could see her friendly face and rolling body

"It rattled, it jerked, it sprang . . ."

on that lost veranda again. What tales of ghosts and haunts, fights and dances, races, crinolined girls and bold young blades in cabbage-tree hats, she could have narrated; what stories of gay and wild doings she could have told. Maybe she was the wife of John, who was a big man six feet tall; maybe of Big John, who was bigger; maybe of John the Boomer, who was so much bigger still that he could quiet a row within reach without getting up from his seat, he was so strong and so long in the arms.

From the inn we went on, the tongues on the box-seat now fluent and the voices fruity where previously both had been short and dry. Words flowed like rivers where aforetime they had been like the clack of an occasional stone from the wheel. And it wasn't all the whisky, it was kinship—the kinship of those who belong even if not related. And who was not related there! Even lately, I found that one of my father's cousins had married Melba's uncle; a girl who was the boast and the toast of the country-side for her beauty. Her beauty has come down in her children and her grandchildren, but not as she had it. The bloom of a colder land is gone; for in Australia, what was rose-leaf in colour and texture yesterday is too often powder today.

After a time we came to our uncle's house—"Sandy Cameron of the Middle Arm"—"Big Sandy"—"Sandy Cameron of the Head of the River." And all the place welcomed us: house, people, dogs, trees, sky, recollection.

"And how old are you, Jean?" asked long, six-foot-four Hugh, when, the elders gone to bed that night, we younger ones all sat round a hearth as big as heaven; and, like heaven, with some inside and some out; but most were inside.

I told him, and as I said it he laid his hand on my knee.

"You have the family knee," he said, startled as he touched it. And then whimsically: "It is time you were married... You have been too long sleeping alone."

It was one of the broad simplicities of an old generation, but not broad to those of its day. The broad of today is coarse; that was of a provocative simplicity... I had become a town girl by that time; my hair nearly stood on end, but I kept my face.

She was a scented land

Even in my own life she was a scented land. In spring the bush used to be a constant choir of song; wings were everywhere; throughout the changing years might be heard the continual flying of birds: curlews, plovers, travelling duck, swans, wandering owls, bitterns, night-jars, and in the swamp the bleat of the snipe. From twenty directions at once you could hear the mopoke; from a hundred the curlew. There were the birds of all seasons, and the birds of the different hours of the day; there were the waders, the runners, the creepers, the carrion-eaters, the killers (kestrels, falcons, eagles), and those like the fantails that caught the fluttering insect on the wing.

In sheltered places where the blue wren was plentiful, he was literally in hundreds, a family flight being like a small jewelled cloud slipping tenuously through the undergrowth. In every bush I dare affirm there was a pigeon or a dove; the grass was a moving mass of parrots and parrakeets; while the trees glistened white with cockatoos, or were flamingo-pink with the galahs. Ants swarmed on the earth and trees; native bees, flies, gnats, beetles, spiders, and butterflies, burst from egg; rose from larvae, emerged from chrysalis. Everywhere things crept, swarmed, climbed, hummed, chirped, whistled, croaked, sang, and flowered. The air was full of the scent of life and honey, of the warm rich smell of feathers and fur.

The Almighty had poured out for plenty, and the black man had guarded that plenty by his care for balance. The black was indeed the unconscious father both of rationing and of the "Five Year Plan."

There were no bad smells about the bush when the kingdom of the wild was its only kingdom; for the army of the small ate corruption before corruption became malodorous. It was not till the settlement came that the earth stank, and sewers burst. Once Australia smelt like the Spice Islands; the winds stooped as they passed because of her blossom; ships knew her before they came to her.

"We are near Australia," said the seamen. "Can't you smell the flowers?"

And people raised their heads and breathed in perfumes as it were

out of heaven, for the land was still invisible, or but a bank low down on the horizon. Now only at the Leeuwin, as ships pass, do people raise their heads and snuff the air for scented winds. And then only for a short time in the year. Soon that, too, will be gone.

"It was a land of flowers!" said my grandmother. "At sea we smelt the rich scent of the country, different from anything we had ever known. We noticed the perfume long before we came to it. Those who had come home from Australia told us of it, and all who went out to Australia looked for it."

So spoke all the grandmothers. But who has said it in the full rich way that makes it live? Has anyone really sung to the world the song of this Scented Land? The thick-nosed and dull-eared derided her, and we accepted their derision. They called her a land of songless birds and scentless flowers. The world believed them; and we for a century followed in the train of the world, even though on our breath her perfumes hung rich.

Indignantly I used to combat the statement:

"But our flowers *are* scented and our birds *do* sing!" I would counter.

"Oh, but your flowers do not smell like *English* flowers, and there are no *nightingales*!" would be the reply. Well, the rose, the lilac, and the nightingales are all Persian. As for our Australian wattle, London now calls it French mimosa . . .

"*She was a scented land . . .*" And we were taught to look otherwise, and looked as taught.

"*She was a scented land . . .*" And only the exile knew her.

In the days of the first-fleeters, in the years of the forthfarers and the forerunners, the hills and shores of Sydney Cove were sheets of flowers.

"There was nowhere that you could step that you did not walk on them. You would see people trying to avoid treading on the blossoms as they walked just as if they were in a garden," my forerunners of that day used to tell me. They also said that, flower-hungry after the long six months voyage with nothing but sea and sky to lengthen sight, and nothing but the ship by which to contract sight, as soon as people set foot on shore they would drop their baggage and run to gather of the abounding loveliness.

"They would be so eager that when their hands were full they would let fall what they had for fresh ones. *And the scent! . . . The scent! . . .*"

Where the streets of Sydney now are, the very stones grew rock-

". . . the continual flying of birds . . ."

lilies; the flannel flower and the boronia covered every inch that was not just bare rock. I had not seen these lilies when my maternal forebears talked to me of their landing in 1837; I was only a child then. But when at sixteen I came to Sydney I walked all around the Quay, along The Rocks, and back through what is now the Tarpeian Way, a thing hacked out of the earth to make a road, trying to see as *they* had seen; trying to reset the Scented Land, the Land of Flowers.

I look back to old kitchens with their sanded floors; I see my elders peeling potatoes, saving the skins cut thick at the "eyes" for planting, and nursing them for more seed; I see them picking over scant bushels of wheat that the best grains might be kept for the sparest of sowings. I hear the glad cry:

"There is *a quart, at least, of fairly good seed*!" as my grandfather, my grandmother, or one of my aunts or uncles would stand up to stretch the tired, down-bent back. I smell the aroma of fire from wood such as we will never cut again in Australia; for the very long-growing are all chopped out and destroyed now. And, as I think, I feel glad that I belonged to those who pioneered and helped set the foundations of this the last of the Wonderful Lands.

In the kitchen that I knew so well hung the bunches of drying and already dry herbs; those whose drying in the air was complete tied in paper or calico bags for winter use; for the habits of older countries, less prodigal and less hospitable than this, still governed the habits of the people who first came here. On the outside walls, under the long veranda, hung the bundles of orchard and vine cuttings; and each kind had its own scent. Even the varieties of vine differed in smell—Isabella, Shiraz, Golden Hamburg, Sweet Water! Old-fashioned kinds? True. But they were old-fashioned times.

They were the years of frontier beginnings even if Sydney and the coast districts had already reached stability, to markets and easy

comfort. From the deep, dark wine cellar comes the winey, earthly smell of all such places; the greater garden at the front of the house gleams with its laurels, its standard roses, its veronica, its laurustinus, lilacs, and oleanders; and the smaller, less formal, flower-beds at each side of the house, set under the sheltering high rose hedges, send out perfumes on every wind that blows. There lavender and pinks, Sweet William and rosemary border the shaped beds in which blaze anemone and ranunculus, petunia, and verbena. But under the quick-set, deep in the shade are love-in-a-mist, periwinkle, balm, and violets.

The peach- and plum- and nectarine-trees run in rows down the front orchard to the lower vineyard; the quince- and apple-trees are by the kitchen, the dairy, and the wine-sheds; and between these and the "old" vineyard the cherries, greengages, and figs, are companioned by more peaches, more plums, and more quinces.

"I put *them* in for shade for the cows on the other side," said Uncle Alfred, but we all knew he did it for the love of flowers and trees. And he put in more that ran between the cow-sheds, stables, workshops, and barns just behind the "new" vineyard.

The old parts near the house I wandered in at will. But the new was forbidden. "You are too small yet," they said, "you might get lost *and not come home to dinner*!" But yet, small as I was, the elders talked to me and told me of the things I have written here; told me because to me it was romance, history, picture, and vision; told it to a mind journeying back into a world where my foot would never go because it was too late a comer. And part of it was even then in the land of things past.

"The Spice Islands—where are they, grandmamma?"

"In the Indies, Borneo, Java, Sumatra, the Celebes. They smelt of nutmeg and allspice, of pepper, oranges, cloves, and cinnamon. Ships put out of their course that they might pass near and smell them."

"And when you came here was Australia like that, grandmamma?"

"Australia was just like that, my child. The very birds carried the perfume of her flowers on their feathers. . . Ships smelt her scents on the winds as they passed. . . She was a land of flowers."

"... when their hands were full they would let fall what they had for fresh ..."

NOTES ON THE LIFE OF DAME MARY GILMORE

Barrie Ovenden

"I have seen the beginnings," said Dame Mary Gilmore in a recording she made for the Australian Book Society shortly before she died, her voice still strong and vibrant, echoing a spirit which her many years had but served to strengthen.

"I began, myself, with a slush lamp, went on to the tallow candle (we used to lend our candle-mould to the neighbours), then to the imported stearine candle, to kerosene lamps, from kerosene to gas, from gas to electric light, and now we have ahead of us the atomic power to cover every mortal thing we can think of."

Mary Jean Cameron was born on 16 August 1865 and died on 3 December 1962. During her long lifetime, spanning more than half of Australia's recorded history, she not only saw and experienced the many profound changes which took place in social and political life, she was one of those who worked and fought for them.

Her acute perception and deep understanding of humanity made her a natural champion of all radical causes, constantly aware of the problems of the generation around her. In her books of prose and verse she has left valuable descriptions of the life of the early settlers and accounts of little-known Aboriginal customs. In her articles and letters to the Press she influenced public opinion on many varied topics for more than seventy years.

"I write for the man leaning on a lamp-post," she told poet Robert FitzGerald. "The ordinary all-round-the-world common man who may sometimes feel the sun and see the moon."

The land around Roslyn, near Goulburn in New South Wales, is still very much as it must have been when Mary was born in the slab cottage with a thatched roof which belonged to her maternal grandfather, Hugh Beattie. The kindly hills and creeks, and the twisting lanes through green pasture lands fringed by tall gum-trees and golden wattle, make it easy to understand why Mary Gilmore's

writings always breathed a love of the land and reflected a fierce regard for the background of its people.

Mary's father, Donald Cameron, was brought from Scotland to the colony of New South Wales by his parents when he was five years old. Their home, "Rosslyn", was "just behind the fence" of the Beattie home, "Merryvale", and in 1864 Donald married Mary Beattie, whose father was an 1833 immigrant from Armagh.

In the garden of "Merryvale" there still stands a clump of tall trees, protecting the house from the harsh winds that blow across the Eastern Highlands. One of these trees, a white poplar, was planted when Mary was born, by her grandfather Beattie. It was a cutting from one of the trees that Mr Macleay had imported for the new Botanic Gardens in Sydney. The Camerons moved to Wagga Wagga when Mary was a few months old and "Merryvale" was taken over by old friends of the family named Nixon. In 1936 Mrs Sarah Nixon Smith wrote to Mary and told her the poplar was still flourishing.

With her love of tradition and intense regards for "roots", Mary arranged that a cutting from the poplar be planted in the "Poets' Corner" of the Sydney Botanic Gardens. Another link in the chain was forged when, on the occasion of Dame Mary's ninety-first birthday in 1956, the daughter of the late Mrs Nixon Smith presented a further cutting, from the tree in Poets' Corner, to the National Library of Canberra. This offshoot of the Macleay poplar was planted in the National Gardens on the site of the proposed Poets' Corner there.

Mary Gilmore came from a line of rebels, says the writer Kylie Tennant. "Her grandfather Beattie on his Hunter River farm at first caused shocked complaint and comment by saying he not only would *not* hunt down black men and women with dogs and guns, but regarded such acts as murder. His neighbours could not believe he was serious. Then they saw that he saved and protected the Aborigines. He was called 'The Abolitionist'. The parson was sent to remonstrate with him. He refused to conform to what his neighbours thought right, and what public opinion of his day regarded as a communal duty—if not jolly good sport.

"Then his fences were burned and his cattle maimed. No one dared work for him. He left the Hunter River financially ruined, because he had not only maintained his own judgment against the opinion of his day, but had done something practical about it—such as trying to save the lives of black people."

Donald Cameron, her father, was, said Mary, "a wanderer", and the family moved about the country a great deal. First a property manager, he later became a building contractor and travelled all over New South Wales and into Queensland with his family, following the building boom which was then taking place.

Sitting beside her father in front of the horse-drawn wagon or sharing his saddle, Mary learned of the hardships endured by the early settlers and the ruthlessness shown towards the Aborigines. She met and talked with the people she has described as "the real carriers of this country in its early movement towards settlement . . . the people who travelled in drays and carts, or who went on foot driving a pig, a calf or a goat ahead of them, the mother helping to carry the bedding, the children bearing the pots and pans. . ."

The things she saw on these long treks across the still undeveloped country, following the rough tracks made by the bullock-teams, and the stories she heard told around the camp fires when the travellers rested for the night, made a lasting impression on her sensitive and inquiring mind.

"The earliest teamsters I recollect," she has written, "carried water in a jar or crock (if the wife or the mother had one), and sometimes in a keg or demijohn, as evaporation was less from these than from a waterbag. Many a carefully measured-out sup of sun-warmed water I have had from these, when, as a child, my father would take me, sometimes in front of him on horseback, sometimes in the wagonette, looking for pine belts on the stations where he built the first 'sawn' house that followed the mud floor, split slabs and bark roof, with which most of the squattages of older Riverina began."

Her sympathies were always with the poor and struggling, for whom she felt a special responsibility which later forced her to continually campaign on their behalf.

"The real makers of our foundation history," she wrote, "lived on possum legs, had no carriages and slept in slab houses. They were the mass of the people. The same holds good today. James Ruse is still planting his little plot of wheat where no man planted wheat before."

Though the Aborigines were fast being wiped out, remnants of some of the tribes still had their camps in the Riverina district when Mary was a small child and she has told how her father was made a "blood brother" of the Waradgery tribe and how, as a "sister" and child of the tribe she played with the children in their camp at Houghlian's Creek, just outside Wagga. Once she lived alone with the tribe, for six weeks, on the banks of the Murrumbidgee:

"I grieved to leave them and they 'wept' me as I left. Being a 'sister', all the men and boys had to be away when this occurred—a rare ceremony and given to very few white people indeed. But as we

rode away, my father carrying me on the front of the saddle, the chief waited by a tree to see us pass, cried a few words of friendship, and waved us farewell. I never saw any of that kind, friendly body of people again. They were raided, and all that were not in hiding were killed. It was because of word that this was to happen that my father had to come for *me*. What warning he *could* give he had given the chief, knowing he took his own life in his hands by even hinting a warning. . . ."

Among her recollections of the ancient traditions and colourful ceremonies of the Aborigines which fed her imaginative young mind, Mary has described how the "Emu ceremony" was performed for her younger brother, George, when he was about six months old. The Aborigines called it "singing the knees" and said it would make him "strong to run and jump, and also enduring".

"The child was to be fully fed after a good sleep and his other physical requirements attended to so that he would be at ease and there would be no taint or urgency about him during the ceremony, in which there must be neither hindrance nor disturbance by any need of the child. At the time named, with the baby fed and washed, in a clean plaid frock, his hair combed and tied up in a roach, father went to the appointed place. My mother wanted to go too, but father had to tell her she would be put to death if she even went near the locality, as it was a man's observance and no woman could be allowed to approach or see it. It was a long ceremony, taking nearly three hours, and the curious thing was that, as had been foretold, this boy became the best runner and 'lepper' of the family."

Mary, or Jeannie as she was then called, first "learned her letters" from an old Cranmer Bible that had belonged to her great-great-grandfather. Sitting on her grandfather's knee she learned to read "In the Beginning was the Word . . . no alphabet, no syllables, nothing as a foundation to start from; nothing but the black letter, with to my mind for long afterwards, capitals like miniature cathedrals and as intricate in form."

Her father taught her the modern alphabet from an ABC book given to him by Mrs Mackay when he was building a house for her at Tooyal in 1870—the year of the earthquake there, when the waters of Lake Tooyal swept right up to the back of the place in which the Camerons were living, rocking the house up and down "like a doll's castle".

An apt pupil, by the time she was six years of age Mary was teaching her brothers to read. "I taught them," she says, "as my father had taught me—by analysis and comparison of form; A—like a tent with a stick across; B—like two D's and so on."

The Camerons were a talented and unconventional family. On one occasion the young parents shocked the Victorian susceptibilities of their neighbours by riding on a merry-go-round when a circus visited the nearby town. "To make matters worse," says Mary in the note appended to her verse describing the incident, "my mother wore a scarlet cloth dolman or cape. Parallels were drawn in which, I remember, the Scarlet Woman and the Apocalypse figured."

At this time the family was living on the Brucedale Road, opposite Brooklyn, in a small place on their own land.

"Talk ran very high. My father, being then an Orangeman, our house hummed with it. We really feared that there would be bloodshed. One man had unearthed and polished up a bayonet used at Sebastopol, another had his grandfather's sword, somebody else had a 'fowling-piece'," she writes in *The Tilted Cart*.

Mary's first formal education was at Brucedale School and so that her education should not be interrupted, her parents left her at Brooklyn with her grandfather Beattie while they went on trek.

"My grandmother's chair was black. It was 'the American chair', and, to my delight, had apples, peaches, plums and cherries painted along the back. My grandfather's was yellow turned and bent wood, with a loopholed cane seat—an exciting interest to small fingers during the kneeling at prayers. It was always known as 'the English chair'. My own seat at this time was a 'creepie', which came and went with me on Sundays in the gig, whenever I stayed with my grandparents, first at Springfield then at Brooklyn. Long forms and stools occupied the middle of the temporary building then used for worship, and later on the weatherboard church which replaced it. Many a time I sat on a hassock and watched the sunbeams fall in round spots through knot-holes to the floor. Sometimes it was the moonlight."

It was at Brucedale School, she has recorded, that she first felt the urge to write. She learned "not merely to make letters and spell words, but to express my own thoughts; and from then on, till I left that school, I spent my dinner hours at the slate in a fury of composition instead of going out to play. I was like something for whom the gates of the world had opened. I had wings. I could not help writing."

At eight years of age she was learning Greek at Mr Pentland's Academy at Wagga Wagga—"the only girl thought worthy of the privilege"—and from there went on to the public school. Although she has described herself as a "pale and sickly child", at twelve years

of age she was sent to act as pupil-teacher at a school in Cootamundra conducted by George Gray, an uncle by marriage. With him she moved to Bungowannah, near Albury, then on to the school of another uncle, John Beattie, at Yerong Creek.

When she sat for the entrance examination as a pupil-teacher at the age of sixteen, she passed highest of all candidates for her year and, given a choice of schools, chose Wagga Wagga as being nearest to her home. The new young teacher, sensitive and self-conscious, described her first day thus:

"I was only a gawky country girl, dressed in a home-made frock, when I entered the school to begin work, and when I went eagerly to an old schoolfellow (she wore a watch and her skirt was weighted down with pennies instead of shot, and afterwards she married a clergyman and wore glasses) she coldly gave me the tips of her fingers and turned away to another girl whose dress had six pearl buttons where mine had one."

After three years as a pupil-teacher in primitive bush schools, Mary contracted tuberculosis and in 1884 had to resign without achieving the status of a classified teacher. She spent a year at home in Wagga Wagga and when she was well again, went to the tiny Beaconsfield Provisional School near Temora, then to Illabo near Bethungra, where she taught in the daytime and studied at night.

It was at Illabo that she first showed her rebellion against unimaginative authority—by reading books to her pupils, a practice forbidden by the school board. Keeping a look out in case the inspector should unexpectedly call, she read to her small class from *Robinson Crusoe, Uncle Tom's Cabin, Pilgrim's Progress,* and Walter Scott's *Marmion*, and introduced the children to the delights of Hans Andersen and Grimm. In this educational pioneering she was following the example of her aunt, Jeannie Lockett, who, as headmistress of William Street, had been the first to teach Domestic Economy in schools.

Mary was as much a wanderer as her father and in 1889 we find her teaching at Silverton, near Broken Hill.

"We have had a great deal of wet weather here," she wrote to her cousin, Mary Ann McLean, "and the place is looking almost green, a thing that happens about once in ten years here. I never saw it looking so green even in winter before.

"The place is very quiet now, has been growing duller and duller ever since the boom went down and everyone complains of the scarcity of money."

Already she was evincing an interest in historical data and

pursuing the origins of her own family. The letter continues:

"Do you remember me asking you to send me any anecdotes you knew about our family or ancestors, such as, for instance, of 'a Cameron being a good son but a bad husband'? And what is that saying that a Cameron should never be rocked in a cradle? Find out all you can and write it out for me please. Also I want you to write out our genealogy (your Mother is sure to know it in Gaelic). If you send me the English (Donal son of Hugh son of ? etc.) I should be so glad . . . ask my Aunt the surnames of Grandpapa Cameron's Father's Mother and his Mother's Mother. Our Grandmother's name was McColl. What was her Mother's maiden name? . . ."

Cousin Mary Ann McLean did not answer this letter. Her son, Mr Donald Baxter, who still lives on the Roslyn property, tells us that his mother would not comply with the request because, she said, "Jeannie always made so much of it." Mary was to complain bitterly, many years later, of how much of Australia's early history was lost because people did not realize the importance of conserving what they knew of the first settlers.

In this same letter, Mary says she hopes "to get to Sydney for good at Christmas". She had already begun to contribute regularly to the Albury and Wagga papers, her articles appearing under a *nom de plume* because schoolteachers were not allowed to write for the Press. Some of her verses were signed "Em Jaycee", a somewhat obvious disguise of the initial letters of her name.

"I remember the port of Sydney as full of masts as a Sunday pincushion of pins. The sky was pierced to heaven with masts, with the purgatory of sailors' years between them and the earth. . ."

So Mary Cameron described the city as she saw it in the seventies but the Sydney to which she returned in 1890 had a less romantic aspect. Poverty and squalor stalked the narrow back streets and close-packed rows of crumbling houses gasped for air in the blazing sunshine. Work, for those who could get it, was ill-paid and hard.

On the land the shearers fought for recognition of their union, while on the waterfront the dockers struggled for a living wage.

Sydney was in a ferment of political and literary activity. Side by side with the growing trade union movement there was developing a creative spirit which looked to Australia for its inspiration. Writers who voiced the hopes and dreams of the working people were expressing themselves in the recently established *Bulletin* and *Worker*. The settlers in the outback were being dramatized by "Banjo" Paterson; the lives of the city workers by Henry Lawson.

With her mother, who was writing a column for the *Daily*

Telegraph under the pseudonym of "Humming Bee", Mary went to live at a boarding-house in Bligh Street. The meeting place for what we would now call the "progressive" young writers and politicians of the day was McNamara's Bookshop in Castlereagh Street. A large reading-room above the shop was used as a debating place where the many and varied political ideologies of the time were investigated and discussed. It was here that the young country schoolteacher probably first met William Lane, John Farrell and A.G. Stephens—"The three people who most shaped my mind and life . . ." she said. "To these three I owe any power of output, any shape in my work, any touch of 'quality'—anything that is good in my work."

A brilliant journalist of considerable personal magnetism, William Lane's utopian-socialist zeal affected Mary as it had the thousands of readers of his articles in the *Boomerang* and Queensland *Worker*. In his teaching she saw the answers to the problems of poverty and inequality that prevailed, the only cure for the many social ills that she saw around her.

John Farrell was, with Henry Lawson and "Banjo" Paterson, one of the group of "Bush Balladists" who were breaking away from the established European-based culture to present a new kind of literature with Australia as its inspiration.

As an established critic, editor of the *Bookfellow* and later of the "Red Page" of the *Bulletin*, A. G. Stephens gave practical help to the budding young writer. He advised her and published her work, setting her firmly on the literary path she was to travel for so many years.

In the political ferment of the time, women, too, were beginning to assert themselves by demanding the right to vote and an equal place in society. In nearby George Street, Louisa Lawson, an ardent feminist, was publishing Australia's first magazine for women, *Dawn*, and Bertha McNamara (the wife of the bookshop's owner) who has been described as "the Mother of the Labor Movement", organised, with Rose Scott, the fight for women's suffrage.

Though working as a teacher at Neutral Bay school, Mary took an active part in the great Maritime Strike of 1890 and the bitter Shearers' Strike that followed. She organized relief for the families of the strikers, raised funds, and assisted the men "on the run" from Queensland.

She was the first woman to join the Australian Workers' Union when it was formed from the Shearers' Union and was co-opted onto its first executive. As a teacher she could not use her own name and was placed on the books under her brother's name, J. G. Cameron.

"In nearby George Street . . ."

When the combined forces of the employers finally brought the Big Strike to an end there was much poverty and bitterness among the workers, with more than 20,000 unemployed in Sydney alone. William Lane had long dreamed of a communist utopia far away from the heartbreaks of capitalist society and in the bitterness of their defeat in this first major conflict between Australia's employers and employees his plan attracted many of the country's best workers and unionists. Mary was one of his most ardent supporters.

Lane formed the New Australia Co-operative Settlement Association with the aim of establishing a colony where the means of production, distribution and exchange would be communally owned. From all over Australia enthusiastic members were recruited, eager to start a new life. Capital of £20,000 was raised and every member was required to put all his assets into the common pool.

Unable to obtain suitable land in Australia, Lane turned to South America where he was eventually granted 450,000 acres, free of all

control, from the Paraguayan Government. A sailing ship, the *Royal Tar*, was built and after many delays and frustrations the first settlers started off for Paraguay early in 1893.

When they finally reached their destination they found the life in the wild, undeveloped country much harder than they had anticipated and many, though honest and hardworking, were totally unsuited for such primitive pioneering.

After a great deal of dissension the colony was divided and with about sixty loyal followers Lane left the original settlement and started another on land obtained on time-payment. At the new settlement, called "Cosme", everyone worked willingly and eagerly and within four months a dining-room, store, galley, butcher shop, tannery and stockyard had been built. Grassland and scrub were cleared and ploughed and a vegetable garden sown. Optimism and enthusiasm made light of all difficulties and it seemed, when Mary sailed from Australia to join the colony, that the fulfilment of their dream was in sight.

Mary taught the children in the colony's small school and edited the handwritten newspaper, *Cosme Evening Notes*, which was read to the assembled colonists after their day's work was done. She also organized the library which, over the years, grew to more than 2,000 books, mostly of a high literary standard.

On 29 May 1897 Mary Cameron was married to William Gilmore, a fellow-colonist from western Victoria, and her son, William Dysart Cameron Gilmore, was born on 21 August 1898, in the neighbouring town of Villa Rica.

In 1899, completely disheartened, Lane left Cosme for good. Soon after, Mary went into Villa Rica to live while her husband found work in Patagonia. From Villa Rica the Gilmores went to Sapucay for two or three months, then to Buenos Aires and on to Gallegos in South Patagonia. In January 1902 they left South America to return to Sydney.

"It was like coming to the backyard of the world," Mary said. "In the Argentine we had seven cable lines to all parts of the world and newspapers in many languages. Our sources of world information were direct. Back home we had but one cable service and we learnt our news from English sources only."

After a short stay in Sydney, the Gilmores went to live at Strathdownie, some twenty miles from Mount Gambier, then at Casterton, Victoria, where, says Mary, she "descended into hell on a lonely farm . . . nearly died in hospital". She wrote nothing until her son, Billy, was turned seven years of age. "I knew that if I started writing again it would take hold of me."

In 1907 Mary wrote to Hector Lamond, editor of the Sydney *Worker*, urging him to include a "Women's Page". Women, she argued, were just as important in Australian politics as men. Lamond wired back, "Start at once", and so the first Australian Labor "Women's Page" was born.

Mary continued to write her page from Casterton until 1912, when she went to live in Sydney while her husband joined his brother in a pastoral venture in Queensland. Her office at the *Worker* building became a regular meeting place for the leading writers of the day and her page gained a tremendous following. It appeared each week in the *Worker* for twenty-four years. She was never paid more than £3 a week, though frequently offered better-paid employment on other newspapers. During these years, through her page and in articles and letters in other papers and magazines, she was a constant partisan of many causes. No issue which affected the people was too small or too big for her attention. Her voice was ever raised on behalf of the inarticulate, the poor and propertyless and the ill-treated Aborigines.

Her attitude towards the Aborigines was never patronizing or sentimental but a straightforward and direct expression that all men are equal. In all her writings there is sincerity and truth. "I believe in truth," she declared. "Truth, to me, is more than powers and principalities and the applause of rogues and fools."

On the recommendation of Bernard O'Dowd, Mary's first collection of verse, *Marri'd*, was published by George Robertson of Melbourne in 1910. The second, *The Passionate Heart*, was described as "the literary sensation of 1918". Her first book of prose, *Hound of the Road*, contained a selection of finely-written essays with an air of mysticism about them. Nevertheless, they dealt with subjects close to the hearts of every human being. *The Tilted Cart*, published in 1925, was a collection of poems recalling her early memories, and, together with the copious notes at the end of the book, gave tantalizing glimpses of life in early Australia. The height of her literary power, it was said, was reached in 1930 with *The Wild Swan*.

By now Mary was sixty-five years of age and had suffered repeated attacks of illness but her life was as full and busy as ever. Hundreds of writers and would-be writers asked her advice and sent manuscripts for her appraisal and she helped them all unstintingly.

"I am devoured still by other people's affairs," she gently

complained, "and I am afraid I shall have to go out into the wilderness to escape them—and I starve in the wilderness for want of people. Only as I grow old do I realize how much I have been and am a hungerer for my kind. . . ."

But she remained in her Sydney flat and despite the many calls upon her generosity and time, the next five years saw an almost annual publication of her work. Two collections of poems, *The Rue Tree* (1931) and *Under the Wilgas* (1932) were followed by two books of prose, *Old Days: Old Ways* (1934) and *More Recollections* (1935), describing in detail the everyday life of the Australia of the nineteenth century. Another collection of verse, *Battlefields*, appeared in 1939. Fittingly, Cecil Hadgraft has described her as ". . . the poet of love, if the word is given a wide meaning—love of woman for child, of wife for husband, of observer for bird and flower, of a human being for the past to which we are all in debt. The objects of her regard are neglected things—the hunted and forgotten aboriginal tribes, the lonely shepherd, even the convict bowed under his task or straining against bonds and blows. She is, then, rather like a national conscience. . . ."

In 1937, in recognition of her contribution to Australian life and literature, Mary Gilmore was made a Dame of the British Empire by the then Prime Minister, Joseph Lyons.

Throughout the Second World War, Mary was again active with her pen on behalf of the men who were fighting, as she had been during the 1914-18 conflict. But in 1945 Mary's husband and son both died tragically within a few months of each other. In her deep sorrow Mary wrote to a friend: "I don't know what life holds for me now that my two, husband and son, are gone. I can only try to get on with the work that will be the monument to all of us. The shock caused some functional paralysis, tips of the fingers, toes and spine . . . However, my brain is still clear."

And, indeed, her brain was still clear, and her spirit as undaunted as ever. Her letters and articles continued to appear regularly in the Press on an amazing variety of subjects.

Despite her many interests, her literary activities and the unique place in society that she had attained, she still firmly believed in the socialist cause. She showed great courage in the face of opposition at the time of the Communist Party Dissolution Referendum in 1951, and made a practical protest, a year later, against the Government's efforts to prevent the Youth Carnival for Peace, by offering to write a weekly column for the Communist newspaper, *Tribune*.

Mary Gilmore's "Arrows" appeared each week in the *Tribune* until a few weeks before her death. She dealt with any subject, not always political, that she thought would interest her readers and she took as much care in writing and re-writing as she had done with her poems. The only "fee" she demanded was a supply of copy paper.

Mary's last years were rich in the honours bestowed upon her in gratitude for her contribution to Australian life and literature. To honour her long association with the trade union movement, in 1956 representatives of the May Day Committees of Melbourne, Sydney and Newcastle instituted a "Mary Gilmore Award" for literature relating to working people. Mary was asked to be its first President—"an honour I am privileged to accept".

Over 600 people attended her ninety-first birthday party, organised by the Fund Committee for a Chair of Australian Literature, and £500 was collected for this project which Mary had long advocated. The Australasian Book Society added their tribute by commissioning William Dobell to paint her portrait which, after its presentation to her by Sir John Northcott, Dame Mary gave to the nation. The portrait, now recognized as one of Dobell's most outstanding works, caused a great deal of controversy and even questions in the Legislative Assembly. It was described, as were other of Dobell's now world-famed paintings, as "a caricature". With more insight than the Honourable Members, Mary herself considered the portrait a great work of art and commented: "The painting is more important than the sitter. This painting will still be carrying my identity when my own work is forgotten."

To honour her as the oldest working journalist in Australia, in 1958 the Australian Journalists' Association, of which she had been a member almost since its inception, presented her with a gold badge. Perhaps one of her proudest moments was when she was declared winner of the "Queen of the May" contest organized by the Sydney May Day Committee in 1961, when she was ninety-six years of age.

During the last years of her life Mary was almost totally confined to her small, simply furnished flat in Darlinghurst Road, King's Cross, looked after by a nurse-housekeeper. Nevertheless she still kept a perceptive finger on the pulse of the world and expressed her forthright views of its happenings.

In the dim quiet of her small oasis in the midst of Sydney's bustling traffic she spent four hours each day at her large desk near the window, then, after a short nap, devoted the rest of the day to receiving visitors. From all over the world scholars, historians,

politicians, artists and journalists came to see and talk to her, and young writers and poets seeking advice and encouragement were never turned away.

Mary Gilmore had grown so much a part of the Australian scene that despite her ninety-seven years her death came as a shock to all of us. "We must go and see Dame Mary," we had said, for long with the unspoken thought that it might soon be too late. And suddenly it was too late and she was gone.

Yet her passing left no idle regret; she had been the match that lighted a torch that burned brightly and by the time that small match had burned itself out, the torch was a beacon for all who believed in right, in truth and in justice.